CNUT THE GR

'The newest and by far the best general-intere
Bolton marshals a greater array of sources, a... ....
energetic creativity, than any previous writer on this king has done.'
—Steve Donoghue, *Open Letters Monthly*

'Bolton has made an exhaustive study of the available sources, both
texts and artefacts. His narrative has the virtues of a well-told story.'
—Nicholas Orme, *Church Times*

'Through judicious use of northern sources, Timothy Bolton gives us a
Cnut firmly rooted in Scandinavia, and a nuanced portrait of an
English monarch and Scandinavian ruler active on a European stage.'
—Pauline Stafford, author of *Queen Emma and Queen Edith*

'Drawing on a range of rich resources from Old Norse sagas and poetry
to charters, chronicles and laws from England, Timothy Bolton presents
a fresh and engaging account of the compelling figure of Cnut in all
his diverse glory.'—Rory Naismith, King's College London, author of
Money and Power in Anglo-Saxon England

'In this stimulating and timely study, Timothy Bolton illuminates a
king and an age of supreme importance. Cnut's forging of an Anglo-
Scandinavian empire and England's place within it are explored in
original and thought-provoking ways – fresh evidence is put forward
and well-known material considered anew. Bolton is a confident guide
through the tangled thicket of sources that surround Cnut, handling
English and Scandinavian texts with insight and sensitivity.'—Martin J.
Ryan, co-author of *The Anglo-Saxon World*

Also in the Yale English Monarchs Series

* Available in the U.S. from University of California Press

CNUT THE GREAT

Timothy Bolton

YALE UNIVERSITY PRESS
NEW HAVEN AND LONDON

Cover image: detail from MS. Ee.3.59, fol. 5r (the sole surviving witness to Matthew Paris' Life of King Edward the Confessor, produced in the second quarter of the thirteenth century) depicting Cnut the Great and Edmund Ironside locked in combat. Reproduced with the permission of Cambridge University Library.

First published in paperback in 2019

For information about this and other Yale University Press publications, please contact:
U.S. Office: sales.press@yale.edu   yalebooks.com
Europe Office: sales@yaleup.co.uk   yalebooks.co.uk

Set in Baskerville by IDSUK (DataConnection) Ltd
Printed in Great Britain by Hobbs the Printers Ltd, Totton, Hampshire

Library of Congress Cataloging-in-Publication Data

Names: Bolton, Timothy.
Title: Cnut the Great / Timothy Bolton.
Description: New Haven : Yale University Press, 2017.
Identifiers: LCCN 2016046797 | ISBN 9780300208337 (cloth : alk. paper)
Subjects: LCSH: Canute I, King of England, 995?–1035. | Great Britain—History—
Canute, 1017–1035. | Great Britain—Kings and rulers—Biography. | Denmark—Kings
and rulers—Biography. | Norway—Kings and rulers—Biography. |
Danes—England—History.
Classification: LCC DA160 .B649 2017 | DDC 942.01/81092 [B] —dc23
LC record available at https://lccn.loc.gov/2016046797

A catalogue record for this book is available from the British Library.

ISBN 978-0-300-24318-5 (pbk)

10 9 8 7 6 5 4 3 2 1

This book is dedicated to the memory of my dear friend Raymond Ian Page (1924–2012), who taught me that with warmth and charm our shared traits of pedantry and curmudgeonliness can be powerful tools rather than social drawbacks.

CONTENTS

PLATES

1. Cnut and Emma present the cross to the New Minster, Winchester, in the New Minster *Liber Vitae*: London, British Library, Stowe MS. 944, fol. 6r © The British Library Board.

2. Detail of the confraternity additions to the Christ Church, Canterbury, Gospel Book, now London, British Library, Royal MS. 1 D. IX, fol. 43r © The British Library Board.

3. Emma receiving the *Encomium Emmae Reginae* from the author, while her two sons look on, the frontispiece of London, British Library, Additional MS. 33,241, fols. 1v–2r © The British Library Board.

4. The obverse and reverse of the carved wooden pencase lid from Lund inscribed with the English name 'Leofwine', Kulturen, Lund, no. 53436:1125. Reproduced with the permission of Kulturen, Lund.

5. Cnut's appearance in the *Miracula Heriberti* in London, British Library, Additional MS. 26,788, fol. 64v © The British Library Board.

6. The London Ringerike Tombstone, found in 1852 during the digging of foundations for a warehouse on the south side of St Paul's Churchyard, now Guildhall Museum 4075. Reproduced with the permission of the Museum of London.

7. Drawing of the gilt bronze mount with Ringerike-style decoration, excavated in Winchester Cathedral. From Fuglesang, *Some Aspects*, no. 54, and drawn by that author. Reproduced here with her permission.

8. London, British Library, Additional MS. 40,000, fol. 10r, the eleventh-century entries of the Thorney *Liber Vitae* © The British Library Board.

9. London, British Library, Cotton Augustus ii 90, a vernacular charter recording Harold Harefoot on his deathbed © The British Library Board.

PREFACE AND ACKNOWLEDGEMENTS

The student of medieval manuscripts has often the words of John Cotgrave in mind: 'That the reading of many Books is wearinesse to the flesh, when there were none but Manuscripts in the world: How much is that wearinesse increased since the Art of printing has so infinitely multiplyed large and vast volums in every place that the longest life of a man is not sufficient to explore so much as the substance of them.'[1] Having produced in 2009 a monograph that studied the mechanisms by which Cnut the Great came to power in England and Scandinavia in the first few decades of the eleventh century, I accepted the offer of Yale University Press to write this book, and find myself now offering the reader a similarly lengthy biography of him. I think that one must have good reason to foist two books or more on the world, and especially so if their subjects are so close to each other. Thus, I beg the indulgence of my readers one more time, and give them my solemn promise that there will not be a third book on Cnut from me.

In 2009 I faced a crucial challenge when writing in English about historical figures from both England and Scandinavia in that, as I said then, 'it is difficult to select a consistent principle by which these names should be spelt. Anglicised spellings, whether modern or medieval, often distort Scandinavian names so that they become almost

---

[1] Cotgrave, *The English Treasury of Wit and Language*, published 1605; the text here is from the second page of the unpaginated and unfoliated introduction entitled 'To the Courteous Reader'.

unintelligible to a modern reader of Scandinavian history (and certainly
to those in linguistic fields such as Old Norse or skaldic verse), and likewise the use of normalized Old Norse or modern Scandinavian forms
garbles Anglo-Saxon names.'[2] This problem has not gone away in the
subsequent years, and indeed to me seems to have become worse, as I
have come to realize that to follow Campbell in his edition of the
Encomium Emmae Reginae and use normalized Old Norse spellings for
Danes and Swedes is to force East Norse names into badly fitting West
Norse forms, which again garble such names nearly to the point of
unintelligibility.[3] Thus, again I propose to 'follow the convention that
seems to me to make the most sense for the readers: in that, the names
of the majority of the historical figures are given here according to the
geographical spheres in which they were most active, with Scandinavian
skalds' names appearing in their normalized Old Norse form and
Anglo-Saxon statesmen in the accepted English form'. To this I will
now add that most figures with lives spent predominantly in Denmark
or Sweden will appear here in their Old Danish or Old Swedish forms
as laid out by Peterson, *Nordiskt Runnamnslexikon.*[4] As before, certain cases
such as Scandinavians who arrived with Cnut and spent most, if not all,
of their careers in England, and those who spent their time between the
two regions, demand individual treatment. Thus, the former will appear
as in English records with various Anglicized spellings, and in addition

[2] Bolton, *Empire*, p. xi.
[3] This topic was a perennial debate between me and Ray Page, who usually expounded
on the terrible effects of adopting normalized West Norse (and usually Icelandic-influenced)
forms of names in source editions. I am not sure that I agree that this is one of the world's
chief ills, but I have never been able to shake off the thought that he may have been, in part
at least, correct to point this out. See, for example, the form of Swen Estrithsson's name in
West Norse sources: Sveinn Ástríðarson. This is a form I have used in some publications for
the sake of the rule, but cannot get comfortable with.
[4] The principal differences are an eschewing of the symbols þ and ð for 'th', a number of
consistent vowel variants, and the dropping of some of the West Norse nominative case
endings. Note that I have dropped the formation of the genitive necessary for patronymics
and matronymics in an '-ar' ending (which often provides the most confusion for a reader
without a solid understanding of Old Norse), as it was certainly not used in Denmark or
Sweden in the thirteenth century when substantial written records begin to survive in sufficient numbers to examine this feature, and it may have already been weakened or absent
from Denmark in the eleventh century.

Cnut, Harthacnut, Harold Harefoot and Thorkell the Tall will appear as here. Furthermore, in order to differentiate between Cnut's first wife, Ælfgifu of Northampton, and his second wife, Emma (who took the name Ælfgifu during her marriage to Æthelred in the opening years of the eleventh century, and is referred to by both names in the sources), I will exclusively use the names Ælfgifu and Emma respectively to differentiate them here.

There are a number of letters or characters that may be unfamiliar to my reader, but were common in Old English and Old Norse. Chief amongst these are Thorn 'Þ' and its lowercase form 'þ', and Eth 'Ð' and its lowercase form 'ð', which are both pronounced as Modern English 'th'. Thus the common Old Norse name Þórkell is pronounced 'Thorkell'. For the pronunciation of other unfamiliar symbols the reader is directed to the various academic textbooks intended to help the student learn Old Norse or Old English.

In addition, as some sources have been edited and translated more than once, and readers in various countries may have easier access to any one of these, I have used here a system of reference to primary sources in which I cite the place within the source text in its original language first, followed by the editor of the edition used by me in brackets, as well as the page reference there. Translations mostly follow the relevant editions cited by me, with occasional adaptations for sense. These are recorded in the notes.

All tasks this large incur substantial personal debts. I would like to thank Yale University Press, and from my perspective its charming and patient representatives in Heather McCallum and Rachael Lonsdale, for placing their trust in me and asking me to undertake this study. They asked for a study that could add something to scholarship as well as be read by the 'man on the Clapham omnibus', and I hope I have lived up to their expectations. As part of this I have consciously returned to the style of Barlow, in his seminal biography of Edward the Confessor. In doing so, I have kept citation in the original to a minimum. It is a happy coincidence that most sources cited in translation for the present task are in unambiguous language, but where the original reading might be easily called into question, I have given that as well in the main text. I also wish to offer my thanks to Richard Mason, whose eagle eye saved me from potentially disastrous errors.

Many others are owed especial thanks, including Michael Benskin, Ian Davis, David Dumville, Roxana Kashani, Kari Maund (many times), Camilla Previté, Peter Stokes and Mary Wellesley, for either listening to and salving my panics on so many occasions or for blocking the slings and arrows of this world to give me the necessary space to work on this book. My wife Ingela and my young son Harald tower over all of these in their patience and fortitude in the face of a book project that grew and grew, demanding far too much of my time and ending some weeks *after* the recent birth of our daughter (and his sister) Estrid, not a few weeks *before* as I had promised – and to them I must offer the greatest thanks, and also apologies.

Timothy Bolton
Stockholm, 2016

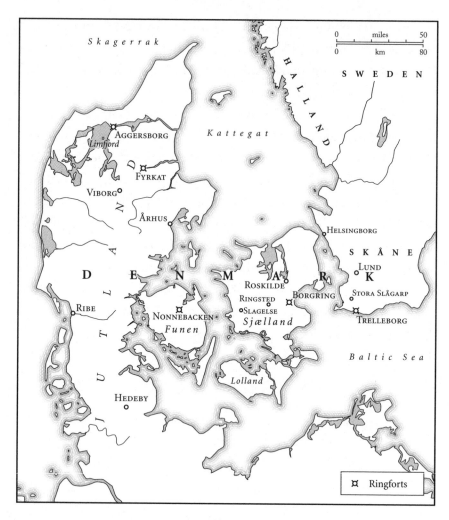

Map 1: Important sites in Denmark in the eleventh century

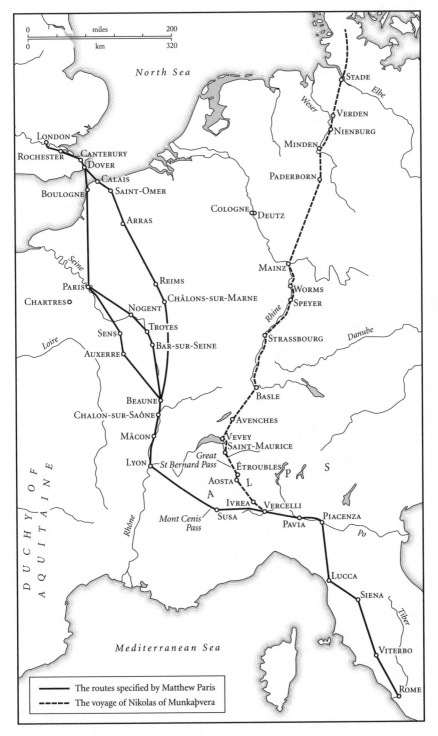

Map 2: Recorded overland travel routes from northern Europe to Rome c. 1026 (following Birch, *Pilgrimage* to Rome, pp. 43–9)

INTRODUCTION

ON THE STUDY OF CNUT

It is unfortunate that, even in the shadow of the millennial anniversary of Cnut's successful invasion of England, most members of the public in Britain and Scandinavia will know this king mainly for the story of his attempts to turn back the tide – and that in a truncated form which removes the essential message of the story and makes him appear foolish or prideful.[1]

He is one of the most fascinating of the pre-Conquest kings of England, and his life presents us with several new ways of examining late Anglo-Saxon England in addition to areas of neighbouring Scandinavia, as well as of questioning the established norms of how an English monarch could and should behave in the eleventh century. Unlike all other pre-Conquest monarchs in this series, his regime spread beyond the British Isles and spanned multiple geographical boundaries in northern Europe. He came to power in England first, following his conquest of the country in 1016, and to full kingship on the death of

---

[1] For the earliest witnesses to this story see Appendix I. The truncated version has its origins in 1587 at least, when it appears in Holinshed, interpreted as a prideful act, albeit followed by a brief note of the act of supplication to God which is normally omitted in popular retellings: 'his intollerable pride in commanding the waters of the flouds not to rise, he humbleth himselfe and confesseth Christ Iesus to be king of kings, he refuseth to weare the crowne during his life'. By the publication of William Slayter, *The History of Great Britaine*, in 1621, the supplication has been further eroded: 'This Cnute commands the seas to shew,/His Sycophants flattering termes vntrew,/And knowledging Christ his only trust,/Return'd from Rome, returnes to dust.' I owe both of these references to Elaine Treharne's 'Performance of Piety', p. 360.

Edmund Ironside on 30 November that year. In c. 1019, after the death of his own brother Harald, he added Denmark to this, and Norway as well by conquest in 1028. In ruling these nations, he had to cross substantial cultural and linguistic boundaries, and appeal to local elites in each region in entirely different ways. The resulting regimes would profoundly change the societies of England and Denmark, and ultimately contribute significantly to the end of the Viking Age in Scandinavia.

That said, the relatively undeveloped nature of the Danish Church, and in particular monasticism there as well as in Scandinavia in general, ensures that the lion's share of the surviving evidence for his life comes from England.[2] What little evidence there is from Scandinavia in a written form is later, or at least is preserved as literary fossils of early oral poetry copied piecemeal within later narratives. This has caused the almost overwhelming focus of modern historical debate on English sources alongside occasional mainland European ones, and on Cnut's activities in England, contributing to some general impressions of him that have done much to hamper comprehensive discussion. The first of these notions presupposes Cnut's barbarity before his takeover in England, and thus his need to be educated by one or more of the English elites. It should be noted that an impression of barbarity and 'otherness' lingers around Scandinavians from Cnut's time and before, most probably perpetuated by the horrors of viking raiding, or accounts of it, as well as by the fact that the Scandinavians up to the eleventh century existed without substantially literate or bureaucratic societies and had so recently Christianized. This is what lies behind the comment of the Anglo-Norman monk and hagiographer Goscelin around 1080, when he wrote to encourage Eve, an English nun who had left to join a hermitage in Angers, saying that 'the daughters of kings and princes, raised from infancy in all delights, knowing nothing beyond the

---

[2] The earliest apparent foundation in Denmark was the Benedictine cathedral chapter of Odense founded by monks from Evesham between 1095 and 1100, with other possible early foundations in Schleswig, Ribe and Lund (for Odense, see King, 'English Influence' and 'The Cathedral Priory'). For a survey of the earliest historical writing in Scandinavia, see Sawyer and Sawyer, 'Adam and Eve'.

splendours and the happiness of their homeland, marry into foreign nations and far-away kingdoms. They are destined to learn barbarous customs and strange languages, and to serve fierce lords and repugnant laws that go against nature, as for instance recently the daughter of the Margrave of Flanders married King Knut of Denmark.'[3] The Knut here is almost certainly Knut 'the Holy', the son of Cnut the Great's nephew Swen Estrithsson, who married Adela, daughter of Robert, count of Flanders, on the accession to the Danish throne in 1080. Much the same sentiment stands behind the tone of surprise in Fulbert of Chartres' letter to Cnut, which praises Cnut's 'wisdom' and 'piety' but explains that Fulbert had previously thought Cnut to be 'a ruler of pagans'.[4] This was written nearly seventy years after Cnut's grandfather had been converted to Christianity, about a decade after Cnut's father had been buried in a church in Roskilde, and at a point at which even though some Danes were of questionable Christian allegiance or still pagan, Cnut himself had Danish bishops and most probably also chaplains in attendance at his court.[5]

Echoes of the same misconceptions are detectable in modern scholarship. Sir Frank Stenton stated in his seminal *Anglo-Saxon England* that '[Cnut's] relations with his bishop and abbots were those of a pupil towards the teachers who had introduced him to the mysteries of a civilization higher than his own. For all their skill in warfare, the intricacy of their decorative art, and the elaboration of their encomiastic verse, the northern peoples of Cnut's age belonged in spirit to a remote, barbaric, world.'[6] The same sentiments stand behind Dorothy Bethurum's explanation of Cnut's ecclesiastical patronage, in which she states that he was a 'brilliant young barbarian . . . [who] put himself under Wulfstan's tutelage', as well as Frank Barlow's similar statements and observation (in error) that Cnut's patronage appears to wane after

---

[3] Goscelin, *Liber Confortatorius* (Talbot, p. 41).
[4] *The Letters and Poems*, no. 37 (Behrends, pp. 66–9).
[5] For these, see below at pp. 36–7, and 137–8, and references there.
[6] Stenton, *Anglo-Saxon England* (3rd edn), p. 411.

the archbishop's death in 1023.[7] Further, and more modern, examples
can be found in Simon Keynes' claim that '[u]nder the tutelage of
Archbishop Wulfstan in particular, Cnut learnt how he was expected to
behave as a good Christian king', as well as M. K. Lawson, who opens
a sub-chapter on 'Cnut's Religious Background' having previously
discussed how Emma may have been of aid in how to deal with the
English Church, with the emphatic 'Cnut must have needed it'.[8] I hope
to show in what follows that such views have no basis in fact, and mask
the very real probability that he was a devout Christian, without much
need of a crash course in Christian worship or 'civilization'.

Similarly, doubt is often cast on the amount of time Cnut spent in
Scandinavia, as well as his commitment to it, with Peter Sawyer stating
the consensus view that 'Cnut spent relatively little of his time in
Scandinavia. He went there when necessary, in 1019 to claim Denmark
and nine years later to claim Norway, in 1022 and 1026 to deal with
enemies who threatened Denmark. England was the source of his
wealth and power and therefore he did not need to dominate Scandinavia
as his father and grandfather had done.'[9] Here there are two issues
rolled up together. Certainly England was the source of the greatest
part of Cnut's wealth and power, and needed his physical presence
more. However, his actions in Scandinavia do not indicate that he went
there only out of necessity, and when we consider sources of evidence
such as skaldic verse and archaeological materials it is clear that he
remained, in part at least, culturally Scandinavian throughout his life.

The Scandinavian sources need extremely sensitive handling, but
they often operate as a check and balance on the preconceptions of
those of England and mainland Europe. We do Cnut an injustice if we
reject them without any attempt to use them, albeit with the necessary
caveats concomitant on their method of survival or distance in time

---

[7] Bethurum, *The Homilies of Wulfstan*, pp. 63–4, Barlow, *The English Church*, p. 41.
[8] Keynes, 'Cnut's Earls', p. 87, and Lawson, *Cnut*, p. 129.
[9] P. H. Sawyer, 'Cnut's Scandinavian Empire', p. 22.

from the events they record.[10] Much of contemporary Scandinavian history is a void, and any facts we can show that bear some weight will contribute greatly to our knowledge there.

Two previous biographies have been written at opposite ends of the twentieth century. The first was that by Laurence M. Larson, his *Canute the Great 995–1035, and the Rise of Danish Imperialism During the Viking Age*, published as part of Putnam's 'Heroes of the Nations' series in 1912. To this should be added two influential academic articles by the same author, his 'The Efforts of the Danish Kings to Recover the English Crown after the Death of Harthacnut', published in the same year, and 'The Political Policies of Cnut as King of England', published in 1910. His work is now quite dated, notably in its uncritical use of late Scandinavian narratives in the monograph of 1912, and suffered badly from the initial attacks on such uses of these sources published by Lauritz Weibull in 1911. However, Larson's work framed much that was to follow, and several lines of enquiry, which were successfully followed up by later historians, have their roots there.[11]

In 1993, M. K. Lawson produced his *Cnut: The Danes in England in the Early Eleventh Century* in Longman's 'Medieval World' series. That book, as well as the conference proceedings published in the following year as A. R. Rumble (ed.), *The Reign of Cnut, King of England, Denmark and Norway*, enabled more than a decade of scholarly activity on Cnut from a diverse range of approaches including numismatics and literary studies of skaldic verse.[12] Lawson's study, however, made little of the Scandinavian evidence or subsequent debate, despite alluding to its importance, and the nature of the collection of individual papers in the

[10] This is discussed much more fully below in the section on sources, at pp. 21–6.
[11] See, for example, Larson's tabulation of the earls who witness Cnut's charters ('The Political Policies', p. 725, with discussion on pp. 725–9), which prefigures Keynes' approaches to the witness-lists of Æthelred (in his *Diplomas*), Cnut (in his 'Cnut's Earls') and his more comprehensive *An Atlas of Attestations*.
[12] In addition to more traditional historical approaches to Cnut's reigns in England and Scandinavia in this volume (those supplied by P. H. Sawyer, 'Cnut's Scandinavian Empire', Lund, 'Cnut's Danish Kingdom', and Keynes, 'Cnut's Earls', amongst others), papers by Jonsson, 'The Coinage of Cnut' and Frank, 'King Cnut in the Verse of his Skalds', made important contributions rarely seen before.

book edited by Alexander Rumble caused much of the discussion of the Scandinavian elements of his life to be dealt with separately.[13] I tried to fill some of this gap myself in 2009 with a monograph on the methods of Cnut's rise to power and control over his 'empire', and since then the awakened scholarly interest in Cnut has continued apace. Thus the moment would appear to be ripe for this biography, with the aim of viewing Cnut 'in the round', wearing both his English and Scandinavian mantles.[14]

ON BIOGRAPHY: 'A BASTARD, AN IMPURE ART'[15]

The problems of this medium are all too easily perceived by the modern student of history. The writer of it must attempt to stand at some distance from his or her subject, and prioritize and organize the surviving sources into a coherent narrative; and, that done, attempt an educated leap of faith to draw out and interpret some of the motives and psychological impulses behind their subject's actions. In doing so, the writer doubtless projects some of their own experiences and psyche into the void; this is not a genre to work in lightly.[16] Readers then follow these arguments and statements, entering into their own discourse with the writer and the subject, sifting and weighing the evidence for them-selves (and as a student of medieval manuscripts with a fascination for scribal practices and marginalia myself, I hope they will then fill the margins of the following pages with their own scribbled observations, thereby entering into a form of discourse with my text). To perform this task for a living person is problematic, when the advanced state of the

[13] Keynes, 'Cnut's Earls', is a notable exception to this, as is Frank, 'King Cnut', when attempting to tie in developments in skaldic verse with events in England.

[14] Bolton, *Empire*, and see also Pratt, 'Kings and Books', Treharne, 'Performance of Piety', Lewis, 'Danish Landowners', Williams, 'Thorkell the Tall', and Insley, 'The Family', for further thought-provoking studies.

[15] Lee, *Virginia Woolf*, p. 10, quoting Woolf's notebooks of October 1934.

[16] Of course, in this lies some of the interest in the genre, as Orson Welles observed in an often quoted retort to one of his own biographers: 'There's no biography so interesting as the one in which the biographer is present.'

study of psychology ensures that even if we could interview our subject we might still suspect that they could obfuscate some of their acts and decisions, and, even worse, would not fully understand all the myriad experiences and impulses that informed each decision they made. To perform it for a subject dead for nearly a millennium, and who lived in two cultures long since disappeared, is difficult to say the least.

This is not to say that such a task should not be undertaken. Such works have a fundamental place in the writing of history, and the parts of biography that make us feel uncomfortable as scholars have a crucial, if often unrecognized, place within most historical writings about individuals or their actions. The discomfort that many modern historians may experience when turning to write or read biographies is fuelled by the fact that up until the nineteenth century, when the modern form of our discipline was born, the writing of history was principally the stories of so-called 'great' men and women. The subsequent revolution in historical writing ended up as a three-pronged attack on biography, with increasingly fierce source criticism, the rise of 'grass-roots history' and the popularity of the *longue durée* approach widening our horizons beyond that of a single life. While quite necessary, this has left us with anxieties about biography, and for a few scholars a complete denial that medieval biography is even possible.[17] For many, it is what we set aside when our discipline began to shape and analyze itself.

However, when ignored by academics, biography did not die in scholarly writing but went underground. It appears in the pages of modern scholarship in snippets of biographical assumptions that modern authors have silently formulated in their own minds, often offered to their readers as uncontested facts. For example, it is clear to us after the abandonment of scientific racial stereotyping in the second half of the twentieth century, that when Larson in 1910 ascribed aspects

---

[17] For a survey of the history of biography see the introduction to Bates, Crick and Hamilton, *Writing Medieval Biography*, pp. 1–13, and in particular the comments on pp. 6–11, including a citation of K. B. MacFarlane's assertion that medieval biography is impossible.

of Cnut's character to his mix of Slavic and Scandinavian blood, this is his and his society's presumption, and a false one at that.[18] However, it is less obvious to the reader that when Bethurum and Barlow make their statements about Cnut seeking out an English mentor in Wulfstan, as discussed above, these are based on a hasty biographical presumption that Cnut came from a barbarian Scandinavian culture, and thus needed guidance. Before the reader has even had the chance to consider it, the notion that Cnut might have actively patronized the English Church for his own reasons, and what those reasons may have been, is swept away from him or her by an unstated conclusion in modern scholars' minds.

Such conclusions infuse our historical writing, and bring much to it: the narrative would be a very dry and patchy thing without them. Moreover, I am not going to argue that we should write biography with all possible choices laid out before us, like one of those Dungeons and Dragons *Endless Quest* multi-choice books that were popular when I was a child, in which each potential decision is explored fully; so that if one believes Cnut needed a tutor in how to deal with the English Church one turns to page 53, and if not then to page 58, or similar. The resulting narrative would be breathtakingly cumbersome, and it is part of the biographer's role to make those decisions. However, they must be made carefully, and with a knowledge of the biographer's relevant 'mental baggage'. For my part, I should state here that my past researches have always revealed to me an active and commanding figure in Cnut, and because of this I am inclined to see his agency in matters rather than his passivity. It is no secret that my previous work has foregrounded the less well-known Scandinavian side of Cnut in an attempt to try and set what we learn from the sources from Scandinavia alongside those of England and mainland Europe, and this study continues in that vein.

[18] Larson, 'The Political Policies', p. 722, where he notes the differences between Cnut and his 'violent and bloodthirsty' father: 'Unlike Sweyn, he was anything but a typical Viking; the lesser excitements of court life appealed to him more than the wild life of the sea-king. These differences may, to some extent, have been due to a strong strain of Slavic blood, for racially Cnut was Danish only in part.'

In recent years biography has found champions. Jacques Le Goff made important contributions, and others have been made by a handful of more modern figures, such as Nicholas Vincent, Robin Fleming, George T. Beech, Pauline Stafford, and perhaps most obviously Frank Barlow and Janet Nelson.[19] The volume entitled *Writing Medieval Biography*, dedicated to Frank Barlow in 2006, was a defiant rallying cry to potential historical biographers, and from the 1970s onwards the series in which I write now, that of Yale University Press' 'English Monarchs', has been a flagship for the medium. It was with the weight of this important publishing series behind me, and with this responsibility to my reader before me, that I accepted Yale's invitation and turned once again to Cnut.

ON THE SOURCES FOR CNUT'S LIFE

A handful of sources make up the lion's share of the narrative for the present work. While comment on specific aspects of them will be made within the relevant parts of this book, a more general comment on their contents and relative weaknesses is needed before we properly begin.

The principal text for the narrative of almost all English history before the Norman Conquest is the series of annals now known collectively as the Anglo-Saxon Chronicle. The twelfth-century Anglo-Norman Gaimar thought that its origins lay in King Alfred's desire to have 'a book written in English about events and laws and about battles in the land and about kings who made war', and it does seem likely that the text we have today has its origins in the late ninth century, probably in the south-west of England, perhaps near the Mercian border.[20] Multiple copies of important records seem to have been deposited in a number of ecclesiastical archives for security in Anglo-Saxon England,

---

[19] See as examples: Vincent, *Peter des Roches*, Beech, 'Biography and the Study of Eleventh-Century Society', Stafford, *Queen Emma and Queen Edith*, Barlow, *Edward the Confessor, William Rufus, The Godwins*, and Nelson, *Charles the Bald*.

[20] Gaimar, *Lestorie des Engles*, lines 3,445–8 (Bell, p. 110) , Sprockel, *The Language of the Parker Chronicle*, I, p. xix.

and this seems to have been the case with the Chronicle, perhaps within Alfred's lifetime. By the tenth century some of these copies were being kept up to date in blocks, often with local material added where relevant, either year by year or more probably in sporadic bursts of composition and copying. Thus the text is not a single uniform set of annals, but after its earliest entries it diverges into a series of branches, each of which draws from and adds to a common stock.[21] The 'A' text is the earliest, and was written at Old Minster, Winchester, in the final decade of the ninth century.[22] The 'B' and 'C' texts both appear to be from Abingdon, where in the second half of the tenth century 'B' was evidently copied, and was used in the mid-eleventh century during the compilation of 'C'.[23] The 'D' text was written in the mid-eleventh century, probably at Worcester.[24] The 'E' text was written in the early twelfth century at Peterborough.[25] The final text here, the 'F' text, is a bilingual composition from about 1100 made at Christ Church, Canterbury, probably by a scribe who made notes in 'A'.[26]

The annals relevant for our purposes here, as contained in C, D, E and F (A is of little use for our period, and B stops in 977), mainly descend from a common stock of Æthelredian material, written up in a single effort of composition most probably in c. 1022.[27] However, the entries before and after 1017 are of a markedly different character (with those before being much fuller and composed as a passionate narrative of the defeat of the English, and those after often reduced to a few brief factual observations with almost no elaborations or authorial opinions),

[21] A comprehensive codicological and paleographical survey of the different surviving manuscripts can be found in the relevant entries in Ker, *Catalogue of Manuscripts*, and see also Keynes, 'Manuscripts of the Anglo-Saxon Chronicle'.

[22] Cambridge, Corpus Christi Cambridge, MS. 173; recently edited by Bately, and available in facsimile in Flower and Smith, *The Parker Chronicle and Laws*.

[23] London, British Library, Cotton MSS. Tiberius A iii and Tiberius B i; recently edited by Taylor. The C-text has been recently edited by O'Brien O'Keeffe.

[24] London, British Library, Cotton MS. Tiberius B iv; recently edited by Cubbin.

[25] Oxford, Bodleian Library, Laud MS. 636; a facsimile exists in Whitelock, *The Peterborough Chronicle*, and the text was edited recently by Clark.

[26] London, British Library, MS. Cotton Domitian A viii; a facsimile exists in Dumville, *The Anglo-Saxon Chronicle*.

[27] Keynes, 'The Declining Reputation', pp. 229–31.

and these most probably descend from a separate source, which over-lapped in chronology with the entries composed c. 1022, and continued the text to the early 1040s. The relationship between C, D, E and F is not straightforward. E and F seem to share a common exemplar that was at St Augustine's, Canterbury, in the mid-eleventh century, while C and D are also connected to this exemplar as well as to each other.[28] None of these agrees exactly with each other, and all appear to have received small additions from local knowledge or other sources. Finally, other material common to D and E may have been added to the Cnut entries in the Canterbury exemplar as late as the 1040s and 1050s.[29] The nearly complete doctoral research by Zhangfeng Xu at Aberdeen University into the common stock of this section of the Chronicle is eagerly awaited.

There is a good translation of these sources in parallel columns by Dorothy Whitelock from 1961, and another in blocks of prose by Michael Swanton from 1996, but the latter can on occasion eliminate what is individual to each text while seeking a common core.[30] I shall reference the various redactions of the Chronicle here as 'ASC' followed by a capital letter that denotes the variant of the Chronicle text, followed by a year (corrected in some editions) and finally the relevant editor and page number in brackets.

The *Encomium Emmae Reginae* was written by a cleric, evidently of St Omer, Flanders, initially in the reign of Harthacnut (d. 1042), at the request of and for the adulation of his mother, Emma, who had been Cnut's wife.[31] It surveys the conquest of England by Swen 'Forkbeard' and Cnut, and ends with an account of the struggle for power after Cnut's death. The early version of the text exists in a single

---

[28] See ibid., pp. 50–3, where Lawson draws on the work of Plummer, *Two of the Saxon Chronicles Parallel*, and Dumville, 'Some Aspects', to set out a comprehensive discussion of the relationship between C, D and E, and their common source.

[29] Lawson, *Cnut*, p. 53.

[30] Whitelock, Douglas and Tucker, *The Anglo-Saxon Chronicle*, and Swanton, *The Anglo-Saxon Chronicle*.

[31] There is an edition by Campbell from 1949, reissued with an extensive introduction by Keynes in 1998.

eleventh-century manuscript (London, British Library, Additional MS. 33241), which has a line-drawn frontispiece showing the author presenting the work to Emma while two of her sons look on.[32] That is probably not the original, but a close copy of it. Another version, updated in Edward the Confessor's favour, after Harthacnut's death, was suggested by a series of extracts from the text in a sixteenth-century manuscript (now Paris, Bibliothèque nationale, Fonds Lat. 6235). A fourteenth-century copy of this revised text came to light in an historical compendium, which was lot 31 in the Sotheby's sale of Western Manuscripts on 3 December 2008. It is now in the National Library of Denmark (their Acc. 2011/5).[33] Modern scholarship has detected more than a little propaganda and conscious distortion in its retelling of events, intended to justify Emma's position, further her agendas and glorify her, but it remains an extremely valuable near-contemporary narrative if handled carefully.[34]

Contemporary writs and charters provide invaluable snapshots of gifts from the royal court and other elites to a range of benefactors, or the involvement of these elites as judges in other transactions or disputes. Writs are commonly in the vernacular and carry direct orders in the form of an administrative letter, while charters of this period are principally in Latin and acknowledge or ratify grants or agreements.[35] Apart from the record of the transfer of land or privileges concerned in the main text, these are of greatest use for our purposes for their witness-lists. The documents may well be in some cases a composition

---

[32] A reproduction of this opening of the volume is given in this book.

[33] Sotheby's, London, sale catalogue for 3 December 2008, lot 31, the variant text subsequently published by me as 'A Newly Emergent' and again with a parallel text and translation by Keynes and Love as part of 'Earl Godwine's Ship'. The manuscript has been digitized by the National Library of Denmark at: http://www.kb.dk/da/nb/materialer/haandskrifter/HA/e-mss/acc-2011_5.html

[34] Stenton called it 'completely unreliable on points of fact' (*Anglo-Saxon England*, p. 697), and a wealth of studies on it and its purposes have followed. See Gransden, *Historical Writing*, pp. 56–60, Körner, *Battle of Hastings*, pp. 47–74, Campbell, 'The *Encomium Emmae*', John, 'The *Encomium Emmae*', Keynes, introduction to 1998 reprint of edition of text, pp. [lxvi]–[lxxi] as examples.

[35] The writs were collected and edited by Harmer, *Anglo-Saxon Writs*, in 1952.

in whole or part of the receiving party, written once he had returned home as a memory of the oral gift by the king; however, they are often provided with lists of witnesses, who are cited according to their social grouping, and could be summoned later to verify the facts. Keynes has shown that regular patterns can be perceived within this body of names from charters deriving from meetings and archives held at different sites and dates, and that the names at the heads of these columns of attestations must have been men who surrounded the king, with the order in which they appear marking their status within that group.[36] The rise and fall of these men within this relative scale can on occasion also be charted alongside their changing fortunes in the narrative sources, and thus their occurrence and relative position over time can indicate their waxing and waning influence at court. The number of surviving charters for Cnut's reign is not large: some thirty-six charters and eight writs, of which seven are most probably later forgeries and nearly half are suspect. The charters were catalogued and organized by Sawyer in 1968, and that work has been substantially revised and published online as the *Electronic Sawyer*.[37] Since 1973 the charters of individual archives have been edited and published as monographs by the British Academy. A concordance of the documents and the relevant editions in this series can be found at the end of this volume, in Appendix II, listing older alternative publications where the archive concerned has not yet been edited and published. References here to such documents are made to the individual documents by an 'S.' and their relevant Sawyer number.

The royal lawcodes promulgated by Cnut in 1018 at Oxford and again c. 1020 in a religious code (I Cnut) and a secular code (II Cnut) are of great importance for our purpose, but the nature of their survival

---

[36] The extensive debate on this matter has been summarized and discussed by Keynes, *The Diplomas*, pp. 14–83, especially 39–79, as a prologue to his own case study of the charters of Æthelred. However, also note Lawson's remarks in his *Cnut*, pp. 65–71, and the study by Snook, *The Anglo-Saxon Chancery*.

[37] P. H. Sawyer, *Anglo-Saxon Charters*; the online extension of this publication can be accessed at: http://www.esawyer.org.uk/about/index.html

makes them complex sources.[38] Their contents appear to come straight
from the monarch himself, giving us a true voice of his wishes within
the English administration. However, as both Patrick Wormald and
Lawson have reminded us, this initial impression is quite far from the
mark.[39] The survival of numerous versions of one of Æthelred's codes,
that for Enham promulgated in 1008, and the differences between
them, is a stark reminder that the law in late Anglo-Saxon England
probably still lay fundamentally in the oral pronouncements of the
king. What we have today are to some unknown degree 'clerical fanta-
sies . . . influenced by the special preoccupation of his [the king's] servants, as well as the carelessness of their scribes'.[40] They must be generally
true to what was promulgated by the king, but many of the written
records that survive may have been committed to writing as notes for
only one individual or an interested group at the assembly. The fact that
Archbishop Wulfstan of York, who was responsible for most of the
material in question here, freely made alterations to these texts later,
perhaps for use in preaching, is a sobering thought.[41] Cnut's letters to
the English were evidently promulgated publicly and thus also fall into
this category as a form of interim legislation from afar.

The letter of 1019–20, which was sent while Cnut was in Denmark,
is a text I should dearly like to place my trust in, but have problems
doing so.[42] Its principal potential inconsistency is Cnut's stated purpose
for the visit.[43] It seems a little much of Cnut to claim in this letter that

---

[38] *Die Gesetze* (Liebermann, I, pp. 278–307 and 308–71). However, that edition reduces the
1018 code to a series of textual variants of the others. Thus, see Whitelock, 'Wulfstan and
the Laws', and Kennedy, 'Cnut's Law Code' for further discussion and an edition of that
text.

[39] Wormald, 'Æthelred the Lawmaker', and Lawson, 'Archbishop Wulfstan'.

[40] Wormald, 'Æthelred the Lawmaker', p. 49.

[41] See ibid., pp. 54–5, and Lawson, 'Archbishop Wulfstan', pp. 154–5 and 159.

[42] *Die Gesetze* (Liebermann, I, pp. 273–5). The manuscript has been published in facsimile
as Barker, *The York Gospels*, fols. 158r–160v. See also Ker, 'The Handwriting of Archbishop
Wulfstan', especially pp. 330–1.

[43] I do not see the problem deduced by Lund, 'Cnut's Danish Kingdom', p. 31, and
Treharne, *Living through Conquest*, pp. 26–7, in Cnut's statement that he has gone to Denmark
to put down a threat to the English from the Danes, in which they see 'a wonderful irony'
in Treharne's words, 'when he himself brought conflict from the former to the latter'. If, as
I have argued below, one of Swen's intentions in invading England was to get it under his

he had gone to Denmark to protect the English from some threat there, and spent his money freely in pursuit of this, when in fact it is more likely that he had gone there to accept the kingship of that country for himself. What is also worrying is the context in which the letter survives. It exists in a single copy, added to the endleaves of a Gospel Book amongst three homilies concerned with the state of the perfect Christian nation, which were copied for Wulfstan onto the last leaves of that codex and annotated in a hand identified as probably his. The letter itself forms part of the homiletic set, providing an example of model Christian kingship, and was prepared for public preaching, ending in an 'AMEN'. Keynes notes that chapters 14–20 of the text (with general injunctions) are close to the material of the homilies and bear strong traces of Wulfstan's style.[44] This document is subject to the same doubts as the formal lawcodes, and the evidence of small tweaks probably made to those by Wulfstan continues to worry me (at least) about this source. Doubtless it is generally correct, and certain features such as its address firstly to Thorkell the Tall make no sense as being the additions of Wulfstan or another, but it has been used for preaching and has probably been subject to additions and contractions in order to make it fit that task.

With Cnut's letter of 1027, sent while he was on the return journey from Rome to Denmark in that year, we are perhaps on safer ground.[45] While it is subject to the same doubts we must apply to any written record of what could have been an oral proclamation, Wulfstan had died in 1023 and had no part in its survival. It survives copied in full into two Anglo-Norman chronicles, which most probably made

---

control and reduce the raiding there that had brought instability to Denmark, then Cnut going to re-establish the authority of his dynasty in Denmark did have the effect of shutting off this raiding. It is a slightly convoluted rationalization of the situation, but most probably Cnut's own. What worries me more is the failure to mention his going to receive the crown, something for which I can think of no reason for him to omit.

[44] Keynes, 'The Additions in Old English', p. 95.

[45] *Die Gesetze* (Liebermann, I, pp. 276–7).

independent use of a manuscript of it, perhaps once at Worcester.[46] John of Worcester claims that Abbot Lyfing of Tavistock brought it to England, and to this Wormald adds the suggestion that he also wrote it down.[47] If the connection to Lyfing is correct, then the fact that he was later bishop of Worcester may explain where the two later chroniclers found a copy.

There are then only sporadic and predominantly hagiographic accounts composed in the late eleventh century, some of great merit and others dubiously so, until the emergence of the Anglo-Norman historians in the early years of the twelfth century. The point at which the last survivors from pre-1066 England began to die out saw an upsurge in the collection of sources and writing of histories by Anglo-Norman ecclesiastics, such as the monks John of Worcester (once thought to have been named Florence), William of Malmesbury, Symeon of Durham, as well as an hereditary archdeacon of Huntingdon named Henry.[48] All were careful researchers, who could compare differing sources and comment on reliability, but who to a greater or lesser extent saw history as an instructive series of stories that could aid their fellow man and so must be read with a note of caution. John of Worcester is the source we shall deal with most closely here, and it is clear that he managed to collect a substantial amount of information and copies of sources in preparation for the writing of his text, some of which no longer survive. His statements, even when independent of other sources, should be considered seriously.

---

[46] It survives in John of Worcester, *Chronicon*, s.a. 1031 (Darlington and McGurk, p. 512), and William of Malmesbury, *Gesta Regum Anglorum*, II: 183 (Mynors, Thomson and Winterbottom, I, pp. 324–8). See Brett, 'John of Worcester', pp. 113–17, on their independence from each other and separate use of sources.

[47] John of Worcester, *Chronicon*, s.a. 1031 (Darlington and McGurk, p. 512); Wormald, *The Making of English Law*, p. 348.

[48] John of Worcester, *Chronicon*, edited by Darlington and McGurk; William of Malmesbury, *Gesta Regum Anglorum*, edited by Mynors, Thomson and Winterbottom, Simeon's work edited in *Symeonis Monachi Opera Omnia* by Arnold, and Henry of Huntingdon, *Historia Anglorum*, edited by Greenway. See also Brett, 'John of Worcester', Thomson, *William of Malmesbury*, and Hunter Blair, 'Some Observations on the "*Historia Regum*"'.

In Scandinavia, the only substantial early narrative source is the late eleventh-century German chronicler Adam of Bremen, who in his history of the archbishops of his own see of Hamburg-Bremen made great mention of Scandinavia and eastern Europe as ecclesiastical subsidiaries to that see. Adam's own words show that he had come to Hamburg in the twenty-fourth year of Archbishop Adalbert (May 1066–April 1067), and he appears to have witnessed a charter of 1069 as master of the school there.[49] Parts of Book Two were written while Swen Estrithsson was alive (d. 1076), but others referred to the king as 'ever to be remembered', and the epilogue makes note of Liemar's mediation in the Saxon war of 1075.[50] Adam's primary aim was to establish the greatness of his see and its ecclesiastical rule over northern and eastern neighbours, as opposed to claims of other missionary sees, such as Cologne, and much material here was adapted to fit with this agenda. His sources were drawn from a wide variety of texts and libraries, with his extensive use of Tacitus' *Germania* arguing for his travelling to Fulda to consult the single manuscript of this text that appears to have survived into the Middle Ages.[51] As such, Adam's work is often a dense literary tissue of oral reports and patched-together written accounts, and it demands extremely sensitive handling. One particularly contentious point is the large number of brief marginal additions that are associated with the text, named *scholia* (sg. *scholion*) by modern scholars, and which contain much additional historical information. However, while many of these can be shown to be connected with the text at an early stage in which Adam or his associates may have written them, other *scholia* cannot, and do not appear in any manuscript until the thirteenth century or later. These were the subject of a study by me

---

[49] Schmeidler's introduction to his edition of this source, pp. lii–liii.

[50] Ibid., pp. lxv–lxvi, but note that Schmeidler (and others following him) have the crucial year of Swen's death wrongly as 1074. He was still alive in April 1075, and most probably died in 1076. See my 'Was the Family', p. 52, n. 27, on this.

[51] See Reynolds, *Texts and Transmissions*, pp. 410–11, on the manuscript tradition of Tacitus' *Germania*, and my 'A Textual-Historical Response' on Adam's dependence on this source as well as Orosius.

some years ago, and alongside a re-examination of the manuscript stemma they will be the subject of a future publication of mine for an international research group currently working on this text.[52] Here I shall give reference to such *scholia* with a statement of the likelihood that they were part of the early tradition, and the earliest dated occurrence of the addition.

An important primary source for both Scandinavia and England during Cnut's reign is skaldic verse. These are praise poems composed for a Scandinavian ruler, which primarily extol his manly virtues and laud his acts of violence, successes over his enemies, and ability to distribute treasure to his followers. They are set in a series of strict metres and linguistically encoded in an intricate and complex fashion that replaces crucial nouns with kennings (sets of words intended to poetically allude to the original subject, such as 'long-planked reindeer of the bench of Solsi [= a sea-king]', i.e. 'ship'), while breaking up normal word order and even subdividing certain words and placing their composite parts in separate places in the stanza in order to obscure the word's true meaning.[53] When explained, I have found that this seemingly obtuse art form most often reminds the casual modern reader of cryptic crossword puzzles. Internal references to recital before patrons make it clear that such verses were composed orally in order to be recited before a Scandinavian patron in the hope of reward, but they now almost exclusively survive as single verses cited as sources within the later saga-narratives from the late twelfth century onwards.[54] The complex form of such verse, in that one cannot easily replace single words or phrases without upsetting the metre or rendering the rest of the verse unreadable, ensures that what survives from the eleventh

---

[52] The paper written some years ago, but still forthcoming, is Bolton, 'Preliminary Investigations into the Scholia of Adam of Bremen's *Gesta Hammaburgensis ecclesiae pontificum*'.

[53] This kenning from Hallvarðr Háreksblesi, *Knútsdrápa*, edited in *Poetry from Treatises on Poetics*, in Gade and Marold (eds.), *Skaldic Poetry of the Scandinavian Middle Ages*, forthcoming.

[54] On the evidence for their recital before patrons, see below at pp. 177–8.

century copied into later narrative sources did so in a more fossilized form than that expected of free prose or verse. As scholarship of the last few decades has noted, whereas some individual verses or clusters of them must be fabrications by the authors of the sagas in order to support their narratives, those that are preserved in King's Sagas or treatises on poetry or grammar, and stated there to be by known authors and perhaps also from named poems, appeal to a collective knowledge of the poem in that text's readership and are thus unlikely to be inventions.[55]

Further linguistic analysis has shored up this position, showing that amongst other aspects, some of the verses composed for Cnut show the influence of Anglo-Saxon and use loanwords from that language, most probably reflecting the *patois*-like language of an Anglo-Scandinavian elite who had been resident partly in England for some time.[56] Russell Poole has even made a tentative argument for *Liðsmannaflokkr's* use of a word that has no surviving example or trace in West Norse (Icelandic and Norwegian), as perhaps indicating the poem was composed by East Norse (Danish and Swedish) speakers.[57] No such poem for the eleventh century survives complete in any saga source, and these poems mostly survive as isolated snippets of verse, often in various later 'host' texts. These have then subsequently been arranged into skeletal remains of the lost poems by modern scholarship.[58] Their complexity, the potential for literary hyperbole by their composers, the range of subsequent modern reinterpretations of their meanings, and their survival within the late and suspect saga sources, kept historians from doing much

[55] See Foote, 'Wrecks and Rhymes', Frank, 'King Cnut', Poole, 'Skaldic Verse and Anglo-Saxon History', and Jesch, 'History in the Political Sagas'.

[56] See Hofmann, *Nordisch-Englische Lehnbeziehungen*, pp. 59–100, and Frank, 'King Cnut', p. 108. Also Poole, 'Skaldic Verse and Anglo-Saxon History', pp. 284–5, and Fidjestøl, *Det Norrøne Fyrstediktet*.

[57] Poole, 'Skaldic Verse and Anglo-Saxon History', p. 286.

[58] The surviving material was arranged and edited first by Finnur Jónsson, *Den Norsk-Islandske Skjaldedigtning*, in 1912–15, and later rearranged and republished by Kock, *Den Norsk-Isländska Skjaldediktningen*, in 1949. See below, n. 65, for details of the recent re-edition of the last few years.

more than occasionally citing them until the last few decades, but they
have been experiencing a renaissance of interest since then.[59]

A recent international project culminating in the re-editing and
re-publication of the verses with modern English translations and
extensive textual appendices does break up the flow of the verse for the
modern reader, but this drawback is far outweighed by their new avail-
ability in a definitive and scholarly format for the English-reading
public, and it is to be expected that future studies and uses of these
verses will experience a boom in interest through these recent publications.[60] Here I have cited these publications by their general editors
(those relevant here: Whaley, Gade and Marold), but in fact the majority
of relevant verse has been edited by Poole (the anonymous
Liðsmannaflokkr), Matthew Townend (almost the entire corpus of poems
for Cnut or his son Swen: Óttarr Svarti's *Knútsdrápa*; Sigvatr Þórðarson's
Knútsdrápa; Þórarinn Loftunga's *Höfuðlausn* and *Tøgdrápa*; Hallvarðr
Hárekblesi's *Knútsdrápa*; and perhaps a fragment of a verse by Arnórr
Jarlaskáld), Jayne Carroll (Þórðr Kolbeinsson's *Eiríksdrápa*) and Judith
Jesch (Sigvatr Þórðarson's *Vestrfararvísur*). Where such verse has been
used by historians this has principally been as a record when they note
an event or person in passing, but some scholars are now beginning to
employ tools developed by literary studies to use poems as indicators of

[59] Lawson, *Cnut*, offers an example of this cautious use of skaldic verse by historians, in
that he cites it very sparingly (only on pp. 7, 26, 74–5, 79, 97–8 and 100; in which those on
pp. 74–9 are part of a section discussing the available sources), and usually only in passing
for its stray historical facts. An early and notable exception to this traditional view of skaldic
verse can be found in Campbell, who had sufficient linguistic skills to master skaldic verse,
leading to his integrated use of these verses alongside other sources in his appendices to his
1949 edition of the *Encomium Emmae* (see pp. 66–87), and his *Skaldic Verse and Anglo-Saxon
History*. The scholarship listed here in the preceding notes as well as Townend,
'Contextualising', attests to the recent renaissance.

[60] The recent project to edit the corpus of extant material has an electronic base at:
http://www.abdn.ac.uk/skaldic/db.php. The publications most relevant for our purposes
already in print are Whaley, *Poetry from the King's Sagas*, 1, and Gade, *Poetry from the King's
Sagas*, 2. I would like to thank Tarrin Wills and other members of the project for making
Hallvarðr Hárekblesi's poem on Cnut from the forthcoming volume in the series, *Poetry from
Treatises on Poetics*, available to me in proof format.

how a ruler wished to be seen by his peers and the ideologies underpinning his rule.[61]

Runic inscriptions on monumental stones provide some information about Scandinavia in the tenth and eleventh centuries, either through their content (as in the Jelling runestones), or through the mapping of their distribution or features on them. However, such inscriptions are necessarily brief, and frequently their content and the meaning of their distribution can be so vague as to be open to being used to draw quite opposing conclusions.[62] I shall refer to the *Danmarks Runeindskrifter* catalogue of Jacobsen and Moltke where these occur in the text, in the abbreviated form 'DR.' followed by a reference number.

The twelfth century saw the emergence of the earliest surviving narrative histories from Scandinavia, with Theodoricus Monachus' *Historia de Antiquitate Regum Norwagiensium* in the decade 1177–87, and the anonymous *Ágrip af Nóregskonungasǫgum*, most probably based in part on Theodoricus' work and thus dated c. 1190.[63] Both are Norwegian narratives, and quite terse in comparison to later saga materials. The majority of these sources, like the longer saga narratives in the *Legendary Saga of St. Óláfr* and Snorri Sturluson's vast compendium *Heimskringla* that followed in the next half century, are focused on events in Norway and Iceland, with only passing reference to Danish affairs. However, there seems to have been significant interest in Danish history in the entourages of six Icelandic bishops in the twelfth century (three from Hólar and three from Skálaholt), who received consecration in Lund, where a substantial historical school had sprung up in that century.[64] The first,

[61] See Frank, 'King Cnut', and Bolton, *Empire*, pp. 289–95.
[62] See Bolton, *Empire*, pp. 189 and 229–30.
[63] Theodoricus Monachus, *Historia de Antiquitate*, edited by Storm, and *Ágrip af Nóregskonungasǫgum*, edited by Driscoll. There is also a sound discussion of these late narrative Scandinavian sources in Sawyer and Sawyer, 'Adam and Eve'.
[64] On this see Bjarni Guðnason's introduction to his *Danakonunga Sǫgur*, and his *Um Skjöldungasögu*. An excellent study in English is Guðrún Nordal, *Tools of Literacy*, pp. 309–38. The school at Lund would produce annalists as well as the historians Sven Aggeson and Saxo Grammaticus in this period, who both refer to and use skaldic verse and Old Norse narrative material. See Mortensen, 'The Nordic Archbishoprics as Literary Centres', on this aspect of Lund under Archbishop Absalon.

Jón Qgmundarsson, brought two teachers back with him to teach grammar and chant at his new school at Hólar.[65] Another, Páll Jónsson of Oddi, bishop of Skálaholt between 1195 and 1211, and it was on his family estate at Oddi that Snorri spent his formative years. The fact that Snorri's family set out their genealogical origins in the Skjöldungar, Cnut's line, in the Uppsala manuscript of the *Snorra Edda*, may point towards the motivation for their interest.[66] This interest produced not only the more consciously historical *Knytlinga saga*, which may or may not have used a lost *Knúts saga ríka*, but also the wild semi-legendary texts of *Jómsvíkinga saga* and *Skjöldunga saga*.[67] It bears noting that the interest of the Icelanders was not exclusively aimed at Norway.

The problems of using the saga narratives of the thirteenth century for the history of the eleventh century were foregrounded in Sweden by the campaign of the Weibull brothers: Lauritz Weibull in 1911 with his *Kritiska Undersökningar i Nordens Historia omkring År 1000*, and Curt Weibull in 1915 with his *Saxo: Kritiska Undersökningar i Danmarks Historia från Sven Estridsens Död till Knut VI*, to bring the more precise approach to historical sources of Leopold von Ranke to Scandinavian history. They were followed in Norway by Halvdan Koht in 1914 with his 'Sagaernes Opfatning av vor Gamle Historie', and their arguments have been rehearsed and augmented ever since.[68] In essence, the late date of these late twelfth- and thirteenth-century narratives makes significant parts of their record of events and especially the interpretations of these events suspect; and where records were wanting in the late twelfth and thirteenth centuries, invention was evidently often used to fill the gap, leaving us with sources which are demonstrably as much invention as they are historical record. However, the last few years have seen a

---

[65] On this specifically, see Bjarni Guðnason's introduction to his *Danakonunga Sǫgur* and Guðrún Nordal, *Tools of Literacy*, p. 310.

[66] Uppsala, De la Gardie, MS. 11 4to; see also Guðrún Nordal, *Tools of Literacy*, pp. 124–6.

[67] The fundamental work on this putative lost *Knúts saga* is that of Bjarni Guðnason in the introduction to his edition of *Knytlinga saga* for the Íslenzk Fornrit series in 1982 (in Icelandic). The best discussion in English remains that of Campbell, 'Knúts saga', with brief comment by Poole, *Viking Poems*, pp. 91, 94 and 97.

[68] See Lindkvist, 'Early Political Organisation (a) Introductory Survey', pp. 161–3.

pushing back by modern scholars such as Michael Gelting, Jón Viðar Sigurðsson and myself against the harsh and uneven source criticism of the Weibulls, and we seem to be entering a period in which the total writing-off of these sources is to be replaced with careful and sensitive use of the aspects of them that we can show to be trustworthy.[69]

This is of especial relevance to Cnut as such studies have yet to make their mark in English or amongst scholars of Cnut's activities in England. Ann Williams represents the case for the traditional group well, when in the last part of her paper on Thorkell the Tall she uses quite reasonable doubt about the reliability of the literary and late *Jómsvíkinga saga* to erase any link between what the English and Scandinavian sources say about Thorkell, writing off all such Scandinavian sources in the process – one with a flourish 'the less said the better'.[70] I cannot bring myself to agree. Certainly we should, as she urges, 'pay more attention to contemporary sources and . . . mistrust anything which cannot be corroborated', but if we wish to be comprehensive in our view of Cnut we have a responsibility to take in as many sources as possible and see what can be done with them.[71] To ignore our Scandinavian sources risks diverting our attention towards only the English part of his realms. While such sources should not be approached lightly, that does not mean we should throw out the baby with the bath-water. The scholar who attempts to use these must strive to understand such sources within their own context first, in order to identify their potential weaknesses, and then employ very careful handling and weighing up to see what they contain that might be of value.

The problem for most modern scholars with accepting these sources as something we might engage with, and see whether they hold weight, is perhaps based on a focus on the surviving sagas. If in trying to say

---

[69] For a recent and inspiring criticism of the Weibulls' approach see Gelting, 'Uløste Opgaver' (with English summary), the same author's 'Saxo Grammaticus in the Archives' and 'Forholdet mellem Liber Daticus og Memoriale Fratrum'. See also Jón Viðar Sigurðsson, 'Tendencies in the Historiography'.

[70] Williams, 'Thorkell the Tall', pp. 151–2.

[71] Ibid., p. 152.

something of the events of the eleventh century, for example, we jump
straight from the contemporary record of the reconstructed skaldic
verse to *Heimskringla*, the best known of the Old Norse thirteenth-
century Kings' Sagas, it is clear that two centuries of storytelling are
missing and a vast break is implied, after which authors might reasonably have filled in many holes with invention. However, this was not the
vantage point of those who wrote the narratives of the late twelfth or
thirteenth centuries. Theodoricus Monachus makes his sources explicit
in his prologue, and implies them at several stages of his narrative. First
he notes that skaldic verse (his 'ancient poems' of the Icelanders) was
his principal source. His comment that his narrative is based on what he
learnt from others – 'audita non visa' ('things not seen but heard') – has
caused much distraction, and an overly literal translation of this phrase
has led in the past to the idea that he was working primarily from oral
material.[72] However, a wide survey of the use of this phrase in medieval
Latin authors finds it often employed to indicate written sources which
the author had 'heard' or learnt from, marking only that the author was
not alive when the events happened, and there are other indications
that lost written material was at his disposal.[73] He notes a written king
list (*catalogus regum norwagiensium*) in the context of his history of Cnut,
and crucially abstains from telling much of the history of St Óláfr
(Cnut's rival in Norway), 'because all these things have been recorded
by several [others]' (presumably in hagiographical accounts).[74] Scholarly
consensus now accepts the widespread use of skaldic verse by the
authors of the Kings' Sagas (and, indeed, many sagas make this clear
with numerous inclusions of such verses as evidence to support their

[72] Theodoricus Monachus, *Historia de Antiquitate*, prologue 9–13 (Storm, p. 3). The misun-
derstanding of 'audita non visa' begins in earnest with the work of Ellehøj, *Studier over den
ældste*, and in response to this Bjarni Guðnason, 'Theodoricus og íslenskir Sagnaritarar',
Gudrun Lange, *Die Anfänge*, and Foote's introduction to McDougall, McDougall and Foote,
Theodoricus Monachus, pp. xiii–xxiii.

[73] See McDougall, McDougall and Foote, *Theodoricus Monachus*, pp. 56–7, n. 11, for a
survey.

[74] Theodoricus Monachus, *Historia de Antiquitate*, 20:53–4; 20:35–45 (Storm, pp. 44 and
43). For discussion of the *catalogus*, see McDougall, McDougall and Foote, *Theodoricus
Monachus*, pp. 92–3, n. 214.

narrative), but little is said about other, most probably written, sources available in the late twelfth or thirteenth centuries. Elsewhere I have written about the repealing of legal clauses by Norwegian kings of the mid- to late eleventh and twelfth centuries, which adds considerable support to the potential veracity of taxes and exactions by Cnut from the Norwegians as recorded by *Ágrip* and *Heimskringla*.[75] The repeals at least must have been in a written form within decades of Cnut's death, and most probably in the second half of the eleventh century. I have also postulated the existence of a now-lost hagiographical source on the death of St Óláfr by comparing the lists of names of those Norwegians involved in his death in the earliest Norwegian and Icelandic narratives.[76] Such a source must have pre-dated Theodoricus' work, and may have been the hagiographical work to which he obliquely alludes. A single leaf from an Old Norse hagiographical collection that included material on St Óláfr's miracles, dating to c. 1155×1165, survives in Copenhagen (A. M. MS. 325 v α 4to), and John of Worcester seems to have known of hagiographical traditions connected with Óláfr in the 1130s, which pre-date the earliest foundations of Norwegian monasteries by monks from northern English houses in the 1140s and following decades. More such fragments remain to be teased from the later narratives. It is clear that neither Theodoricus, the author of *Ágrip*, or any of the saga-authors who followed in the next half century, worked from skaldic verse and oral history alone, and they used material that can occasionally be traced back into the eleventh century or the first half of the twelfth century. Such material was probably never extensive, but any tiny threads that can be argued as having a probable basis in fact add much to the near vacuum of our knowledge of Cnut's activities in Scandinavia. Rather than take a Weibullian approach, and uniformly cast out all such material, I would argue instead for a calm consideration of it to see which parts might plausibly bear weight. There is no

---

[75] See Bolton, *Empire*, pp. 276–85.
[76] Ibid., pp. 252–62.

apparent simple and comprehensive methodology of working with
such sources, and all such material must be presumed guilty until proven
(or at least reasonably argued) innocent. However, the focus on individual aspects of the narratives, and use of comparisons between them
and across all other supporting Scandinavian sources, can produce
(after an often arduous and hard-fought uphill struggle) probable new
lights on the eleventh century. On a small number of occasions saga
material includes the only extant reference to an event that seems plausible. These are included here with the proper caveats.

Archaeology and numismatics have an important role to play in our
assessment of England, and a crucial role to play in Denmark in the
absence of written sources. The foundation and extension of urban
sites in Denmark by Cnut and his predecessors, as well as royal mints,
allow us to determine much from the survival of individual artefacts –
such as a pen-case lid of apparent English manufacture, with the name
'Leofwine' carved into it, in layers of Lund dated to the years of Cnut's
and Harthacnut's rule – as well as wide comparative surveys of the
data.[77] Traditionally archaeology has taken a *longue durée* approach to
medieval studies, and has problems focusing on the reigns of individual
rulers. However, the fact that Cnut and his predecessors chose to found
their own urban centres often on virgin sites, and to produce their own
coinage (as opposed to copies of English or German models), enables
us to distinguish such trends at their point of origin more easily than if
they had existed within a longer tradition. The research that led up to
the Middelalderbyen project in Denmark (monographs on each town,
published from 1985 to 1992) added greatly to this, supplementing individual publications on excavations of urban sites, churches and coin
hoards.[78] Of particular interest are the micro-level archaeological
methods used in the most recent excavations at Viborg, which, while
time-consuming and expensive, allowed the dating to seasons within

---

[77] For the pen-case lid, see pp. 142–3 below. The urban sites in Denmark are discussed
below at pp. 47–9.
[78] See references to this project at: http://dendigitalebyport.byhistorie.dk/medieval/

individual years of floor layers within a building apparently used by royal officials.[79]

Some of these sources lend themselves to working together, and some do not. Several, such as the more literary applications of skaldic verse and archaeological materials, must often be employed on their own, and the conclusions reached be set within the context of other conclusions from different sources and weighed up there for what they add to and what they change about our perceptions of the past.

[79] The results of this can be consulted in Iversen et al., *Viborg Søndersø 1018–1030*.

Chapter 1

CNUT'S CHILDHOOD AND YOUTH
THE BEGINNINGS OF A CONQUEROR

This area of Cnut's life has the least solid evidence for it, and almost all modern historians have shied away from it. Little can be known with certainty of Cnut's acts or whereabouts before he arrived in England as part of his father's invasion force in 1013, but these years were formative. What can be said points to the fundamental forces that drove him throughout the rest of his life.

We can make some comment about the country into which Cnut was born. Denmark in the late Viking Age was formed of three landmasses arranged in a horizontal band across southern Scandinavia: the Jutland peninsula in the west formed from a northwards extension of the coastline of mainland Europe, with the islands of Funen and Sjælland to its east, the latter forming the central landmass of the region, and Skåne (a promotory of the Swedish landmass and now a region of southern Sweden) to the far east. It was a profoundly agrarian society, with the vast majority of the population based on rural estates.[1] Economic life revolved around agricultural production, fishing and trade, with viking raiding in England and the Baltic bringing occasional windfalls to local elite-groups and economies. Christianity was a recent imposition on some of the elites by a number of German missions from various centres, and what urban centres were functioning had only been doing so for a short time. There was little writing, apart from runic inscriptions

[1] For the best general discussion of Denmark in this period, see Roesdahl, *Viking Age Denmark*, and her references there.

28

(both monumental on large erected stones, and on more mundane objects such as spoons or runesticks) and apparently no governmental bureaucracy or written lawcodes. What coins there were that had been struck locally were limited in number and probably used more as emblems than as currency (a small number were struck c. 995–c. 997 for Cnut's father, with perhaps other scattered examples of earlier coins from the reign of his grandfather if these can be securely localized to Hedeby-Schleswig). These mostly copied the models of Denmark's better politically organized neighbours.

Political structures appear to have been near-bewilderingly complex and profoundly decentralized, and as they loomed so large in the life of a man who would one day be king of Denmark, they deserve special mention here.[2] While foreign sources occasionally refer to 'the king of Denmark' in the eighth, ninth and tenth centuries, modern scholarship has deduced that these were usually references to only one of many contemporary rulers.[3] Attempts have been made to see these recorded 'kings' as the overlords of many other petty-kings and nobles within some form of social structure, but such attempts are based on little evidence, and it seems more likely that this society was far from stable and organized.[4] Little can be known with certainty, but the picture that emerges in the briefest of thumbnail sketches is of a society composed of many different types of group (predominantly geographical), ruled over by leaders with a wide variety of titles without any apparent arrangement of these titles and the roles their holders held in a neat and ordered system. These were most probably distinguished from each other primarily by their military might, political influence and access to natural resources, and formed ad hoc alliances or competed with each other according to individual, local or dynastic reasons. There is no consensus even on the titles of the highest office-holders in this system.

[2] See ibid., Sawyer and Sawyer, 'A Gormless Dynasty', and Maund, '"A Turmoil of Warring Princes"'.
[3] See in particular Maund, '"A Turmoil of Warring Princes"'.
[4] Ibid., p. 32.

The term *konungr* (the cognate for Anglo-Saxon *kyning* = king) was used
to describe the petty-king *Sigerich/Sigtrigg*, whose family held power in
the Hedeby-Schleswig region before the arrival of Cnut's dynasty, as
well as Cnut's own grandfather on the Jelling runestones. In skaldic verse
it was also used for Norwegian and Swedish rulers who held royal power
contemporary with Cnut. Yet this term was actively avoided by poets
when addressing Cnut.[5] The overall rulers of Western Norway in the
tenth and early eleventh centuries used the term *jarl* (a cognate of 'earl',
an important but subordinate figure to the king in later Scandinavian
sources) as their title, despite wielding royal authority and claiming in
skaldic verse to rule over sixteen others in Norway with the same title.[6]
However, while we would wish to know more about their motives for
doing so, explanations of these are recorded only in late sources and
must be taken with a large pinch of salt.[7] The choice of title by each
ruler with apparent royal power seems to have been guided by tradition,
ethnic boundaries, or perhaps even to set themselves apart from other
dynasties. It is likely that this disorganization continued down throughout
the social strata. Moreover, as Peter Sawyer has noted when addressing
the same question, it is revealing that in the late ninth century, Norwegian
exiles brought to Iceland a pattern of government based on varying
numbers of lords or chieftains of significantly differing levels of power
and influence, but referred to by a single uniform title (*goðar*).[8] However,
to search for this title in Scandinavia outside of Iceland is a nearly fruit-
less exercise, and intriguingly it is found only on three tenth-century

---

[5] As noted by Frank, 'When Poets Address Princes', pp. 193–4. This would seem to have
been a political decision, probably intended to set Cnut apart from his Norwegian
and Swedish contemporaries, but it lays bare the fluidity of such titles. Cnut clearly
did not need to be called *konungr* by his skalds, and suffered no apparent
reputational damage from the absence of the term. The relevant *Sigerich/Sigtrigg* runestone
is DR. 4.

[6] For these Jarls of Hlaðir, see pp. 74–5 below and the references there. The claim to rule
over sixteen other jarls is found in the skaldic poem *Vellelkla*, verse 32 (Whaley, p. 323) by
Einarr skálaglamm.

[7] See *Ágrip af Nóregskonungasǫgum*, ch. 11 (Driscoll, p. 20), and references there to a twelfth-
century discussion of this dynasty's adherence to the title 'jarl'.

[8] P. H. Sawyer, 'Cnut's Scandinavian Empire', p. 10.

runestones from the Danish island of Funen.[9] Unfortunately, rulership titles on runestones in general are few and far between, and beyond *konungr* and *jarl* they reveal more local variations than Scandinavian-wide agreements, while skaldic verse alike resists attempts to use it constructively to address this question. Other titles denoting some form of ruling authority survive sporadically in the sources, such as that of the *holdr*, but what we might learn from them remains tentative and isolated. This last title was given in northern English sources to a Scandinavian, or at least Scandinavian-descended, leader named Thurbrand, and is also attested in the Anglo-Saxon Chronicle for the leaders of certain viking armies.[10] We also might suspect that some similar title or leadership role stands behind the strange title 'princeps regis' given to the Halfdan who appears above all other secular witnesses after Cnut in a document claiming to be a record of Cnut's confirmation of privileges for the monastery of Christ Church, Canterbury, in 1018.[11] However, those suspicions remain just that.

We can, however, comment on the general nature of this system in which Cnut grew up, as well as on some of its strengths and weaknesses. This disorganized form of political structure was dynamic and thus overall robust, guaranteeing that the strongest and best connected candidates for rule held power at any time. It enabled great social mobility, allowing successful and resourceful individuals to surge up through its ranks. However, it also promoted rivalry and conflict, especially in a society in which raiding and conflict played such key roles.

In addition, some details of Cnut's year of birth and his immediate family can be teased from the sources. The skaldic poet Óttarr svarti notes Cnut's youth ('you launched ships forward at no great age') when describing his initial military conflicts, presumably either the English

[9] DR. 190, 192 and 209.

[10] See Bolton, *Empire*, p. 114, for Thurbrand's title. ASC 904 A (Bately, p. 63) records the existence of a Hold Ysopa and a Hold Oscytel as well as 'their king Eohric' at the head of viking armies. It is worth noting that this term is not recorded anywhere in the runic corpus.

[11] Keynes, 'Cnut's Earls', p. 62, and Bolton, *Empire*, pp. 19 and 17.

campaigns of 1013–14 or 1015–16, and suggests that he was the youngest leader of that campaign ('no ruler younger than you went from home'); thus he was probably born in the decade immediately before 1000.[12] His father was Swen 'Forkbeard', the king of Denmark, and his mother is described by the contemporary German chronicler Thietmar of Merseburg as an unnamed sister of King Bolesław I Chrobry of Poland, the head of the Piast dynasty there.[13] Thietmar goes on to note that this anonymous sister had already been married to Erik 'the Victorious' of Sweden (d. before 995), before marrying Swen and giving him two sons named Cnut and Harald. Adam of Bremen confirms this, noting in his main text that Swen did marry Erik's widow and that Cnut was their son, and adding in a *scholion* that Erik did marry a sister or daughter of Bolesław Chrobry.[14] Some later Scandinavian sources name her as Sigrið stórráða (the haughty), but we can probably set aside the developments there as the product of artistic licence.[15] Swen may already have had a daughter named Gytha, who must have been born about 980, as she later married Jarl Eiríkr Hákonarson of Hlaðir (perhaps c. 997) and was the mother of his son Hákon who himself witnessed Cnut's charters in England from 1019 onwards.[16] Cnut and Harald had a full sister named Estrith, and both sisters later became instrumental in forging alliances with other ruling dynasties through

---

[12] Óttarr svarti, *Knútsdrápa*, verse 1 (Whaley, p. 769). New discussion of the marriages attested in our narrative sources by Lund opens the possibility that Cnut could be a decade older than thought (Lund, 'Svend Estridsens Blodskam'). However, this flies in the face of the contemporary statements of skaldic verse.

[13] Thietmar, *Chronicon*, VII:39(28) (Holtzman, p. 446).

[14] Adam of Bremen, *Gesta*, scholion 24(25) (Schmeidler, p. 95). Note that this is an addition to Adam's text which I have identified as not of a form indicating that it was part of the earliest reconstructable manuscript witness to the text, and thus is probably not the work of Adam or contributors who worked with him (see my forthcoming 'Preliminary Investigations into the Scholia of Adam of Bremen's *Gesta Hammaburgensis ecclesiae pontificum*'). It is first attested in a manuscript of the late thirteenth century (Copenhagen, Royal Library, GKS MS. 2296).

[15] For the fundamental discussion of these later accretions see Weibull, *Kritiska Undersökningar*, pp. 106–10.

[16] Lund, 'Cnut's Danish Kingdom', p. 27, and P. H. Sawyer, 'Swein Forkbeard and the Historians', pp. 27–40.

marriages (in Estrith's case several times).[17] In addition to these, the *Liber Vitae* of New Minster, Winchester, records a noblewoman with the garbled name *Santslave* as 'sister of Cnut, our king'. It has been suggested that this strange name was written by an English scribe trying to convey the Polish name Świętosława, which was common amongst members of the Piast dynasty.[18] She may, or may not, have been the unnamed daughter of Swen whom John of Worcester records as married to an equally garbled King *Wyrtgeorn* of the Wends.[19] A final anonymous sibling might be implied by the reference to a further dynastic link in the thirteenth-century *Chronicle of the Bishops of Ribe*, in which a contemporary Danish nobleman and bishop named Othinkar 'the younger' is described as a 'close relative of King Cnut the Old' (i.e. Cnut the Great).[20] The Latin term *nepos* for 'close relative' here is too imprecise to see how this Othinkar was related to Cnut, but most probably he or another member of his family had married into Cnut's family.

It was common for Scandinavian elites throughout this period to form liaisons between elite men and women which, while socially

---

[17] For Estrith see Adam of Bremen, *Gesta* II:54(52) (Schmeidler, p. 114). There Adam records that Estrith (under the name of Margaret in the main text, presumably a baptismal name; she is named as 'Estrid' in a *scholion*) was married to Jarl Ulf of Denmark, while Ulf's sister was married to Earl Godwine of Wessex. The main text and the following *scholion* record that she was also married to Count Richard of Normandy (II:54[52] and *scholion* 40[41] [Schmeidler, pp. 114–15], with the same problems as that discussed in n. 14 above). This is partly in error, and instead she may have married his son, Robert I of Normandy. A further *scholion* there claims yet another marriage, of her to the 'son of the king of Russia' (*scholion* 39[40]; an addition with the same problems as that discussed in n. 14 above). Campbell, following Freeman, places the order of Estrith's marriages as first to Ulf, then to Robert of Normandy, and finally to the Russian prince (*Encomium*, pp. 85–6, and this argument followed in turn by Keynes, 'Cnut's Earls', p. 73, n. 166). However, this is based on weak saga-evidence, and if the identification of the Russian as Ilja, prince of Novgorod, is correct (see below at p. 169) then that was her first marriage as he died in late 1019 or early 1020. Robert of Normandy would have been in his early twenties at this time, and may have been her next intended suitor, with her repudiation by Robert a few years later leaving her free to marry Ulf. Both marriages, to the Russian prince and the Norman duke, may have been little more than diplomatic exercises, and the parties may not have even met before the liaisons were dissolved.

[18] Gerchow, *Gedenküberlieferung*, p. 325 (entry 30). See Uspenskij, 'Dynastic Names in Medieval Scandinavia and Russia', pp. 17 and 20, for the most likely Polish name that stands behind *Santslave*. See also Hare, 'Cnut and Lotharingia', pp. 265–6, n. 23.

[19] John of Worcester, *Chronicon*, s.a. 1029 (Darlington et al., 510).

[20] *Chronicle of the Bishops of Ribe* (Jørgensen, pp. 26–7); see also Bolton, *Empire*, pp. 186–7, on this.

accepted as a full marriage and with equal status to that, could be easily dissolved should the union cease to be politically expedient.[21] The link between Swen and Gytha's mother was probably of this form. Thietmar of Merseburg states that Cnut's mother was repudiated by Swen many years before her death and returned to Poland.[22] Thus, these last siblings may be from a third and subsequent union of Swen's, or may just have been overlooked by the historical sources as their part in history was minor. The research of Jenny Jochens into the production of heirs by medieval Norwegian kings has cast a long shadow over our under-standing of the liaisons of Scandinavian kings.[23] She showed that they seem to have had sexual access to numerous women outside of marriage, often apparently at the instigation of the women or their family. As in England before the arrival of the Normans, Scandinavia had no system of primogeniture (the inheritance of the eldest son above all other claimants), and after the death of a king the crown might pass to any of his living male relatives.[24] Thus, each sexual act might produce an heir who could bring later prosperity and success to the family as a royal candidate. In general, Jochens is correct, but there is little sign of this in Swen's life.[25] It is possible that the inherent weaknesses of such a system of inheritance caused him to exert a greater degree of control than his peers in order to limit the numbers of legitimate claimants to the throne.

Whether as children or as young adults Cnut and his brother Harald appear to have stayed in Denmark when their mother returned to

---

[21] See Bolton, 'Ælfgifu of Northampton', pp. 252–8, on this distinctively Scandinavian type of medieval marriage.

[22] Thietmar, *Chronicon*, VII:39(28) (Holtzman, p. 446).

[23] Jochens, 'The Politics of Reproduction'.

[24] See ibid.

[25] Moreover, we might compare his descendant Swen Estrithsson, who ruled Denmark from the late 1040s until his death in 1076. William of Malmesbury, *Gesta Regum Anglorum*, II: 261 (Mynors, Thomson and Winterbottom, p. 480), claimed that he had fourteen sons, and Saxo Grammaticus lists twelve, while *Knytlinga saga* lists fourteen sons (and two daugh-ters), by at least five women. See below at p. 44, n. 64, for details of these. To this can be added the Helena 'known as Gunhild' recorded on the Gunhild Cross in the National Museum, Copenhagen (noted by Christiansen, *Saxo Grammaticus*, p. 232). The various tradi-tions are discussed and assessed by Christiansen, *Saxo*, II, pp. 230–2, n. 23.

Poland. It also seems likely that they were either raised in Swen's court or fostered into the courts of other Danish noblemen.[26]

We can be sure that Christianity played a significant part in court life. Adam of Bremen's history denounced Swen as a pagan, but Swen is one of the chief villains of Adam's retelling of the story, having opposed the supremacy that Adam's diocese claimed over Denmark, and is damned in his narrative for it.[27] This so-called paganism probably amounted to little more than a refusal to accept Hamburg-Bremen's brand of Christianity, twisted by Adam to infer that the rejection of the proselytizing of that see (and the political control that came with it) was a rejection of Christianity in general. The *Encomium* paints a picture of him as a spiritual man, who enjoyed an 'end much happier from both the spiritual and the worldly point of view', and who on his deathbed exhorted Cnut to exercise 'the zealous practice of Christianity' alongside matters of correct government, after which he was buried in an ecclesiastical construction of his own foundation in a sepulchre that he had prepared for himself.[28] Much of this must be laudatory hyperbole, but the audience of the *Encomium* was partly Danish, if only by recent descent, and facts such as Swen's construction of a mausoleum in a church for himself would surely have been glaring if they were total invention.

Moreover, Cnut was a Christian from birth.[29] His grandfather, Harald Gormsson, had famously converted to Christianity in 963/5, and seems to have ordered the excavation of his own father's pagan

[26] The late so-called 'Supplement to *Jómsvíkinga saga*', edited as an appendix to Campbell, *Encomium Emmae Reginae*, pp. 92–3, claims that Thorkell the Tall fostered Cnut, but this is the sole source to claim this, and as it heightens the later conflict between Cnut and Thorkell and shifts it towards a family drama, this has probably more to do with Icelandic literary themes than actual events and should be set aside.

[27] Adam of Bremen, *Gesta*, II:27 (Schmeidler, p. 87). Adam's hostility to Swen and Swen's so-called 'paganism' have been comprehensively studied by P. H. Sawyer, 'Swein Forkbeard and the Historians'.

[28] *Encomium Emmae Reginae*, I:1 and 5; II:3 (Campbell, pp. 8, 14 and 18).

[29] On the conversion of Scandinavia in general see P. H. Sawyer, 'The Process of Scandinavian Christianization', and the recent study by Winroth, *The Conversion of Scandinavia*.

grave mound, reburying him in a Christian monument at Jelling alongside runestones declaring the power and new religious affiliations of the dynasty.[30] Further echoes of Christian appropriations of earlier cult sites have also been discerned in the defacing and damaging of the remains and fabric of the Oseberg and Gokstad ship burials in the region of southern Norway most probably under Harald's command.[31] In these, dendrochronological dating of the wooden shovels and sledges left behind by the desecrators of the graves to 'not earlier than AD 953' in the case of Oseberg, and 'after AD 939' in the case of Gokstad, falls securely into his period of influence over the area. In addition, Harald was an active builder of new Christian constructions. Adam of Bremen notes that he was buried in a tomb that he had prepared for himself in a church dedicated to the Holy Trinity.[32] As noted above, Swen seems to have kept up the new religious traditions, and may even have been quite zealous in his Christian observations. Cnut was clearly baptized, and took the baptismal name of Lambert, most probably from his mother's family, the Piast dynasty of Poland, who were passionately Christian from the mid-tenth century onwards.[33]

While they are nearly invisible to us now, it also seems most probable that Cnut's Danish household had attendant priests. Adam of Bremen records that a Danish ecclesiastic with the name Tymmo (who also used the variant German name Thietmar) accompanied Cnut's daughter

[30] A wealth of literature exists on these: see Krogh, 'The Royal Viking-Age Monuments' and *Gåden om Kong Gorms Grav*; Pedersen, 'Jelling im 10. Jahrhundert'; Holst, Jessen and Pedersen, 'Runestenens Jelling'; and Holst et al., 'Kongens Gård i Jelling?'; as well as the extremely lengthy bibliography of works on Jelling published online at: http://velkom-menihistorien.dk/Sider/litteratur1.html. See also Gelting, 'Poppo's Ordeals', and p. 40–1 below.

[31] Bill and Daly, 'The Plundering of the Ship Graves'.

[32] Adam of Bremen, *Gesta*, II:28 (Schmeidler, pp. 87–8). It may have been the same construction that the *Encomium Emmae Reginae*, II:3 (Campbell, p. 18) credits to Swen, perhaps as the latter completed it or substantially added to it. See below, at pp. 48–9, for fuller disscussion.

[33] Gerchow, 'Prayers', pp. 235–6, and Hare, 'Cnut and Lotharingia', pp. 261–8.

Gunhild to Germany in 1036.[34] He was most likely her chaplain, or a royal priest serving much the same function. It is clear that he was educated for higher clerical office, since after Gunhild's untimely death he served as a royal chaplain, perhaps to the imperial house; and after the death of Bishop Godehard of Hildesheim on 5 May 1038, he was appointed as bishop there, and remained in that office until his death in 1044.[35] It seems unlikely that this figure would have been trusted with the key role of accompanying Gunhild had he only been in the service of Cnut for a few years. Tymmo's appointment as a bishop in 1038 ensures that he was born as early as 1008 (that is, the earliest point that would allow him to have been thirty years old and so permitted to take up the office), and perhaps much earlier (he appears to have died of natural causes in 1044, and thus may well have been much older). Therefore, his attachment to the Danish court would appear to pre-date Cnut's appointments of bishops in Denmark and the influx of Englishmen to Denmark, and conceivably he may have served Cnut's father and brother.

While the Danish royal family was wholeheartedly Christian, the same could not be said of the country they ruled over. There were other ecclesiastics, most probably German-trained, who operated in Denmark in the early eleventh century (such as Othinkar the elder and his nephew and namesake, Othinkar the younger), or who were members of Danish elite families but resided in Germany (Othinkar the younger had a sister named Asa who lived as a nun in Bremen).[36] These figures or their families may have been responsible for some early wooden churches in outlying areas, such as that detected by archaeology at Sebbersund on a lower arm of the Limfjord in north Jutland, which can be dated by

---

[34] Adam of Bremen, *Gesta*, II:79 (Schmeidler, p. 136). See also Olrik, 'Den Danske Biskop Tymme'.

[35] Wolfhere, *Vita Godehardi episcopi posterior*, ch. 33 (Pertz, pp. 215–16).

[36] Adam of Bremen, *Gesta*, II: 26, 36 and accompanying scholia 25(26) and 35(37) (Schmeidler, pp. 85, 96–7 and 110) (both an early part of the tradition; see my forthcoming 'Preliminary Investigations into the Scholia of Adam of Bremen's *Gesta Hammaburgensis ecclesiae pontificum*'). For Asa see ibid., scholion 45(46) (not recorded in any manuscript before the fifteenth century) (Schmeidler, p. 124). See also Gelting, 'Elusive Bishops'.

radiocarbon testing to 1000 (±10).[37] However, in the main, churches of such early date appear to have been few in number and were mostly located in royal urban centres.[38]

While some of the skaldic verse from poets close to the zealous Christianizing Norwegian kings presents paganism and Christianity as mutually exclusive and easily identifiable from each other, the matter was probably not so easily discernible on the ground for much of the population of Scandinavia, and certainly not so in Denmark.[39] The account of Widukind, which was written by 968, 'that the Danes were Christian since ancient times, but nevertheless worshipping idols with pagan rites', has received recent support. It would appear to attest to a mixed religious landscape in tenth-century Denmark, in which Danes were familiar with Christianity, and syncretically adopted the Christian God into their older pantheons as another deity or supernatural force to receive their appeals.[40] In the ninth century, Rimbert in his *Vita Anskarii* records that some Scandinavians underwent a form of initial Christianization ceremony, elsewhere known as 'primsigning', in order to interact with Christian society and enter churches during masses, but they put off actual baptism until near the point of death.[41] This of course allowed them to pass between both religious communities without actually committing to either. Without going too deeply into the subject, the flexibility of pre-Christian religion also encouraged this 'patchwork' religious activity, and one suspects that several other

[37] Birkedahl, 'Sebbersund', Nielsen, 'Sebbersund', and Bolton, *Empire*, pp. 197–8, for an attempt to give this some historical context.

[38] See Roesdahl, 'Hvornår blev Kirkene Bygget?', and Thaastrup-Leith, 'Trækirker i det Middelalderlige Danmark', and note that they conclude that a campaign of widespread building of churches, certainly those in stone, belongs to the mid- to later eleventh century. See also pp. 140–1 below for comments on the churches that can be dated to Cnut's reign.

[39] See Hallfreðr vandræðaskáld's verses on his conversion by Óláfr Tryggvason. Poole, 'The "Conversion Verses"', provides an edition and excellent discussion, and see also Edwards, 'Christian and Pagan References', on these.

[40] Widukind of Corvey, *Rerum Gestarum Saxonicarum*, III:65 (Lohmann and Hirsch, pp. 140–1). For this support see Gelting, 'Poppo's Ordeal'. See also Lund, 'Mission i Danmark', Refskou, 'Ottonernes Missionsvirksomhed', and Roesdahl, 'En Gravplads'.

[41] Rimbert, *Vita Anskarii*, ch. 24 (Waitz, p. 53). The practice is also attested in *Egils saga skallagrimsonar*, ch. 50 (Sigurður Nordal, p. 128).

possible grey areas and middle grounds existed but have not been recorded in our sources.

By contrast, the pace of conversion seems markedly relaxed in parts of Denmark, notably in northern Jutland.[42] A resurgence of burials with the apparently pagan trappings of military and equestrian equipment (some even with entire horses) can be traced in north-east Jutland in the late tenth and early eleventh centuries. Strangely, this seems to coexist side by side with the church built at neighbouring Sebbersund. Similarly, using the grave goods and spatial alignment of graves from a cemetery attached to the nearby ringfort at Fyrkat, Else Roesdahl has painted a complementary picture of beliefs there c. 980, which suggests a high degree of tolerance for pagan symbols and practices, perhaps even co-existing alongside Christian practices.[43] In addition, at Hørning, near Randers in the centre of northern Jutland, traces of two wooden churches have been discerned beneath the present twelfth-century fabric.[44] A single decorated plank from one of these structures, which was reused in the later building, dates dendro-chronologically to 1070. If it is from the later of the two churches, then we might reasonably date the initial ecclesiastical structure on the site to the first half of the eleventh century, leaving at least a few decades before this church was torn down and replaced. What is most surprising here is that these church buildings are sited on top of a pagan gravemound, which was levelled so that the grave slab lay directly under the entrance to the nave, forcing parishioners to walk over the grave in order to enter the church. This was evidently the intention of the builders. The grave held a single female body and was a high-status burial of the tenth century, and so it is likely that when the grave mound was levelled there were members of the community who could remember the burial, and without doubt there must have been local elites who traced close descent from the deceased. As at Jelling,

---

[42] Nielsen, 'Hedenskab og Kristendom', and Bolton, *Empire*, p. 198.
[43] Roesdahl, 'En Gravplads'.
[44] Krogh and Voss, 'Fra Hedenskab til Kristendom', and Bolton, *Empire*, pp. 199–200.

the alignment of these pagan and Christian structures suggests much about the pace of Christianization, indicating that it was not a rapid process leading to a clean break with the past. Denmark in Cnut's day would appear to have still retained this calmer pace of religious change in some areas, and within them elements of the older beliefs and syncretic blendings of belief systems could exist in the first few decades of the eleventh century.

Cnut's dynasty are usually regarded with hindsight as well-established and secure rulers, but from the position of Cnut's childhood quite the reverse seems to have been true. Cnut was the product of half a century of power expansion and consolidation by a dynasty who appear to have begun in Denmark as petty-kings in the region of mid-Jutland, but they were relative newcomers to Denmark and their grip on power was not without moments of crisis.

Cnut's grandfather, Harald 'Bluetooth' or 'the Good' Gormsson, is the earliest figure for whom we can paint a relatively comprehensive picture of his life, as well as the figure who appears to have overseen the initial leaps forward by the dynasty in political power. Harald was converted to Christianity by the missionary Poppo in either 963 or 965.[45] Without doubt Harald embraced the new religion, and the traditional archaeological interpretation of the runestones and grave-mound complex at Jelling in eastern mid-Jutland shows that while Harald's father was buried in a pagan gravemound there in the winter of 958–9, he was exhumed within a few years and reburied in a church at the same site in the 960s.[46] Harald was married to a Slavic woman, and was named on the runic monument at Jelling in a celebrated

[45] The traditional date ascribed to this conversion is 965. However, Gelting in his 'Poppo's Ordeal' has redated this to 963, and identified Poppo as Folkmar of Cologne (also known as Poppo in contemporary sources), the deputy of the archbishop of Cologne, who like Hamburg-Bremen also claimed Scandinavia as his suffragan see. Thus Harald's conversion was most probably a political act, and as Widukind notes (see p. 38 above), the Danes had been familiar with Christianity and some had adopted it into the pantheon of their gods for some time. This article changes much of what we thought we knew of Adam's account of early Christianity in Denmark, and places Cologne's claims at its inception.

[46] See Krogh, *Gåden om Kong Gorms*, and Krogh and Leth-Larsen, *Hedensk og Kristent*, but for dissent note Gelting, 'Poppo's Ordeal', pp. 113–15, and references there.

statement of his power as having 'won the whole of Denmark for himself, and Norway, and made the Danes Christian'.[47] He expanded his control over Denmark through building projects, fought against the Germans on his southern border in 974 and lost, but drove these out in 983 through an alliance with the Slavic Obodrites. His claim to over-lordship of Norway is attested by the Jelling inscription and Adam of Bremen.[48] This may have meant either Danish rule over the Viken (the coastal regions of the Oslofjord that face the tip of Jutland), which some Danish rulers may already have exerted authority over during parts of the previous half-century; or rule of the northern and western regions of Norway, through an advantageous alliance with the Jarls of Hlaðir, who controlled the area around Trondheim, and according to the skaldic verse *Vellekla* were themselves the overlords of all of Norway north of the Viken, receiving homage from sixteen jarls there.[49] Harald was driven out of Denmark by a rebellion headed by his son Swen 'Forkbeard', apparently in 987, and fled to his Slavic allies where he died of his wounds.[50]

It is when we push back one more generation that we encounter problems, but we must persevere as the results of these have some bearing on important events that would have been a recent memory when Cnut was born. The larger Jelling runestone names Harald's father as Gorm, and this finds some agreement in Adam of Bremen's account.[51] The earliest figure from this family introduced to us by Adam is named *Hardecnudth Vurm* ('Harða-Knútr worm', with the last word an apparent play on Gorm, as Adam then declares him 'crudelissimus, inquam, vermis' – 'a most cruel worm, I say').[52] A few lines later in the same account this *Vurm* has a son named Harald who is recognizable as

---

[47] DR. 42; see Moltke, *Runes and their Origin*, pp. 206–7, for the modern English translation. See also Jesch, 'Reading the Jelling Inscription'.
[48] DR. 42, and *Gesta*, II:25 (Schmeidler, p. 83).
[49] Einarr Helgason, *Vellekla*, verses 16 and 32 (Whaley, pp. 304 and 323).
[50] On the date of his death see Refskou, ' "In marca vel regno Danorum" '.
[51] DR. 42.
[52] Adam of Bremen, *Gesta*, I:55 (Schmeidler, p. 56).

Harald Gormsson.[53] However, earlier in his account, Adam sets out
details of men who had once ruled over the region of Hedeby-Schleswig,
which he claims he heard from King Swen Estrithsson (Cnut's nephew,
who ruled Denmark from 1042 to 1076 and was thus probably narrating
his own genealogy).[54] This section states that during the office of
Archbishop Hoger (909–16) the local rulers were overthrown by a
'Hardegon, son of Sveinn, who came from *Nortmannia*' (either Norway
or Normandy). We are probably on safe ground if we agree with the
existing consensus view, here stated by Sawyer, that 'the most satisfac-
tory interpretation . . . appears to be that Hardegon was a mistaken
form of Hardeknud'.[55] However, I am less certain of the next clause in
Sawyer's sentence, 'and that he was the father of Gorm'. An argument
about how to interpret these statements of Adam's has raged since the
early 1900s, with the current consensus view using an additional word
in some of the manuscripts of Adam's text for the first of his statements
here, to stitch together these two statements to produce a genealogical
line that proceeds from father to son: Hartheknut–Gorm–Harald–
Swen–Cnut.[56] In short, manuscripts from the two later groups of
Adam's text add the word 'son' (*filius*) before *Hardecnudth Vurm*, perhaps
suggesting that *Hardecnudth* was the father of *Vurm*.

The other view, with which I find myself in agreement, was first
championed in 1929 by Lis Jacobsen, who pointed out that the word
filius is not in the earliest group of copies of Adam's text, and there the
name of *Hardecnudth Vurm* is given in the variant form 'Hardewigh
Gorm', 'Hardewigh Gorem' or 'Hardewich Gwrm'.[57] She proposed
that *Hardecnudth* and *Vurm* were one man with a name and a nickname,

[53] Ibid., I:59 (Schmeidler, p. 57).

[54] Ibid., I:52 (Schmeidler, p. 53).

[55] P. H. Sawyer, 'Konger og Kongemakt', p. 279; his own translation following his Danish
'Man kan ikke i alle detaljer stole på Adam af Bremens beretning . . . [men] Den mest
tilfredsstillende tolkning af Adams beretning synes at være, at Hardegon er en misforstået
form for Hardeknud, og at han var far til Gorm.' For more detailed discussion of the debate
see Sawyer and Sawyer, 'A Gormless Dynasty', p. 690, and the references there.

[56] See Sawyer and Sawyer, 'A Gormless Dynasty', p. 690, nn. 9 and 10, for details of the
debate.

[57] Jacobsen, *Svenskevældets Fald*, pp. 23–8.

misunderstood by later copyists of Adam's text. The whole of her study has not stood up to later criticism, but here I think she may have a point. The word-order in the Latin construction of 'filius Hardecnudth Vurm' with the term for 'son' before the two names is as awkward in Latin as in Modern English, and it is hard to imagine a competent and well-read Latinist such as Adam creating such a construction.[58] Furthermore, neither of the other contemporary German chroniclers to discuss Denmark, Widukind of Corvey or Thietmar of Merseburg, mentions Gorm at all.[59] Lastly and most convincingly, there is a source of circumstantial evidence not apparently noted elsewhere in the debate that supports Jacobsen's case. It appears that elite naming practices of male children in southern Scandinavia in the Viking Age often involved the naming of the first son after his father, the second son after his grandfather, and so on.[60] Thus Cnut's recorded male children were Swen, Harold Harefoot and Harthacnut, respectively named after Cnut's father (Swen), his grandfather (Harald) and presumably his great-grandfather.

Crucially, Swen 'Forkbeard' named his recorded male children according to the same pattern: Harald (after his own father) and Cnut (with Cnut as a variant of Harthacnut: Cnut + a regional or adjectival epithet).[61]

We are left, if the reader will forgive the pun, quite Gormless.[62] The evidence is slight, but the overall agreement of the pattern here endorses

[58] It is worth noting that the variant I prefer here has been followed by both the editor of Adam's Latin text, Schmeidler (p. 56), and its modern English translator Tschan (p. 49), where the latter preserves 'Harthacanute Gorm' in his main text, only admitting another identification on p. 47, n. 155.

[59] He does appear in the late *Jómsvíkinga saga* and *Óláfs saga Tryggvasonar en mesta*, but the details there are manifestly based on Adam's account. I do not follow Jacobsen, *Svenskeveldets Fald*, pp. 58–82, in any suggestion that there was a *Gormssaga*.

[60] This is the subject of a paper I have in preparation, and appears to be a southern Scandinavian practice, perhaps even restricted to Denmark and Danes overseas.

[61] The name Harthacnut occurs on his Jewel Cross and Arm-and-Sceptre type coins, minted in England, in the form Cnut (see Jonsson, 'Coinage', p. 202), confirming that these were interchangeable name forms.

[62] As with most good jokes the pun here is someone else's, repeated by me. See the title of Sawyer and Sawyer, 'A Gormless Dynasty', for my source.

this impression of such naming practices, and otherwise we must make the wild suggestion that two children named Gorm were born between Cnut and his elder brother Harald and between Harold Harefoot and Harthacnut, and that both children died in infancy.[63]

It is hard to explain how both lines here omit Gorm, especially when he is accorded such renown on the Jelling runestones, and perhaps we must conclude that Gorm is present here under a different name. Adam of Bremen drew his material from numerous sources, both written and oral, and it is simplest to conclude that he became confused when dealing with two sources of evidence, perhaps collected and incorporated into his work in different places and even decades apart, and that Gorm/ *Vurm* was a nickname given to a figure named *Hardecnudth/ Hardegon*.

Thus *Hardecnudth/ Hardegon* was then the son of a Swen, who came to the region of Hedeby-Schleswig from *Nortmannia* only three generations before Cnut's birth, seized control there and died in the winter of 958–9. In this context, it is of passing interest that the epithet 'Hartha-' could be derived as the adjective 'hard' or the genitive plural of the ethnonym *Hörðar*, meaning 'of the people of Hordaland', in western

---

[63] That said, the weak spot in my argument here are the records of the sons of Swen Estrithson. He may have had up to fourteen sons and four daughters, by at least five separate women, and those not perhaps one after another. The order of seniority of the sons is recited differently by Saxo Grammaticus, *Danorum Regum Heroumque Historia*, X:7 (Christiansen, II, p. 58) and *Knytlinga saga*, ch. 23 (Bjarni Guðnason, pp. 135–6). See Christiansen, *Saxo Grammaticus*, pp. 230–2, n. 23, for the most comprehensive discussion of this problem. Saxo attests to a son named *Gormo* who shared a mother with Haraldus, and the latter does seem to have been the eldest surviving heir on his father's death. However, the *Sveno* and *Kanutus* recorded there have different mothers to *Gormo* and Haraldus as well as to each other, and both are implied to have been born later than *Gormo* and Haraldus. *Knytlinga saga* enumerates the children in this order (with irrelevant names removed): 1. Knut (predeceased father); 2. Harald; 3. St Knut, then after a son who is not relevant here; 5. Swen, and after some six others; 11. Guthorm (probably for Gorm, and so much later than Harald). I do not think it is possible to reconcile these two lists, and perhaps we must just accept that while the pattern holds true for Cnut and his father's naming practices, those of Swen Estrithson's sons were quite different in that they do not appear to follow the order of genealogical descent and do include a Gorm. Perhaps I am clutching at straws, but if we entertain the notion that this Gorm was the eleventh son, then he may not even be named after Harald Gormsson's father. The name is also attested on DR. 295 and perhaps Sö 74 in contexts that are unlikely to be a member of Cnut's dynasty.

coastal Norway, perhaps resolving how to translate *Nortmannia*.[64] The implication of this is that Cnut's dynasty may have been established on Danish soil for as few as sixty years when he was born, and Cnut may have grown up amongst the last of the elderly men who could remember their arrival.

His grandfather and father spent the decades up to his birth and those of his youth in constant activity, expanding their authority over the petty-kings and chieftains who were their neighbours. What set these rulers apart from their immediate peers was the understanding that conquests far from the seat of their authority could be controlled through the building-up of infrastructure. Rather than continually involving themselves in minor border squabbles, either gaining or losing land when their power waxed or waned, they began systematically to extend their control as a form of conquest, eroding the power of pre-existing local elites. Both invested in quite novel constructions to hold onto their ever-growing areas of influence in Denmark. Despite the grand and propagandistic statements of the Jelling runestones, much was still to be achieved in the second half of the tenth century. Harald Gormsson's expanding authority must be behind the series of uniform ringforts built towards the end of his reign on the periphery of the heartland of his powerbase at Jelling, in north Jutland (Fyrkat near Viborg, and Aggersborg, at the northernmost opening of the Limfjord), on Funen (Nonnebacken in Odense) and Sjælland (Trelleborg and a fort discovered in 2014 some 30 miles south of Copenhagen).[65] Both Fyrkat and Trelleborg can be shown to have been built in 979–81, and they are all near-identical, bespeaking central planning on a royal scale. That at Trelleborg in Skåne is similar enough to be identified as another member of the group, but it has differences that suggest an indirect control of the construction there, and perhaps also of that region. It is not clear whether these were intended to secure control of localities far

[64] My thanks to John Hines for the proposal of this derivation.
[65] Roesdahl, *Viking Age Denmark*, pp. 47–9 and 147–55, and P. H. Sawyer, 'Cnut's Scandinavian Empire', p. 13.

from the royal seat of power, or be used as bases in the event of external attack, but they do attest to Harald's growing presence throughout the kingdom. Similarly, runestones also seem to attest to a process of political upheaval and possible consolidation of power in Harald and Swen's hands in northern Jutland and south-western Skåne in the late tenth and early eleventh centuries – whether we interpret them as monuments erected by traditional elites to assert themselves in the face of powerful new royal agents or as statements of power by these incoming agents.[66]

The foundation of urban sites, early towns, played a substantial role in this process of power assertion. Towns had been founded in Denmark and functioned as central places for trade, minting of coins, and secular and religious control long before Cnut's dynasty came to power. Three such towns existed in the late tenth century, in Århus in the north-east of Jutland (a site dating from c. 900), and in the older sites of Ribe and Hedeby-Schleswig on the west and east coasts of southern Jutland (in existence from the eighth century onwards).[67] However, each of these places dwindled under Cnut's father and grandfather, seemingly ignored by them in preference to sites more under their control, and the impression gained from the available sources of evidence points to the rapid and total collapse of urban functions in these sites in the last decades of the tenth century. Ribe appears to have been almost abandoned throughout the period, and is without any archaeological layers that can be dated between c. 900 and 1077.[68] For the reigns of Swen and his sons, there are almost no archaeological deposits in any of these three towns. Moreover, Adam of Bremen states that after the death of Archbishop Adaldag of Hamburg-Bremen in 988, the episcopal see at Århus passed out of existence, presumably along with the functioning

---

[66] Bolton, *Empire*, pp. 189–90 and 229–32, drawing on the arguments of Randsborg, *Viking Age*, and B. Sawyer, 'Viking-Age Rune-Stones as a Crisis Symptom'.

[67] For general discussion of these sites see Clarke and Ambrosiani, *Towns in the Viking Age*, pp. 50–4 and 56–63. For more specific discussion of Århus see Madsen, 'Introduction to Viking Århus'; for Ribe see Nielsen, *Middelalderbyen Ribe*, pp. 35–6.

[68] Feveile, *Ribe Studier*.

of the urban site there, and the *Vita Bernwardi* records that c. 1000 Bishop Ekkihard (or Esico) of Hedeby-Schleswig left his see and went into exile in Germany, declaring the town deserted and the church destroyed.[69] The other bishops appear to have accompanied Ekkihard, along with an otherwise unattested bishop of Odense. They are all recorded in an imperial privilege of 18 March 988 granting them rights in Germany, implying that they could no longer support themselves from their Danish dioceses, or perhaps even return there safely.[70] This state of affairs appears to have continued into Cnut's reign, and while Hedeby-Schleswig had minted coins in the middle of the tenth century and Ribe probably also served as a mint site in the same period, none of these sites produced coins in Cnut's name throughout his reign.[71]

To fill the gaps left in the infrastructure by the abandonment of these sites, three other towns were founded during the reign of Swen: Viborg in northern Jutland, Roskilde on Sjælland and Lund in south-western Skåne. All three are located in northern Denmark, almost evenly spaced across the region, but crucially away from the other pre-existing urban sites and the border with Germany and the regions under direct or indirect German control. With the exception of Århus on the eastern coastline of mid-Jutland the pre-existing urban sites were placed in the south of Jutland, close to the southern border. The forts at Trelleborg and Fyrkat also fell into disrepair during Swen's reign, and part of their intended functions was perhaps thereafter played by the concentrations of population in the vicinity of the new towns, which like the forts were

---

[69] Adam of Bremen, *Gesta*, II:46 (Schmeidler, p. 106); Thangmar, *Vita Sancti Bernwardi*, ch. 33 (Pertz, cols. 418–19).

[70] The document was issued in the name of Otto III, and has been edited by Sickel, *Die Urkunden der Deutschen Könige*, no. 41, pp. 440–1. See Gelting, 'Elusive Bishops', for discussion.

[71] On earlier coinages in these sites, see Malmer, *Nordiska Mynt*, pp. 7–12 and 246–8. Note that Swen's coinage appeared with the legend 'ZVEN REX AD DENAR / GODÞINE M-AN DNER' ('Swen, king among the Danes / Godwine, moneyer among the Danes') without mentioning any specific site. Only one small and tight-knit group of coins minted in Cnut's name has been possibly identified as from Ribe (with the town name in very garbled forms), and this appears to be a very doubtful attribution. See Jonsson, 'Coinage', p. 226, and Jensen, 'Ribes Mønter i 1000-tallet', p. 48, for differing opinions on these coins.

evenly spaced across the regions of Denmark.[72] Viborg's archaeology
begins with deposits that can be precisely dated through dendrochronology to the last decade of the tenth century and the years around
1000, and the only man-made features on the site that pre-date the
urban structures are the remains of a number of Viking-Age farm
buildings with some associated ploughmarks.[73] Roskilde has little
surviving early archaeology, but again there are traces of Viking-Age
farm buildings beneath the modern town, and its earliest urban structures existed by 987×1014.[74] Adam of Bremen some decades later would
identify it as the largest urban site on Sjælland, and 'the seat of Danish
royalty'.[75] He also records that Harald Gormsson was buried in a tomb
that he had prepared for himself in a church dedicated to the Holy
Trinity in Roskilde.[76] It was most probably this same royal mausoleum
that the *Encomium* claims received the body of Swen.[77] The *Encomium*
states that this construction was erected at Swen's instigation, not his
father's, and that it was a monastery (*monasterium*), but the fact that both
sources note the dedication of the building to the Holy Trinity identifies
it as the same. The author of the *Encomium* appears to have been an
inhabitant of Flanders who had spent time in England, where burial in
monasteries was common, and he perhaps did not know that there
were no monasteries in Scandinavia in the early eleventh century, and
made a small error in transferring the mausoleum he was discussing
into a non-existent monastic foundation. F. Birkbæck has suggested that
this church was built during the reign of Swen, and its construction

[72] For the lack of maintenance of the forts at Trelleborg and Fyrkat in Swen's reign, see
Roesdahl, *Viking Age Denmark*, pp. 147–55.
[73] See Kristensen, 'A Viking-Period and Medieval Settlement', p. 193, his 'A Viking-
Period', p. 191, as well as his *Middelalderbyen Viborg*, pp. 38–9.
[74] See Andersen, Højog and Sørensen, 'Et Vikingetidshus fra Bredgade'.
[75] Adam of Bremen, *Gesta*, IV:5 (ed. Schmeidler, p. 233).
[76] Adam of Bremen, *Gesta*, II:28 (ed. Schmeidler, pp. 87–8).
[77] *Encomium Emmae Reginae*, II:3 (Campbell, p. 18). Cinthio in *De Första Stadsborna*, pp. 33–5,
and most recently again in 'Trinitatiskyrkan, Gravarna och de förste Lundaborna', pp.
159–63, has argued that this Church of the Holy Trinity is to be identified with the church
of the same name excavated in Lund, but such an error about a royal mausoleum of significant importance to Harthacnut and many of the Danes resident in England, who were the
Encomium's primary audience, would appear glaring.

backdated by Adam of Bremen in an attempt to avoid connecting any such activity to Swen, who is the villain of his account. However, it is equally possible that both Harald and Swen had sufficient input into its construction to feel that in the state in which they each saw the building they were its founder.[78]

Archaeological excavations in the 1970s at Lund unearthed a large cemetery from the period of the earliest occupation layers, with bodies buried in wooden coffins datable by dendrochronology to the period from 994(±5)–1048(±5).[79] The earliest traces of structures from Lund date to the period from 1010(±5)–1023(±5).[80] In addition, the Church of St Clements there was excavated by Ragnar Blomkvist in 1932.[81] This revealed fragments of an early wooden church beneath the earliest and eleventh-century stone construction. A recent dating of the wooden church to the early part of that century opens the possibility that it was built during the reign of Swen.[82]

Similarly, Swen began to fill the gaps in the episcopal structures with his supporters. He enthroned a missionary bishop named Gotebald, who had previously preached in Norway and Sweden, to a see based on Skåne (and presumably thus in Lund).[83] The only remaining bishops in Denmark after the flight of the Germans were the elderly missionary Poppo and a single bishop plucked from the Danish nobility, Othinkar 'the younger'.[84] Other senior ecclesiastical duties were perhaps performed by the royal chaplains or other lesser clergy attached to the royal court.

---

[78] Birkbæck, *13 Bidrag til Roskilde By*, pp. 64–5. For details of Adam's distortion of events to present Harald Gormsson and Swen 'Forkbeard' in contrasting lights, see P. H. Sawyer, 'Sven Forkbeard and the Historians'.

[79] Andrén, 'Stadsbilden', p. 24, and Mårtensson, 'Gravar och Kyrkor', pp. 88–90.

[80] Andrén, 'Stadsbilden', p. 24.

[81] Blomkvist, *Tusentalets Lund*, and Cinthio, 'The Churches of St. Clemens', p. 104.

[82] Cinthio, 'Trinitatiskyrkan, Gravarna och de förste Lundboarna', p. 168.

[83] See Gelting, 'Elusive Bishops', pp. 175–6. Adam claims he was English (*Gesta*, II:41 [Schmeidler, p. 101]).

[84] Adam of Bremen, *Gesta*, II:49 (Schmeidler, p. 110). See Gelting, 'Elusive Bishops', pp. 174–5 and 177, and Bolton, *Empire*, pp. 177, n. 85, and pp. 179–80.

All of this gives the impression of a stable dynasty slowly accumulating authority and consolidating its hold on power in the regions. However, at the midpoint of this process, in the mid-980s, perhaps only years before Cnut's birth, his family would turn on itself, unleashing a brief civil war that ended in a scandalous regicide and apparently leaving a deep scar on Danish memory. In the last days of Archbishop Adaldag (d. 988), Swen turned against his father Harald, and, as Adam states, 'set on foot many plots against his father' so that 'of a sudden, the Danes entered into a conspiracy . . . to make Swen king, to declare war on Harald'.[85] Adam sought to portray Swen falsely as a pagan, and we might cast significant doubt on his other statements that this revolt was that of a pagan son wishing to oust his Christian father, and that Swen's followers were reluctant and repentant converts to Christianity.[86] However, we can probably draw from these brief statements the facts that Swen did have the support of sections of the Danish nobility, and that at the root of the matter were tensions created by some unknown aspects of Harald's rule. Swen's forces were stronger, and when they met in battle Harald was defeated and fled to his allies on the Baltic coastline, where he died from his injuries.[87] The *Encomium*, coming from the camp of Swen's son Cnut half a century later, gives its own version of these events as partisan as that of Adam of Bremen, claiming that 'even as a boy he [Swen] was held by all in close affection, and was hated only by his father'.[88] That source goes on to note that Harald's 'envy increased more and more, so that he wished, not in secret, but openly, to cast him out, affirming by oath that he should not rule after him'. This source frequently reshapes history to serve as a moral warning for its own times, which had also seen the murder of a member of the royal family (Edward the Confessor's elder brother, Alfred) and needed to stress royal

[85] Adam of Bremen, *Gesta*, II:27(25)–28(26) (Schmeidler, pp. 87–91).

[86] See P. H. Sawyer, 'Swein Forkbeard and the Historians'.

[87] The support of some part of the Danes (there the army), the battle, and Harald's death from wounds amongst the Slavs are all confirmed by the *Encomium Emmae Reginae* I:1 (Campbell, p. 8).

[88] *Encomium Emmae Reginae*, I:1 (Campbell, p. 8).

unity between the two half-brothers Harthacnut and Edward, but the comments here are introduced without the characteristic moral lesson. Instead, the choice to give a rose-tinted view of this rebellion and royal patricide may suggest that even in the 1040s this act was still felt to be sufficiently shocking to warrant an elaborate explanation.

Much of this instability must have informed Cnut's character and later decisions. He grew up in a society where his family's grasp on power was one of conquest, and that only recent, most probably just on the edge of living memory. This was supported by innovations that for the most part must have been achieved in the face of local outrage. Power is rarely taken from local rulers with their consent, and sections of the nobility must have been hostile to Cnut's dynasty, and wished for a return to the way things were before Cnut's grandfather and father extended their control. Almost all of Harald's long-term supporters, and some, if not many, of the Danish elites must have been scandalized by Swen's rebellion, and the blood this left on his hands. From birth Cnut had learnt to strive and fight for his achievements, even when that led to morally shocking decisions and dark, murderous actions to further his aims. He grew up under the cloud of the death of his grandfather, Harald, could probably securely count on few people for unquestioned support, and was keenly aware that fortune could drag men down just as easily as raise them up.

It is of equal importance in our assessment of what drove him to bear in mind that Cnut was the second of Swen's sons. The *Encomium* states that he was the elder brother, but as Lund has rightly concluded this goes against the grain of all our other sources, and was most probably a detail added by the author of that text retrospectively to promote Cnut and his sons' rights to rule over any surviving heir of his brother.[89] The senior position amongst the siblings was clearly that of his brother Harald. It was this Harald whom Swen left in charge of Denmark when he and Cnut went to England in 1013, and as the *Encomium* is forced to

<hr>

[89] Lund, 'Cnut's Danish Kingdom', p. 28. See also Campbell, *Encomium Emmae Reginae*, pp. lvi–lvii, and my comments in Bolton, *Empire*, p. 155, n. 1.

concede, when Cnut returned to Denmark after his father's sudden death, he had to ask his brother for, and was refused, a share of the kingdom.[90] The only evidence to suggest that they had some form of joint kingship or that Cnut had any measure of rule there before his re-invasion of England is the earliest series of coins minted in Lund, which may date to 1014–15; however, the dating is based solely on their following of English types of that date and is far from secure.[91]

In the opening years of the second decade of the eleventh century, when Cnut became a young man and began to build his own networks of alliances and draw on them for support, he could not have known that his brother would be dead within a few years. At that point, Cnut could expect little beyond the role of an understudy in the rule of Denmark, and when he returned there in 1014 his brother seems to have been so entrenched that Cnut could not challenge him openly. In addition, the country probably could not have withstood another scandalous murder within its new royal house. It must have been painfully clear to him that like those of his great-grandfather and grandfather his fortunes had to be made elsewhere through conquest, and won by his own efforts. There may be a grain of truth in the *Encomium*'s statement that Swen, when considering an invasion of England, 'summoned Cnut . . . [and] began to inquire what were his views concerning the matter'.[92] The conquest of England would offer him a region to inherit from his father, one that was far wealthier than that which was to be his brother's lot. Doubtless Cnut joined the rank and file of Swen's invading army on the boats that would take them to the English coast with a sense that his time had come and so he had to make the most of this opportunity.

[90] *Encomium Emmae Reginae*, II:2 (Campbell, pp. 16–18).

[91] Blackburn, 'Do Cnut the Great's First Coins'. Blackburn's principal arguments focus on the fact that Scandinavian copies of English coins tend to copy the current English issue-type, or the issue-type in use in England during the immediately preceding years. All the early Lund coins that bear Cnut's name are copies of King Æthelred the Unready's Last Small Cross issue, current between c. 1009 and 1015. This idea was criticized by Lund, 'Cnut's Danish Kingdom', pp. 29–30, but supported by me in *Empire*, p. 155, n. 3. However, doubt has crept into my mind since 2009, and certainly these coins cannot be securely dated with any accuracy.

[92] *Encomium Emmae Reginae* I:3 (Campbell, p. 10).

Chapter 2

THE INVASIONS OF ENGLAND IN 1013 AND 1016

Scandinavian ships and their raiding parties were all too familiar to the inhabitants of England who must have watched Swen and Cnut's fleet appear on the horizon and draw up their longships on the beach at Sandwich. The English, or Anglo-Saxons, were themselves invaders who had arrived in the fifth century from parts of Saxony, Frisia and Jutland, and seized control over the crumbling remains of post-Roman Britain. Moreover, they still composed and sung songs of a heroic age in Denmark, and the *Beowulf* manuscript, containing the sole substantial composition of that type to survive, dates to the opening decades of the eleventh century. However, half a millennium had passed since the invading barbarians of the fifth century had assembled themselves into highly organized kingdoms and produced a distinctive language and culture all of their own.[1] They may have been prepared to accept that in a far distant past they were not so unlike the invading Scandinavians, but centuries of Christianization, legal developments and codifications, urbanization, social stratigraphization and the development of a scribal bureaucracy, separated them from the invaders.

It is important to note that Swen and Cnut's arrival in 1013 came at the end of some thirty-five years of devastating Scandinavian raids on English territory. The Anglo-Saxon Chronicle is normally a rather dry account, reading like a sparse bulletin of events, condensing even the most emotive of acts into a few blank words, but here it descends slowly

[1] For an excellent study of the early stages of this see Yorke, *Kings and Kingdoms*.

into a deeply impassioned narrative describing the violence of the
invaders and the collapse of a society.[2] These events left substantial
scars on the memories of the English, and a century later John of
Worcester, presumably working from oral accounts, would describe
harrowing scenes of violence and the systematic murder of every man
the warbands encountered.[3] Confronted with this tide of destruction
many of the English seem to have despaired, and turned towards prayer
and public appeals to God to rid them of the raiders.[4]

The invaders came first in 981, striking Southampton, and this force
was followed, until 1001, by numerous small raiding armies that struck
at coastal sites or headed inland on raiding campaigns.[5] In 991 a larger
raiding party arrived and remained in England until 1005, closely
followed by another in 1006–7. Then in 1009 a 'great army' headed by
the warlord Thorkell the Tall (about whom much will be said later)
arrived at Sandwich and appears to have received reinforcements in
August of the same year from another immense fleet, apparently under
the control of Thorkell's brother and close associate.[6] This force seized
the archiepiscopal see of Canterbury and pillaged the southern coastline, before making a winter camp on the River Thames and seizing
provisions from the surrounding Essex countryside. From that site they
struck into Oxfordshire and East Anglia in 1010, burning Thetford and
Cambridge, before returning to Oxfordshire and proceeding to lay
waste the counties of Buckinghamshire, Bedfordshire and Hertfordshire,
and burning the town of Northampton. At the peak of this orgy of
carnage, they took the archbishop of Canterbury prisoner along with
many inhabitants of the town. The archbishop was imprisoned for
several months, and then executed on 19 April 1012 (perhaps by

[2] ASC 991–1013 CDE (O'Brien O'Keeffe, pp. 86–98).
[3] John of Worcester, *Chronicon*, s.a. 1011 and 1013 (Darlington and McGurk, pp. 468 and 474).
[4] See Lawson, 'Archbishop Wulfstan', pp. 152–6, Keynes and Naismith, 'The *Agnus Dei* Pennies', and Woods, 'The *Agnus Dei* Penny'.
[5] ASC 981–1008 D (Cubbin, pp. 48–54).
[6] ASC 1009–1013 D (Cubbin, pp. 54–8), and John of Worcester, *Chronicon*, s.a. 1009 (Darlington and McGurk, pp. 462–4). For Thorkell the Tall, see pp. 59–65 here.

accident, and according to one version of the Anglo-Saxon Chronicle, by bones and heads of cattle thrown at him by a drunken mob after he refused to pay any ransom); the other captives were presumably sold into slavery.[7] For the author of this part of the Anglo-Saxon Chronicle, this was an inversion of all that was good and normal: 'Then he was a roped thing, who was earlier the head of the English race and of Christendom. There might be seen wretchedness where earlier was seen bliss, in that wretched town from where there first came Christendom [to us] and bliss before God and before the world.'

Æthelred 'the Unready' had been king of the English since 978, and was a descendant of the West Saxon line of Alfred the Great who had reconquered the various kingdoms of Anglo-Saxon England after the viking raids of the ninth century.[8] Despite the unfortunate byname that history gave to him, Æthelred appears to have been a strong and effective ruler, and more ill-counselled (as the Anglo-Saxon *unræd* means) than not up to the task.[9] However, he was powerless in the face of such large and mobile forces, and had to resort to paying the bulk of the invaders off and hiring the remaining crews of forty-five ships under Thorkell the Tall to stay on as mercenaries in his service. Within months the weaknesses of this arrangement were tested and found wanting, as early in 1013 Swen and Cnut's vast fleet appeared, and the English, broken, beaten and at the end of their tether, capitulated to Swen's seizure of power.[10]

Swen led his fleet northwards up the eastern coastline from Sandwich, past East Anglia and into the River Humber and River Trent up to Gainsborough. There he met with representatives of Northumbria and Lindsey, the Five Boroughs of the north of England and soon after all the regions north of Watling Street to accept their homage. From here, and

[7] ASC 1012 E (Irvine, p. 69).

[8] Molyneaux, *Formation of the English Kingdom*, p. 18 *et passim*, prefers 'Cerdicing' (i.e. descendants of Cerdic, the supposed founder of the dynasty) to the geographically specific 'West Saxon line'.

[9] On this see Keynes, 'The Declining Reputation' and *Diplomas*, as well as Roach's biography of Æthelred in this series.

[10] ASC 1013 D (Cubbin, p. 58), and John of Worcester, *Chronicon*, s.a. 1013 (Darlington and McGurk, pp. 472–4).

with English auxiliaries, horses and provisions, Swen marched on Oxford and Winchester, subjugating those towns before attacking London (unsuccessfully, with his forces never breaching the city), then turning towards Wallingford and Bath to receive homage from the nobles of those places. The defeat was overwhelming and Æthelred withdrew with his wife and heirs to London, and then after the submission of that city, to a fleet in the Thames, from where he sent his wife and children to safety in exile in Normandy, joining them after Christmas in 1013.[11]

It is crucial to note that Swen's arrival in 1013 was quite different from that of the other Scandinavian raiders, including several earlier attacks in which he appears to have played a part. Here his aim was conquest not raiding. He sought to seize control at the level of central and local government and permanently rule the country, rather than just raise wealth through pillage and ransoms. It is probable he had taken part in earlier attacks intent on just raiding. Swen is documented by the Anglo-Saxon Chronicle at the head of a force attacking London in 994, which raided widely in Kent, Essex, Sussex and Hampshire, alongside an Óláfr who may be identifiable as Óláfr Tryggvason the future ruler of Norway.[12] The two ravaged widely in the south-east and along the southern coast before accepting a Danegeld payment of £16,000 and departing. Swen appears to have taken his fleet into the Irish Sea, where a 'Swen son of Harald' is recorded by the *Annales Cambriae* as harrying the Isle of Man.[13] He may have been present at the Battle of Maldon in 991, and at the great Scandinavian raid on Saxony in 994.[14] By this time he was most probably already the king of the Danes, and as such represents a new evolutionary phase of viking raiding in the late tenth century in which the armies could be led by the ruler of a Scandinavian nation. Indeed, it was very likely a by-product of the development of the machinery of

[11] ASC 1013 CDE (O'Brien O'Keeffe, p. 98), and John of Worcester, *Chronicon*, s.a. 1013 (Darlington and McGurk, p. 474).

[12] ASC 994 CDE (O'Brien O'Keeffe, p. 87), and John of Worcester, *Chronicon*, s.a. 994 (Darlington and McGurk, pp. 442–4).

[13] *Annales Cambriae* (Williams, p. 20), and Lawson, *Cnut*, p. 23.

[14] Lund, 'The Danish Perspective', although there is no direct evidence that Swen was in Saxony. Perhaps see also Howard, *Swein Forkbeard's Invasions*, pp. 32–5.

royal control in Denmark, which enabled Swen to be, in Lund's words, 'probably the first ruler of a Scandinavian country who was able to take his army abroad on a viking expedition without, apparently, having to fear for his position at home'.[15] However, 1013 was different again, and represents another evolutionary step away from simple viking raiding. William of Jumièges' record that Swen negotiated a treaty of alliance and mutual assistance with Duke Richard II of Normandy before invading England in that year, suggests an attempt to head off at the pass any potential Norman response. Emma, Richard's sister, had married Æthelred in 1002, and could have appealed to him for aid on behalf of her husband.[16] Swen appears to have intended to stay after his conquest.

Medieval legends generally explain Swen's change of intention from raiding to conquest as revenge for the dead of the St Brice's Day massacre of Danes in England in 1002, which by the thirteenth century identified a sister of Swen amongst those killed.[17] This viewpoint was adopted by a generation of historians in the mid- to later twentieth century, but I am not sure it stands up to much scrutiny, and has the ring of a later rationalization about it.[18] It is also possible that Swen may have needed the wealth from such raids following the conflict with his own father, but this event was long distant in 1013. Moreover, neither of these two theories explains why Swen specifically invaded and seized power in 1013, rather than attempting to avenge his sister or just harrying and pillaging. Instead, we might speculate that this invasion was an attempt to control viking raiding and stabilize its effects on Scandinavian society.[19] The

---

[15] Lund, 'The Danish Perspective', p. 133.

[16] William of Jumièges, *Gesta Normannorum Ducum*, V:6 (Van Houts, 16–18).

[17] The earliest reference known to me to the St Brice's Day massacre inducing Swen's invasion is that of William of Jumièges, *Gesta Normannorum Ducum*, V:6 (Van Houts, pp. 14–16). In the thirteenth century John of Wallingford in his chronicle names Swen's sister as a victim of this as well as the motivation for his attack (Vaughan, pp. 60–1). On the event in general see Keynes, 'The Massacre of St. Brice's Day'.

[18] For an example see Stenton, *Anglo-Saxon England*, p. 380.

[19] Similarly, Swen and Cnut's Norwegian contemporary Óláfr Haraldsson would be praised in skaldic poetry for suppressing raiding within Norway and abroad in order to strengthen peace in that society: see Sigvatr Þórðarson, *Erfidrápa Óláfs Helga*, verses 4–6 (Whaley, pp. 669–73).

vast majority of such raids were most probably performed without the presence of a king or grand ruler, and when successful they injected large amounts of movable wealth into the elite groups in Scandinavia, empowering local magnates at the expense of the central government. Enough examples survive in contemporary and later sources of young Scandinavian nobles who were cast out or fled authority only to raise wealth by raiding, and return home at the head of mercenary armies to seize control, to suggest the dangerous influences such sources of wealth could bring.[20] Denmark was only recently under the grip of Swen, and had only just begun to reorganize itself around a centralized government and single ruler, therefore such destabilizing influences cannot have been welcome. Swen's participation in and then his seizure of command of these late tenth-century raids may have been a necessity forced on him by the involvement of some of his subordinates, which eventually compelled him to take control of this river of money at its source.

From the English perspective, Swen's Christianity must have set him apart from many previous viking raiders, and may have made him a more palatable figure to accept as an overlord. This was not an invading army whose leader could be baptized and sent home pacified once his men had been defeated or paid off, as Alfred had done with Guthrum in 878 and Æthelred with Óláfr Tryggvason in 994.[21] Many of the rank and file of the forces must have retained pagan beliefs, or worshipped Christ only as one amongst a pantheon of gods, but Swen was unequivocally Christian, and most probably travelled with a retinue that included chaplains.[22] So much of what we can know of Swen's invasion comes from the partisan voice of the writer of this section of the Anglo-Saxon Chronicle, who viewed his arrival as an inversion of all that was natural and right, and one wonders whether other figures, such as secular elites, were more comfortable with him.

---

[20] Two contemporary examples are discussed in Bolton, *Empire*, p. 214.
[21] ASC 878 A (Bately, p. 51), and ASC 994 E (Irvine, pp. 61–2).
[22] See pp. 35–7.

A figure who looms large in this period, and was to be one of the key players in Cnut's life, was Thorkell the Tall. A few words should be said here by way of his introduction.[23] As briefly mentioned above, Thorkell had led a vast raiding army into England in 1009, which had been disbanded only in 1012 when Thorkell and the men of forty-five ships had switched sides and entered Æthelred's service. In fact, this may have been the trigger for Swen's invasion. The employment of Scandinavian armies as mercenaries was not new, but the employment of one by a reigning monarch gave Thorkell access to vast English revenues, and he was far from just an ordinary raider. The saga traditions identify him as son of Jarl Strut-Harald (probably died c. 986/8), the ruler of Skåne in eastern Denmark in the late decades of the tenth century.[24] By about 980, Thorkell's elder brother, Sigwaldi, was reported to have taken over the title, and the narratives describe his part in the semi-legendary battle of *Hjörungavágr* as the jarl of the region. The so-called 'Supplement to *Jómsvíkinga saga*' states that another of Thorkell's brothers, Hemming, held the jarldom immediately before his own death in England in 1014, and Sigwaldi may have died by then.[25]

However, the connection between these later traditions and the Thorkell named in our contemporary English sources has recently been called into question by Ann Williams, and it is perhaps worthwhile to pause momentarily here to re-examine the evidence.[26] Williams' argument is founded on the late date and unreliability of what she uses as the

---

[23] For this figure see Campbell, *Encomium Emmae Reginae*, Appendix III, pp. 73–82, Keynes, 'Cnut's Earls', pp. 54–7, and Williams, 'Thorkell the Tall', as well as references there.

[24] The late saga-source, *Fagrskinna*, ch. 19 (Bjarni Einarsson, p. 122), is the only witness to Strut-Harald's date of death. See also *Heimskringla Óláfs Saga Tryggvasonar*, ch. 34 (Bjarni Aðalbjarnarson, I, pp. 272–3). Note that Campbell, *Encomium Emmae Reginae*, p. 73, erroneously followed the late *Jómsvíkinga saga* in giving him the title of Jarl of Sjaelland. This is in error, and the family are identified in better sources as the Jarls of Skåne.

[25] This source, a *þáttr* found at the end of the version of *Jómsvíkinga saga* in *Flateyjarbók*, has been edited by Campbell, *Encomium Emmae Reginae*, pp. 92–3.

[26] Williams' paper ('Thorkell the Tall') was first delivered in 2011 at a conference in Gregynog (Powys), was subsequently made widely available in an electronic format via academia.edu, and then revised for print publication in 2016. See also my comment on her criticisms of a historical method involving both contemporary sources and sensitively handled later sources at pp. 22–6 above.

principal source in this genre for him: *Jómsvíkinga saga*, and the lack of prominence of Thorkell in the narratives of the earliest saga sources in which he is only ever a supporting actor in the drama there.[27] The implication of this slight role is that the links between Thorkell and the Scandinavian elites reported in the late sources may be inventions or so subject to doubt that they should be set aside.[28] Williams is quite right to point out the problems of *Jómsvíkinga saga*, which should eliminate it from use as a historical witness. I think no one would now claim that *Jómsvíkinga saga* is free of legendary and literary accretions, exaggerations and outright inventions, and elsewhere I have set it aside.[29] However, I am not sure that I can follow the jump to her notion that because Thorkell's part in the saga narratives is slight, it is of sufficient doubt for us to sweep it away. Williams is wrong to focus on *Jómsvíkinga saga* and she misses a number of sources that identify him (or at least someone of his name, understood by writers in the thirteenth century to be him) as a member of this ruling dynasty of Jarls of Skåne. The so-called 'Supplement to *Jómsvíkinga saga*' is a difficult and troubling source that survives attached to *Jómsvíkinga saga* in a single manuscript, but we must note that it contains a surprising amount of accurate material and clearly pre-dates the fourteenth-century manuscript in which it survives.[30]

Snorri Sturluson's *Heimskringla* includes some sparse comments on this ruling dynasty, including Thorkell's part in it, but we might presume that this source is dependent on the traditions set out in *Jómsvíkinga saga*.[31] Yet to do this we must account for that text's

---

[27] Williams, 'Thorkell the Tall', pp. 151–2.

[28] While Williams does not actually state this clearly, this is the upshot of the last section of her published paper, which begins by observing Thorkell's slight role in the saga narratives, explained as 'by the time of writing, Thorkell was regarded as the brother of Sigvaldi', and 'Thorkell's alleged relationship with Sigwaldi takes us out of history and into legend' (both p. 151).

[29] She may be responding to Campbell, *Encomium Emmae Reginae*, pp. 73–82 and 87–91, especially p. 73. Keynes, 'Cnut's Earls', follows Campbell's discussion of the Scandinavian parts of Thorkell's life on p. 54 of his account.

[30] See Bolton, *Empire*, pp. 211–12, especially n. 28.

[31] *Heimskringla, Óláfs Saga Tryggvasonar*, chs. 34–5 and 43 (Bjarni Aðalbjarnarson, I, pp. 272–4, and II, p. 54).

independent aside on the career of the skaldic poet Þórðr Sigvaldaskáld as being another invention.[32] This poet is identified there as Sigwaldi's permanent court poet, who was later in attendance of 'Thorkell the Tall, his brother; and after the fall of the jarl Þórðr became a merchant'. This poet was the father of perhaps the most celebrated and prolific skald of this period, Sigvatr Þórðarson, who served both Ólafr Haraldsson and Cnut, and he is an improbable candidate to choose if one wished to fabricate parts of his life a century after his death. In addition, another source, the *Skáldatal*, also links Thorkell to this dynasty.[33] This source is a list of known skaldic poets arranged by the rulers they composed for, compiled in the early thirteenth century apparently as part of the research materials behind the composition of *Heimskringla*. The manuscript witnesses to this list, which descend from the redaction of the text once in the *Kringla* manuscript, place a Harald Thorkelsson and his poet Þióðólfr Arnórsson at the end of the list of the Jarls of Skåne, immediately after Sigwaldi.[34] There could have been another Thorkell in the dynasty of the Jarls of Skåne who was not the namesake in Cnut's following, but clearly Snorri believed this to be Thorkell the Tall, as he identifies both him and his son in his narrative.[35] In addition, the chronology of the poet Þióðólfr Arnórsson,

---

[32] *Heimskringla, Ólafs Saga Helga*, ch. 43 (Bjarni Aðalbjarnarson, II, p. 54). This would suggest that Williams' statement, 'no skald seems to have felt moved to compose eulogies for Thorkell' ('Thorkell the Tall', p. 149), is inaccurate, although such poetry is not recorded in any surviving account or in *Skáldatal*.

[33] The *Skáldatal* has been edited by Finnur Jónsson in his *Snorra Edda*, on pp. 259, 268 and 284, but is greatly wanting; a facsimile of the Uppsala manuscript (De la Gardie 11) has been published as Grape, Kallstenius and Thorell, *Snorre Sturlasons Edda*.

[34] The relevant parts of the manuscripts are Reykjavík, A.M. MS. 761a 4to, fols. 16v–17r (paper transcript of c. 1700), and Uppsala, Universitetsbibliothek, MS. R. 685, f. 25v (early eighteenth-century paper transcript of the Swedish antiquary Peter Salan); I have given their readings in Bolton, *Empire*, pp. 206–7. See Guðrún Nordal, 'Skáldatal and its Manuscript Context', for discussion of this source. The *Kringla* manuscript of c. 1260 was destroyed in the Copenhagen fire of 1728, apart from a single leaf surviving since the late seventeenth century in the Royal Library, Stockholm; it was presented to Iceland in 1975 by King Carl Gustaf XVI, and is now in Reykjavík, Landsbókasafn Íslands fragm. 82.

[35] *Heimskringla, Ólafs Saga Helga*, chs. 183 and 239 (Bjarni Aðalbjarnarson, II, pp. 333 and 399).

who is also recorded as composing for Magnús Ólafsson (r. Norway c. 1035–47), agrees with the possible dates in which a son of Thorkell might have lived.

None of these sources falls very far from each other, and we could strike through all this, as Williams suggests, as being too late and too complex to include, but I think we would be at risk of throwing out the baby with the bathwater. What strikes me here is that the link between Thorkell and this dynasty of the Jarls of Skåne is not just the mere brotherhood of Thorkell and Sigwaldi, upon which Williams focuses as a potential invention by a later writer wishing to locate Thorkell within the Scandinavian elites, which would have been easy to forge. If we presume that this brotherly link was invented in the very late twelfth century when *Jómsvíkinga saga* was composed, we must also presume that by the time Snorri began to research *Heimskringla* a handful of decades later, the forger(s) had gone to the trouble of inventing stories about the father of one of the most famous skalds of this golden age of the art linking him to Thorkell as well as composing an entire skaldic poem on Thorkell's son. A simple assertion of brotherhood might be an invention, but these further details push the boundaries of what was probable for a forger to pull off quite beyond their limits. Alternatively, we could suggest that another Thorkell who had a son named Harald was a member of the dynasty of the Jarls of Skåne, but was not Thorkell the Tall, and a misidentification was made in the late twelfth century. However, no source suggests or even supports this, and we should probably be economical with the number of 'what ifs' we create. Much more reasonably, we should take the cluster of references to Thorkell's relationship to the Jarls of Skåne and the supporting detail of a court poet of his brother Sigwaldi passing into his employ, as well as the naming of Thorkell's son as a member of this dynasty by the *Skáldatal*, as representing an accurate historical tradition, albeit written down about two centuries after Thorkell's death.

We can also say a few words about the power of the Jarls of Skåne in Denmark in the late tenth and eleventh centuries. While no verse now survives, it is telling that this dynasty appears to have had court poets. Like most forms of any intricate and highly skilled art, skaldic poetry seems to have been costly for the patron, and the existence of poems thus presupposes a level of wealth and influence for the patron. In the surviving corpus of verses, patrons with skalds attached to their retinue for some time are always of royal or quasi-royal status.[36] Due to the Icelandic and Norwegian focus of the saga traditions, Danish verse survives in substantially smaller quantities, and commonly only in isolated fragments.[37] However, the various manuscript witnesses to *Skáldatal* do ascribe to Strut-Harald a poet named Þjóðólfr or Hvíni, perhaps in error for another now lost name, and to Sigwaldi a poet named Þórðr Sigvaldaskáld (whose epithet suggests a long association with that patron), as well as noting the relationship between Harald Thorkelsson and Þjóðólfr Arnórsson.[38]

The position of Skåne is also of importance for charting the authority and influence of Thorkell's dynasty. As a promontory of the Swedish landmass it juts out into the Baltic, separating that body of water from the Øresund and Kattegat and access to the western regions of Denmark and the North Sea. We can only speculate here, but it seems likely that substantial taxes could be claimed by the elites of this region on goods passing through these waters. Moreover, the location of this region at the furthest point away from the traditional centre of royal power in central Jutland most probably gave these elites greater independence than other ruling dynasties in Denmark.

The fruits of this commanding position perhaps can be seen in the archaeological excavations at Uppåkra on the western coast of Skåne, at about the midpoint of the part of the coastline facing Sjælland. This site

---

[36] Gade, *The Structure*, p. 3, Fidjestøl, 'Norse-Icelandic Composition', p. 321, and Kuhn, *Das Dróttkvætt*, p. 228.

[37] See also Townend, 'Whatever Happened', for discussion of another corpus of lost skaldic verse.

[38] Þjóðólfr or Hvíni is otherwise recorded in the ninth century, and I have argued elsewhere that his name here is probably an error introduced during the copying of a lost ancestral version of the list. See Bolton, *Empire*, pp. 206–7.

has produced artefacts (particularly bronze and precious metalwork, votive objects, and a staggering number of 'sacrificed' weapons) that identify it as the main central place in this landscape with wide trade links across the region and Europe.[39] It was the most important site in western Skåne in the Migration and Viking Ages, and a natural fortress on top of a large and densely occupied hill in a wide marshy landscape between the mainland and the seafront, and must have been a crucial site in the power of the Jarls of Skåne. The lion's share of the grand metalwork objects discovered there come from the Migration and Viking Ages up to the eighth or ninth centuries, with the last great find being that of an ornate silver animal statue with inlaid glass eyes, perhaps a lion fighting with two snakes taken from a reliquary made in western Europe and brought to Uppåkra in the ninth century. However, in the tenth and eleventh centuries we still find occupation layers, as well as indications of trade and commerce, such as Arabic dirhams (coins) of the tenth century, three coins of Æthelred, and general metal-detector finds such as weights.[40] The site, or the road network that supplied it, clearly still held a commanding presence in the landscape, and necessitated the founding of Lund on the adjacent mainland at the centre of this road network. The foundation of Lund was linked to Swen and Cnut's power in the region, and almost certainly played a part in the final reduction in size and importance in the last years of the tenth century of Uppåkra, which lay almost abandoned by the middle of the eleventh century.[41]

Thus, Thorkell looks to have been a potential problem for both Swen and Cnut. He had access to wealth and must have had substantial influence within sections of the Scandinavian nobility. In addition, in his youth Thorkell had probably experienced first hand his dynasty's humbling by Harald Gormsson and Swen, and by 1013 he had already had a long career as a warlord and must have been at his wealthiest, loaded with the

---

[39] See Bolton, *Empire*, pp. 224–9. See also Larsson and Hårdh, 'Uppåkra'.

[40] Branca et al., 'Detektorfunna', Silvegren, 'Mynten från Uppåkra', and Gustin, 'Vikter'. See Helgeson, 'Helge', for the silver animal statue.

[41] Along with the smaller settlements in its vicinity. See Bolton, *Empire*, p. 226 and n. 88 there.

proceeds of raiding and payoffs from his three years of campaigning in England. He was clearly not under Swen and Cnut's control, and was perhaps for the first time in a position to challenge Swen for control of some, if not all, of Denmark. Whether he wished to do so or not, he must have been a considerable source of worry for Swen and Cnut.

Let us return to the invasion of England in 1013. Just as Swen's invasion differed greatly from the viking raiding that had preceded it, so his intentions about what to do with the country when it was finally under his sway differed greatly from all previous models of rule. The West Saxon line of Æthelred was exclusively that of southern men, whose interests centred on Wessex, a vast region in the middle of the southern coastline, with its northernmost border along the line of the towns of Bath, Abingdon and Reading. To the west lay Cornwall and to the east London and Kent, over which they had progressively extended their grip since the ninth century. This was the region in which these rulers spent most of their time. Less familiar, but under significant control, were the Midland regions of East Anglia, Mercia and Lindsey, which were less frequented by southern rulers the further north they lay. George Molyneaux has recently shown that legal reforms, reforms of coinage production and imposition of royal agents from the mid-tenth century onwards, drew all these regions together as a kingdom, giving the monarch powers to 'monitor, constrain, and direct significant aspects of the behaviour of even quite ordinary people throughout the area from the Channel to the Tees'.[42] That said, such reforms were still a recent phenomenon when we turn northwards to the region of York, and royal authority there seems to have been established by the imposition of a handful of royally appointed officials.[43] The ability to call such

[42] Molyneaux, *Formation of the English Kingdom*, the quotation here from p. 11. See also Campbell, 'Some Agents' and 'The Late Anglo-Saxon State'.

[43] Molyneaux, *Formation of the English Kingdom*, pp. 177–9. My comments about the chaotic nature of authority in Northumbria in this period (see Bolton, *Empire*, pp. 117–18) work with rather than against Molyneaux's conclusions. Whereas I have focused on the 'bewildering array of competing and co-operating' power blocs of varying sizes in the region, he focuses on the ties that bound individual elements of these structures to the royal court in the south.

officials southwards to attend a royal meeting is not the same thing as
uniform control over the population of the region, and accounts of the
feud between Thurbrand the Hold and Styr Ulfsson suggest that local
lords in the north may have operated with a greater degree of autonomy
than their counterparts in the south.[44] Æthelred did visit the north in
c. 1000 and again in 1014, but these were fleeting visits. As William of
Malmesbury stated in the early twelfth century, the king of England,
although content with an escort of his own men while in the south,
'takes with him a large company of auxiliaries' when in the North.[45]
Northwards of York lay Durham and an area under the control of an
aristocratic family based at Bamburgh, both of which were semi-
autonomous regions.[46]

　　Swen may have felt drawn to the north of England by the greater
number of Scandinavian settlers or the looser governing structures that
may have resembled those of Denmark, or both, and he focused his
attentions there. He commanded his men from, and died at, his camp
in Gainsborough near Lincoln, and as noted by Jonathan Wilcox there
is evidence that he intended to have himself crowned at nearby York.[47]
The D text of the Anglo-Saxon Chronicle records the appointment at
York of Ælfwig as bishop of London on 16 February 1014, only thirteen
days after Swen's sudden death. Such an election could only be made at
a national assembly, or *witenagemot* (literally 'meeting of the wise'), and
as thirteen days is hardly enough to call a nationwide meeting it seems
most likely that Swen summoned it to have his rule formalized, but died
while most of the dignitaries were in transit.[48] The choice of York is

---

[44] See Fletcher, *Bloodfeud*, pp. 51–3, Kapelle, *The Norman Conquest*, pp. 19–20, and Bolton,
Empire, pp. 113–17, with a map of the estates of Thurbrand's grandsons showing their clus-
tering around York on p. 116.

[45] William of Malmesbury, *Gesta Pontificum Anglorum*, ch. 99 (Winterbottom and Thomson,
p. 326).

[46] Whitelock, 'The Dealings of the Kings of England', pp. 77 and 82–3, Kapelle, *The
Norman Conquest*, pp. 24–6, Bolton, *Empire*, p. 110, and Molyneaux, *Formation of the English
Kingdom*, p. 199.

[47] Wilcox, 'Wulfstan's *Sermo Lupi*'.

[48] On the functions of a *witenagemot* see Liebermann, *National Assembly*, pp. 63–4, Oleson,
The Witenagemot, pp. 91–3, and the important recent work of Roach, *Kingship and Consent*.

startling, because no such meeting had previously been recorded there, and no northern *witenagemot* at all since the mid-ninth century, unless one counts the northern Midland meetings at Tamworth in 855 and 857 and Nottingham in 930.[49] Indeed, rulers after Swen would focus their attentions on the south, and the only recorded northern *witenagemot* that follows the period under concern here was that at Lincoln in 1045, and perhaps that at Northampton in the north Midlands in 1065.[50] This York meeting must have been intended to set Swen's rule quite at odds with the earlier regime based in southern England.

Moreover, Cnut's marriage to Ælfgifu of Northampton also dates to this period, and firmly tied Swen and Cnut into the ruling elites of the Midlands and northern England.[51] Ælfgifu was Cnut's first wife. Despite nearly a millennium of misrepresentation as merely his concubine, this was a form of union that was common and recognized by Scandinavian and Scandinavian-descended contemporaries as an elite practice used to unite dynasties. It could be set aside when the political benefits dwindled, but with the offspring retaining legal rights.[52] The slur of 'concubine', with its suggestion of sexual slavery and illegitimacy of offspring, is found first in the *Encomium*, a narrative initially written for the edification and pleasure of Cnut's second wife (Emma of Normandy). The term is there given alongside the slanderous claim that one of Ælfgifu's offspring by Cnut was in fact the child of a servant smuggled into her bed and passed off by her as a royal heir.[53] The

[49] See Liebermann, *National Assembly*, pp. 45–7, n. 21, for a full list of all recorded *witenagemot* (in which he does record one at York for 685, but this is highly unlikely to have a basis in fact), and for an updated list of those held 900–1066, ordered alphabetically by site, see Keynes, 'Church Councils', appendix I (where he notes for York that while no *witenagemot* are recorded there, a number of tenth-century royal meetings with groups of elites are).

[50] Liebermann, *National Assembly*, pp. 150–1 and 153.

[51] See Bolton, 'Ælfgifu of Northampton', and Insley, 'The Family of Wulfric Spott'.

[52] Bolton, 'Ælfgifu of Northampton', pp. 253–8.

[53] *Encomium Emmae Reginae*, III:1 (Campbell, p. 40). Note that Emma and her supporters appear to have been quite active in this smear campaign. John of Worcester, *Chronicon*, s.a. 1035 (Darlington and McGurk, p. 520), reports that he knew of allegations that this heir was in fact the son of a cobbler, and that his elder brother (who was dead by the 1040s and thus omitted by the *Encomium*) was the son of a priest's concubine.

paucity of sources that even mention Ælfgifu doubtless forces the reliance of modern historians on the *Encomium* – but as a rule of thumb it is perhaps sound practice when one wants to understand a man's first wife to take all comments from the second wife (or produced for her) with a pinch of salt.

Ælfgifu was a member of a powerful Mercian family, who rose to prominence when one of its members named Wulfric Spott entered the inner circle of Æthelred in 980.[54] From then until 1002 he witnessed royal charters as one of the king's closest advisors, and around 993 his brother, Ælfhelm, was appointed the ealdorman of Northumbria, an office he held until his death in 1006. Wulfric Spott founded Burton Abbey, and one of the charters preserved in its medieval archive reveals a clique of powerful northern nobles associated with this Mercian family. The witnesses at the head of the secular ministers in the witness-list of Æthelred's confirmation of the endowment of Burton Abbey (a document that must have been produced at its founder's, Wulfric Spott's, request) are revealing about the connections of this family.[55] The names of Æthelmær and Ordulf head the list and are recognizable as Æthelred's close family members and principal advisors.[56] These are followed by Wulfgeat and Wulfheah, who are most probably the sons of Ealdorman Ælfhelm, Wulfric Spott's brother. After an individual named Wulfstan who defies simple identification, these are in turn followed by the rare northern names Styr and Morcar, who would seem to be northern English allies of this family. Styr also appears amongst the witnesses on another Burton document dated 1009, and he appears again in the company of this family in a charter dated 996, from the

[54] See Keynes, *Diplomas*, pp. 188–9, P. H. Sawyer, *Charters of Burton Abbey*, pp. xxxviii–xliii, Whitelock, 'The Dealings', pp. 80–1, and Insley 'The Family of Wulfric Spott' for discussion of Wulfric and some of his family members.

[55] S. 906. Edited in P. H. Sawyer, *Charters of Burton Abbey*, no. 28. The term 'secular ministers' here is a literal translation of the Latin *ministri*, and in modern English perhaps implies too much of a government role. The men with such titles from high up the witness lists should be seen as royal agents with no apparent fixed portfolio, with some of these attached to the royal court, and those further down the lists merely important landholders from the localities. See Keynes, *Diplomas*, pp. 84–231, and Bolton, *Empire*, pp. 14–15.

[56] See Keynes, *Diplomas*, pp. 132, n. 165, and 209.

archive of the New Minster, Winchester: 'Ælfhelm and Wulfheah and Wulfric Wulfrun's son and Stir Wulf's son and Nafena and Norþman his brother', in which Wulfric Spott is listed with his matronym rather than his nickname.[57] The use of a patronym for Styr here also allows us to identify him with a supporter of Æthelred based around Durham, and one of the two key players in what is perhaps the most famous feud in Anglo-Saxon history.[58] A number of eleventh- and twelfth-century narratives from Durham Cathedral, notably the *De Obsessione Dunelmi*, record the details of a bitter feud between two influential Northumbrian nobles named Styr Ulfsson and Thurbrand the Hold.[59] These narratives suggest that while Styr held no formal office in Northumbria, he was an influential figure who wielded some considerable authority. The fact that he donated seven estates to the community at Durham, in both the northern and southern parts of Northumbria, but concentrated on the north-eastern region around Durham, confirms that he was a man of significant influence and wealth.[60]

Morcar was an equally influential northerner, and was named the 'thegn of the Seven Boroughs' by the Anglo-Saxon Chronicle on his death in 1015.[61] He appears to have held authority over these 'Seven Boroughs' with his brother Sigeferth, and they probably encompassed a region of the northern Midlands elsewhere referred to as the Five Boroughs (Leicester, Lincoln, Nottingham, Stamford and Derby), with the addition of York and Torksey.[62] Morcar was one of the beneficiaries of Wulfric

[57] S. 922; edited by P. H. Sawyer, *Charters of Burton Abbey*, no. 32. S. 877.

[58] See Fletcher, *Bloodfeud*, pp. 51–3, and Kapelle, *Norman Conquest*, pp. 19–20.

[59] *De Obsessione Dunelmi*, edited in *Symeonis Monachi Opera Omnia: Historia Ecclesiae Dunhelmensis* (Arnold, I, pp. 215–20).

[60] A grant by one *Stir filius Ulfi* to Durham, which evidently was entered into a Gospel Book there, is in the late eleventh-century *Historia de Sancto Cuthberto*, ch. 29 (Johnson South, p. 66), Symeon of Durham's twelfth-century *Historia Dunelmensis Ecclesiae*, edited in *Symeonis Monachi Opera Omnia: Historia Ecclesiae Dunhelmensis* (Arnold, I, p. 83); and the fifteenth-century *Liber Ruber*, edited by Craster in his 'The Red Book of Durham', p. 526.

[61] ASC 1015 CDE (O'Brien O'Keeffe, p. 99).

[62] Morcar and Sigeferth are identified as brothers (sons of one Earngrim) by John of Worcester, *Chronicon*, s.a. 1015 (Darlington and McGurk, p. 478). For the 'Seven Boroughs' see Whitelock, *Anglo-Saxon Chronicle*, p. 94, n. 2.

Spott's will, and Peter Sawyer has shown that it is likely he was married to Wulfric's niece (the daughter of Wulfric and Ælfhelm's sister, Ælfthryth).[63]

Moreover, the last two names that follow Styr Ulfsson in the document from the archive of the New Minster, Winchester, are also easily identifiable as northern nobles. Northman must have been the 'Norðman miles' to whom Æthelred gave estates in Twywell, Northamptonshire, in 1013, and he is probably the namesake whose landholdings link him to the community at Durham.[64] The late eleventh-century *Historia de Sancto Cuthberto* records a Northman as one of three earls who was able to forcibly abstract from the community twenty-four estates in the vicinity of Durham during the episcopate of Bishop Aldhun (990–1018), with one of these estates, at Escomb, subsequently returned by the donation of a 'Norðman eorl' recorded in an addition to Durham's *Liber Vitae*.[65] Nafena appears later in the Anglo-Saxon Chronicle as the father of a Thurcetel who was executed alongside Earl Uhtred in 1016, apparently as his associate, and this association leads us even further northwards.[66] This Uhtred was yet another significant figure in the north, who held an office, comparable to an earldom, from a stronghold at Bamburgh, wielding authority over the northern region of Northumbria, or at least the north-eastern coastline from the Scottish border to the River Tees, from some point in the 990s until his death.[67] He was a supporter of Æthelred, and in c. 1004 he repudiated his first wife in order to marry Styr's daughter, Sige, and subsequently was remarried to one of Æthelred's daughters (also named Ælfgifu).[68] No more than these threads can now be recovered from history,

---

[63] P. H. Sawyer, *Charters of Burton Abbey*, p. xliii.

[64] S. 931.

[65] *Historia de Sancto Cuthberto*, ch. 31 (Johnson South, pp. 66–8), states that the bishop gave these estates to his supporters. However, Symeon of Durham, *Historia Dunelmensis Ecclesiae*, edited in *Symeonis Monachi Opera Omnia: Historia Ecclesiae Dunhelmensis* (Arnold, I, p. 83), and the *Liber Ruber* (Craster, pp. 526–7) claim that these were loaned to these men through necessity and were subsequently held by force. The reference within the *Liber Vitae* is *Liber Vitae Ecclesiae Dunelmensis* (Stevenson, p. 57).

[66] ASC 1016 CDE (O'Brien O'Keeffe, p. 101).

[67] Kapelle, *Norman Conquest*, pp. 14–26.

[68] *De Obsessione Dunelmi*, ch. 2, edited in *Symeonis Monachi Opera Omnia: Historia Ecclesiae Dunhelmensis* (Arnold, I, 216).

but it does appear that the family of Ælfgifu of Northampton were aristocrats of wealth and influence based in the Midlands, who by design or accident had strong ties to elites throughout the north of England right up to the Scottish border.

Importantly, while the family of Wulfric Spott were amongst Æthelred's closest advisors from 980 to the early years of the eleventh century, they fell dramatically from favour in 1005.[69] As Simon Keynes notes, it was then that their subscriptions of royal charters ceased abruptly, and the Anglo-Saxon Chronicle reports that in 1006 Ealdorman Ælfhelm was killed, his sons Wulfheah and Ufegeat were blinded, and Wulfgeat was deprived of all his territory.[70] John of Worcester adds that their downfall was orchestrated by Eadric streona, and that the blinding of Wulfheah and Ufegeat was ordered by Æthelred himself.[71] They presumably retired to their Midland estates, and their valuable northern connections must have withdrawn from the royal court at the same time. The proposed union of the family with Swen and Cnut must have seemed like a reprieve to them, and offered the conquerors access to Midland and northern political circles.

Swen died suddenly on 3 February 1014, bringing these plans to an abrupt stop.[72] The various notices of Swen's death have been extensively studied, with Lene Demidoff devoting an entire paper to them. However, one such notice, and perhaps the most touching and poignant, is, to my knowledge, always omitted from modern scholarship – that of a half-stanza in Þórðr Kolbeinsson's poem for Swen's son-in-law, Eiríkr Hákonarson, composed in the years immediately after 1016.[73] There the

---

[69] Keynes, *Diplomas*, pp. 188–9 and 209–13.

[70] Ibid., pp. 210–11.

[71] John of Worcester, *Chronicon*, s.a. 1006 (Darlington and McGurk, pp. 456–8). Boyle, 'A Welsh Record' discusses the report of this in a Welsh chronicle.

[72] The *Encomium Emmae Reginae*, II,3 (Campbell, p. 18), and Thietmar of Merseburg, *Chronicon* VII, 39(28) (Holtzmann, p. 446), both note that his body was left in England, and then carried to Denmark later by a unnamed woman, who was warned of Æthelred's intentions to disinter the corpse. On this see Bolton, 'Ælfgifu of Northampton', p. 259.

[73] On Swen's death see Demidoff, 'The Death of Sven Forkbeard' and P. H. Sawyer, 'Swein Forkbeard and the Historians'.

poet states: 'King Swen is reported from the south to be dead, and his dwellings to have been desolate; misfortune scarcely spares most men.'[74]

Swen's focus on the north and apparent wish for unprecedented change in how England was run may now have sealed the immediate fate of his dynasty in England. I think we might safely postulate that such a dramatic sea change and proposed removal of power from the hands of the nobility of southern England did not sit well with them. It is hardly surprising that on Swen's death the Anglo-Saxon Chronicle states 'all the councillors', backed in John of Worcester's words 'by general agreement', sent to Normandy for Æthelred to ask whether he would return from exile to govern them 'more justly than before'.[75] Æthelred sent his son Edward and an entourage to England to negotiate, and afterwards the same council 'declared every Danish king outlawed from England forever'. The embassy returned to Normandy with an accord agreed, and brought back Æthelred during Lent of 1014.[76] Cnut, however, still remained in the north, and reached his own settlement with the inhabitants of the north-east region of Lindsey, while semingly in command of the invading forces.

Æthelred had been given a second chance, and could not afford to allow Cnut further time to regroup. Thus, on his return, Æthelred struck immediately at Lindsey and exacted violent revenge for their support of the Danes, and 'all human kind that could be got at were raided and

---

[74] Þórðr Kolbeinsson, *Eiríksdrápa*, verse 10 (Whaley, p. 503; the translation is Carroll's, published there). The first two lines are especially well crafted to evoke emotion, opening with the king's name, 'En Sveinn konungr sunnan / sagðr es dauðr, en auðir', and including in the second line a repeating half-rhyme, which initially continues the alliteration on 's' (and Swen's name) from the first line, before drawing our attention to the phrase 'reported to be dead'. The last word in this half-rhyme ends the line on *auðir* (desolate). The text here is so touching within the context of an otherwise violent and swashbuckling poem that Fidjestøl (*Det Norrønne Fyrstediktet*, p. 116) concluded that it and another fragment, recorded as the work of Þórðr Kolbeinsson for Eiríkr, must in fact have been from an *erfidrápa* (a memorial poem composed post-mortem) for Swen instead. However, they fit well within the rest of Þórðr's composition for Eiríkr, and instead most probably record the great respect and tenderness of affection of the latter for his father-in-law.

[75] ASC 1014 CDE (O'Brien O'Keeffe, p. 98); John of Worcester, *Chronicon*, s.a. 1014 (Darlington and McGurk, pp. 476–8).

[76] This is dated solely by John of Worcester, *Chronicon*, s.a. 1014 (Darlington and McGurk, pp. 476–8).

burned and killed'.[77] Cnut was forced to take to sea with his fleet, apparently so quickly that his father's body had to be left behind and brought later, perhaps by 'a certain English woman' sometimes identified as Cnut's first wife, Ælfgifu of Northampton.[78] They sailed southwards as far as Sandwich, where they put ashore the hostages who had been surrendered to Cnut's father (doubtless to ensure the loyalty of the English who had sworn allegiance to Swen during his takeover), after mutilation by the cutting off of their hands, ears and noses.[79] From here the fleet turned eastwards to the open sea, and returned to Denmark.

Cnut could not now afford to rest. While he must have been an experienced operator within the Danish political system, and had had his first taste of the English political machinery, he was Swen's second son. His elder brother, Harald, was firmly in control of Denmark. In a hyperbolic tone the *Encomium* narrates the reuniting of Cnut and his brother as a tearful embrace, with each brother pressing kisses on the other's cheeks.[80] This we might set aside as an exaggeration composed some two decades later, but what may be accurate here is the record of Cnut's intention to return to England with another force. Certainly, he wasted no time in Denmark, and began to forge another network of Scandinavian warlords from which to draw another vast invading army. There appears to have been no standing army at this time in Denmark, and the social infrastructure was not yet centralized to the point where a ruler could call up such a force.[81] Thus, Cnut had to build a large network of personal supporters from the most important elites of the kingdom, balancing their egos, wants and various pre-existing rivalries and alliances to place himself at the centre of this network. Each of

---

[77] The Anglo-Saxon Chronicle is followed here (ASC 1014 CDE [O'Brien O'Keeffe, p. 99]).

[78] *Encomium Emmae Reginae*, II:3 (Campbell, pp. 18).

[79] The details of the Anglo-Saxon Chronicle are followed here (as n. 77 above), while John of Worcester states that the hostages lost their hands and ears, and had their nostrils slit (*Chronicon*, s.a. 1014 [Darlington and McGurk, pp. 476–8]).

[80] *Encomium Emmae Reginae*, II:2 (Campbell, pp. 16–18).

[81] See Lund, 'The Armies' and 'The Danish Perspective', pp. 114–42, and 'Cnut's Danish Kingdom', pp. 32–3.

these men had their own followings of lesser nobles, and so on, forming a sunflower-like structure, with a single sturdy stem above ground but a huge array of branching roots beneath the surface. Thus, when the stem was pulled the entire root network followed.

I have mentioned Thorkell the Tall above, and it now seems fitting to discuss the other main Scandinavian influence on Cnut during this period of his life: the Norwegian Eiríkr Hákonarson, Jarl of Hlaðir (Modern Norwegian: Lade, a large rural estate now on the eastern outskirts of Trondheim). The Jarls of Hlaðir had ruled the northern coastal regions of Norway in the second half of the tenth century, and maintained close relationships with Cnut's dynasty.[82] Jarl Hákon Sigurðsson (r. c. 961–95; Eiríkr's father) had brought Norwegian military forces to the aid of Harald Gormsson on at least one occasion in the late tenth century, and members of the jarl's family had sought refuge in the Danish court during the periods of exile forced on the jarls by the Norwegian rulers Óláfr Tryggvason and Óláfr Haraldsson.[83] Eiríkr himself married Cnut's elder half-sister Gytha, most probably while Cnut was still a child. The seizure of power by the Norwegian king Óláfr Tryggvason c. 995 indirectly contributed to the death of Eiríkr's father and forced him and his brother Sveinn into exile in Sweden, and thence perhaps to raiding in the Baltic. They ambushed Óláfr Tryggvason at the Battle of Svolder in 999/1000 at which Óláfr died, leaving them to return home to their family's old allies.

Thus, Eiríkr was a middle-aged man in 1015, with experience of rule and substantial personal contacts throughout the elites of Scandinavia. In addition, he was a trusted ally, married to Cnut's half-sister, and whose dynasty had relied on Cnut's for aid on several occasions in the recent past. Importantly, his area of political interest was also

---

[82] This dynasty has yet to find a modern political historian with a strong interest in it. See Koht's entry for 'Haakon Sigurdsson' in *Norsk Biografisk Leksikon*, pp. 187–91, Davidson's entry for 'Hákon jarl ("earl") Sigurðarson' in Pulsiano, *Medieval Scandinavia*, p. 259, Andersen, *Samlingen av Norge*, pp. 99–101, Ström, 'Poetry as an Instrument', and Jon Vidar Sigurdsson, *Det Norrøne Samfunnet*, pp. 27–34.

[83] See Einarr Helgason, *Vellekla*, verses 25–28 (Whaley, pp. 314–18).

sufficiently far enough removed from Cnut's to avoid any serious overlap of authority and thus potential conflict. Eiríkr seems to have been a stable and experienced influence on Cnut, and most probably understood and shared Cnut's need to seize territory outside of Scandinavia. Eiríkr and his brother's rule in Norway would appear to have already been under threat when he joined Cnut, and the collapse of their authority there began with Sveinn Hákonarson's loss of the Battle of Nesjar to Óláfr Haraldsson on 25 March 1016.[84] Sveinn retreated again to Sweden, and died there soon after, perhaps of injuries sustained in the battle, leaving Eiríkr as head of his dynasty but without a Norwegian territorial foothold. Like Cnut, therefore, Eiríkr may also have been searching for a new region to rule.

As we might expect from what has been said above, Thorkell the Tall's alliances with Cnut appear to have been quite the opposite of those that Cnut shared with Eiríkr. Like Eiríkr, Thorkell was probably middle-aged in 1015. We do not know what he did when Swen successfully invaded England in 1013. Thorkell had been hired as a mercenary by Æthelred, and he may well have escorted him to safety, or abandoned his new employer as soon as his fate became clear. The *Encomium* narrates how, after Æthelred's return to England, Thorkell resurfaced in Denmark (having been dispensed with by Æthelred), approaching the shore cautiously and only when permission had been secured by intermediaries.[85] This done, he asked for mercy, and offered his local knowledge of England in the event of another invasion.[86]

---

[84] Sigvatr Þórðarson, *Nesjavísur* (Whaley, pp. 556–78), and Hellberg, 'Slaget vid Nesjar'.

[85] *Encomium Emmae Reginae*, II:3 (Campbell, p. 18).

[86] It has been noted, but not studied in any detail, that the *Encomium* contains several parts that are clearly written to pander to pro-Thorkell elites in its intended audience, and yet few such factions can have remained in Cnut's court after the 1020s. Thorkell's son, Harald, did appear to enter or remain in Cnut's service after his father's expulsion in 1021 and subsequent death in Scandinavia, attesting charters in the 1030s and 1042 (for this see Keynes, 'Cnut's Earls', p. 66, and Williams, ' "Cockles amongst the Wheat" ', pp. 9–11; but also note that Williams, 'Thorkell the Tall', p. 157, n. 82, subsequently rejects this, perhaps following the view found in a footnote to Tschan, *History of the Archbishops*, p. 109, n. 274, citing Steindorff, *Jahrbücher*, I, p. 277), as well as perhaps holding a key role in the rule of Norway. Perhaps Harald, or followers of his, were the intended recipients of this rose-tinted view of his father's actions.

It was from the men of these two quite different warlords, as well as many others, that Cnut forged his invasion fleet. The breaks with tradition of skaldic verse in this period suggest how fragile the balance of power was. Skaldic verse is an overwhelmingly conservative genre, and changes in its format are rare and always surprising. The earliest surviving verse for Cnut, the anonymous *Liðsmannaflokkr*, narrates the invasion of 1015–16 and the fall of London, and must date to between 1017 and 1021.[87] It is almost unique amongst the skaldic corpus in appearing to have two patrons, Thorkell and Cnut. As the principal function of such verses was to extoll the virtues of one particular ruler over all others, this deviation from the norm must have been obvious to its Scandinavian audience. It opens with an extremely unconventional address not to a single patron, but to the anonymous invading armies in general, urging them to strike swiftly before the English realize their presence, to put on 'that kind of shirt which the hammer sews' and 'nourish the raven on the blood of Englishmen'. Only in verse four is a possible patron introduced in the identification of part of the forces as 'Thorkell's men', and in the next verse the impression that he is the subject of the poem is strengthened by an apparently conventional direct address to him followed by laudatory statement: 'The earl, who briskly broke the ravens' fast, seems to me outstanding' (the final word, *hár*, punning on Thorkell's nickname, 'the tall', and attesting to the contemporary usage of this epithet). Only at the end of the next verse is it quickly noted that during the campaign 'dissent arose', setting up for the decisive turning point in the opening of verse seven, in which 'Cnut decided, and commanded all the Danes to wait'. This short phrase creates tension, and implicitly hands authority in the verse to Cnut.[88]

[87] *Liðsmannaflokkr* (Whaley, pp. 1014–28). See also Poole, *Viking Poems*, pp. 86–115, and Townend, 'Contextualising' p. 163, in which he dates this verse to c. 1016–17. I would add to this the observation that as Thorkell is named as a 'jarl' in verse 5 of *Liðsmannaflokkr* (Whaley, p. 1022), this poem should probably be dated to 1017 at least, when Cnut appointed him to an earldom. There are no indications that, like several of his brothers, he held the jarldom of Skåne at any stage.
[88] *Liðsmannaflokkr*, verses 6–7 (Whaley, pp. 1023–5).

We might have swept this aside, and concluded it was a short-lived experiment in patronless poetry in this period, but for the fact that another near-contemporary skaldic poem also reflects similar trends, and that it was composed for Eiríkr.[89] Soon after the conquest, a poet named Þórðr Kolbeinsson composed a lengthy verse in his honour, *Eiríksdrápa*, which in its second section narrates the invasion of England. In verse nine it alludes to the 'marriage alliance' between him and Cnut and the fact that this has proved its worth, and verse ten opens with 'Moreover, Cnut, the Scylding, who sailed over the sea, let his warships sail out to the shallow of the shore', a line that in the original alliterates three times with Cnut's name. This verse then discusses the peaceful meeting of the 'helmeted earl' (Eiríkr) and the 'prince' (Cnut), which 'came about easily on the day when both men wished to come over the sea'. Superficially this mention of Cnut assigns the following events to his invasion, but the mention of a ruler in a praise poem other than its obvious patron is again almost unprecedented, and the naming of that ruler as a peaceful ally as opposed to a sworn and vanquished enemy is markedly unconventional.

It should be noted that these two poems were not independent sources, and indeed the poet of one consciously echoes the other, with the notably similar opening lines of stanzas: 'Gongum upp, áðr Engla' (*Liðsmannaflokkr*, verse 1, line 1), and 'Gengu upp, þeirs Englum' (*Eiríksdrápa*, verse 16, line 1), as well as setting up the verbal opposition of the two patrons as *jarl* and *hilmir*.[90] *Eiríksdrápa* has the wider proposed date range of 1016 to the probable death of the patron c. 1023, as opposed to *Liðsmannaflokkr*'s 1017–21, but it is not clear which came first, and the two may have been composed within weeks or months of each other immediately after the end of the campaign.[91] Contemporary skaldic poets frequently echoed or appropriated each other's works,

[89] Þórðr Kolbeinsson, *Eiríksdrápa* (Whaley, pp. 487–513).

[90] *Liðsmannaflokkr*, verses 1 and 5; Þórðr Kolbeinsson, *Eiríksdrápa*, verses 16 and 13 (Whaley, pp. 1016 and 1022, and 511 and 507).

[91] See Townend, 'Contextualising', pp. 161–4, for the current dating of these poems, as well as my comments above in n. 87.

and we can most probably read into these ambiguities of literary patronage a knowledge by the poet of actual ambiguities in the leadership of Cnut's forces. The subtle differences within the works (with Eiríkr having an easy alliance with Cnut, whereas Thorkell has a competitive role) also most probably reflect the actual nature of Cnut's alliances.[92]

Cnut sat at the centre of this spider's web of personal compacts and competing interests, and waited for a crisis in England that would give his attack an edge. This was provided in 1015 by Æthelred and his son Edmund Ironside, when they placed themselves at odds with each other over the executions of the northern lords Morcar and Sigeferth.[93] The Anglo-Saxon Chronicle states that these men were denounced at a great public meeting in Oxford by one of Æthelred's most powerful, acquisitive and probably corrupt councillors, Eadric streona (his byname meaning 'the grasper').[94] They may have been exposed as playing some part in Swen's invasion, or as sympathizing with it.[95] The Chronicle states that they were killed 'dishonourably' and the king seized 'all their property' and ordered Sigeferth's widow, Ealdgyth, to be imprisoned in Malmesbury Abbey. More than any other region of England, Edmund Ironside seems to have formed bonds with the eastern Danelaw, and these appear to have dragged him into this

---

[92] Poole reached similar conclusions in his 'Skaldic Verse and Anglo-Saxon History', p. 283, and *Viking Poems*, pp. 99–100.

[93] On this see Stafford, 'The Reign', pp. 35–6.

[94] ASC 1015 CDE (O'Brien O'Keeffe, pp. 99–100). This source as well as John of Worcester's *Chronicon* (Darlington and McGurk) forms the backbone of the following narrative here. On Eadric streona, see Keynes, 'Cnut's Earls', p. 67, *Deerhurst, A.D. 1016* and 'A Tale of Two Kings', pp. 211–17; Stafford, 'The Reign of Æthelred II', pp. 35–7; and on tensions between Eadric and the family of Cnut's first wife, Ælfgifu of Northampton, see Insley, 'Politics, Conflict and Kinship'.

[95] Stafford ('The Reign of Æthelred II', p. 36) suggests instead that Edmund may have been reacting to the political machinations of Æthelred's wife since 1002: Emma, in having her own children anointed and promoted over him, thus leading him into revolt. She further suggests that Sigeferth and Morcar's crimes may have been a part of this revolt, not that of Swen's invasion. However, there is no further indication of tension between Edmund and his father or half-brothers, and after Cnut's marriage to Ælfgifu of Northampton, Sigeferth and Morcar, as her family's allies, must have looked dangerously close to Cnut.

conflict on the opposing side to his father, the king.[96] Only two charters in Edmund's name survive, one of which is a grant to Thorney Abbey from 1015–16, and the other a grant of land to Peterborough Abbey, made for the souls of Edmund, his wife and Sigeferth.[97] While the ætheling Æthelstan left decorated weaponry and valuable horses to both of his living brothers, only Edmund received land, specifically estates in East Anglia and farther north in the Danelaw.[98] Thus, Edmund would appear to have been obliged to act when his father struck at elites from this region, and came to the defence of the families of these men in defiance of his father and the royal court. Between the Feast of the Assumption and the Nativity of St Mary (15 August–8 September 1015), he released Sigeferth's widow and gave her the ultimate protection he could, by marrying her, then moving northwards to occupy her deceased husband's estates and accept the formal submission of the dependants of the executed men.[99] He now stood at the head of the persecuted kin-groups, directly facing off with his father, the king.

Cnut must have been waiting eagerly for news from England, and immediately after these events he struck swiftly at the port of Sandwich with a great fleet, sailing around Kent and entering the River Frome to raid in Dorset, Somerset and Wiltshire. He then had a stroke of luck, as the ageing Æthelred became seriously ill. The king took refuge at Cosham, leaving Edmund Ironside to rally the English forces. Early in 1016, Cnut and his armies entered Warwickshire, and when Edmund tried to assemble the forces in the area, the local militia refused to support him unless he had the support of his father and the London garrison. These Edmund had secured by 6 January, but still the full penalty and force of the law had to be threatened to mobilize this army, and Æthelred himself was forced to travel to Mercia to show his public

---

[96] His mother may have had her origins there. See Whitelock, 'Dealings', p. 80. See also Stafford, 'The Reign of Æthelred II', p. 36.

[97] S. 947 and 948.

[98] S. 1503; Whitelock, *Anglo-Saxon Wills*, no. 20, pp. 56–63 and 167–74.

[99] John of Worcester gives the date here: *Chronicon*, s.a. 1015 (Darlington and McGurk, pp. 478–80).

support. It is perhaps telling of the fears or even beginnings of paranoia of the elderly king at this stage that, having heard that an unnamed follower or some auxiliary troops would betray him there, he fled back to London and this force immediately disbanded.[100] Edmund then played his trump card and rode to the far north to seek the support of Earl Uhtred. The presence of the royal heir apparent was enough to draw Uhtred and his forces into the battle in the south, but evidently these were still not enough, and Edmund had to use these forces to make an example of Staffordshire, Shropshire and Leicestershire by raiding and harrying amongst the English there 'because they would not go into battle against the Danish army'.[101] Cnut continued to devastate along the eastern coastline, raiding in Buckinghamshire, Bedfordshire, Huntingdonshire, Northamptonshire, Lincolnshire and Nottinghamshire. Skaldic verse composed for Eiríkr and Cnut record that Eiríkr's forces slaughtered an English army (perhaps that of Ulfcetyl) at a site named *Hringmaraheiðr*, and most probably to be identified with Ringmere Pit, near Thetford, while Cnut's forces caused bloodshed in an engagement with soldiers inside the town of Norwich.[102] Following this, Cnut and Eiríkr turned northwards through the open countryside to York and Northumbria. This detour was a tactical manoeuvre in that the invaders seized the region quickly (probably as Uhtred's march south had emptied it of troops loyal to the crown), and here Cnut installed Eiríkr as regional governor. Again skaldic verse composed for Cnut adds to this picture, noting that he and Eiríkr

---

[100] ASC 1016 CDE (O' Brien O'Keeffe, p. 100). The Anglo-Saxon Chronicle states that the threat came from the unnamed follower, whereas John of Worcester (*Chronicon*, s.a. 1016 [Darlington and McGurk, p. 482]) states that it came from the auxiliaries.

[101] John of Worcester, *Chronicon*, s.a. 1016 (Darlington and McGurk, p. 482).

[102] Þórðr Kolbeinsson, *Eiríksdrápa*, verse 15 (Whaley, p. 510), and Óttarr svarti, *Hǫfuðlausn*, verse 9 (Whaley, p. 752). These verses were dismissed by Campbell ('Skaldic Verse', pp. 3–4, 13 and 15) as improbable given the battle-lines of 1015–16, on no more evidence than the lack of the mention of such battles in English sources. On the partisan nature of such English sources, see Keynes, 'Declining Reputation', pp. 229–33, and for a defence of the veracity of the verse see Poole, 'Skaldic Verse', especially pp. 276–9. On the Anglo-Saxon nobleman Ulfcytel see Marten, 'The Shiring of East Anglia', pp. 14–16, Williams, *Æthelred the Unready*, p. 52, Poole, 'Skaldic Verse', pp. 288–9, and Campbell, *Encomium Emmae Reginae*, p. 93.

brought sorrow to the people in *Hemmingaborg*, west of the River Ouse (probably Hemingbrough, East Yorkshire), and killed English some distance northwards nearby the River Tees, most probably recording the northernmost extent of this harrying of Uhtred's lands.[103] Messengers seeking Uhtred were probably allowed to pass freely southwards, and Uhtred abandoned his joint action with Edmund and fled back home. There he submitted to Cnut out of necessity, and gave him hostages, probably trying to curry favour. Cnut appears not to have been reassured by these manoeuvres and, as noted above, Eiríkr needed a new territorial base. Therefore, Uhtred was summarily executed.

Edmund withdrew to London where his father had already sought refuge, and Cnut returned south through the western parts of the country, returning to his ships and main forces before Easter 1016. Fortune then dealt Cnut another stroke of luck as Æthelred died on 23 April. Confusion reigned, with the Anglo-Saxon Chronicle noting that the nobles who were holed up within London's walls, along with the garrison there, elected Edmund Ironside king; whereas John of Worcester states that 'the bishops, abbots, ealdormen and all the nobles of England [presumably with the exception of those in London], assembled together and, by general agreement, elected Cnut as their lord and king, and coming to him at Southampton, renounced and repudiated in his presence all the descendants of King Æthelred'.[104] Edmund marched into Wessex, receiving the submission of the region and raising troops there, but these forces joined him perhaps not so much out of a sense of duty but because he arrived at the head of an army. Cnut besieged Edmund's long-time stronghold of London. Attempts to take the city failed, and Cnut turned back to Wessex, meeting Edmund's forces at Penselwood in Dorset, where the English won the day. The forces met again at Sherston in the days after

[103] Óttarr svarti, *Knútsdrápa*, verses 5 and 6 (Whaley, pp. 772–4). See also Poole, 'Skaldic Verse', pp. 272–3, for further discussion.

[104] ASC 1016 CDE (O'Brien O'Keeffe, p. 101); John of Worcester, *Chronicon*, s.a. 1016 (Darlington and McGurk, p. 484).

midsummer for a battle lasting two days, with the *Encomium* and Gaimar in his Anglo-Norman translation of the Anglo-Saxon Chronicle attributing much of the actual fighting to Thorkell's forces.[105] There was no apparent victor here, but crucially this is the first time that the sources report English defectors and their armies fighting in support of the Danes. This is perhaps what Æthelred had feared in the first few days of January when he fled Mercia for the safety of London, and it seems to have been the crucial tipping point of the campaign, when we can first see the turning of events in Cnut's favour. The Anglo-Saxon Chronicle names the self-interested politician Eadric streona amongst these turncoats at Sherston, as well as a more mysterious Ælfmær deorling, and to these John of Worcester adds an *Algarus filius Meauues* (who must be Ælfgar, son of [Æthelweard] mæw), as well as the forces from Hampshire and Wiltshire.[106] The psychological impact of these acts of treachery on the English as well as the Danish side must have been great. Eadric streona seems to have played the part of the serial traitor, swinging between political opposites whenever each or other side seemed in the ascendant, and his appearance here is no surprise. Ælfmær deorling is otherwise unknown, and much more will be said about Ælfgar, son of Æthelweard mæw, below. However, none of these men appears to have been in charge of the forces called up from the Wessex heartlands of Hampshire and Wiltshire, regions that we might have thought to be stalwart supporters of any member of the West Saxon dynasty, and their inclusion here by John of Worcester points towards a wider shift of support away from Edmund and towards Cnut.

At this stage we must pause briefly to consider a crucial factor in this war: Cnut's use of English collaborators. As noted in the section on sources above, the uppermost names of each column of types of

---

[105] John of Worcester, *Chronicon*, s.a. 1016 (Darlington and McGurk, pp. 486–8), records the length of the battle. On the part played by Thorkell's forces, see *Encomium Emmae Reginae*, II:6–7 (Campbell, pp. 20–4); Gaimar, *Lestorie des Engles*, lines 4229–56 (Bell, pp. 134–5). This crucial battle is also recorded by Óttarr svarti's *Knútsdrápa*, verse 6 (Whaley, p. 774), as the opening of a new southern part of the campaign. See Poole, 'Skaldic Verse', pp. 273–4.

[106] John of Worcester, *Chronicon*, s.a. 1016 (Darlington and McGurk, p. 486).

signatory in witness-lists appended to royal charters represent in some
form a record of those figures at the royal court, and the order of those
names appears to record some hierarchies and relationships within that
court. Two groups of English nobles can be discerned in the last of
Æthelred's charters and again in the first of Cnut's in positions indicating that these men did not merely survive the conquest in 1016 but
thrived under its pressures.[107] They all appear consistently in lowly positions within Æthelred's charters, and rise immediately after Cnut's
takeover to positions of the greatest prominence, immediately beneath
the newly imposed Scandinavians in the court. The first group circu-
lated around a figure with the rare name of Odda, who occurs initially
amongst the secular ministers of Æthelred's court in a charter
from 1013.[108] He resurfaces in documents from 1014 and 1015, and
after the silence of 1016 and 1017 from which almost no charters
survive, Odda is recognizable by his associates there as the same man in
witness-lists attached to documents produced in the archive of Exeter
Cathedral.[109]

S. 931b	S. 951	S. 953
(Barking)	(Exeter)	(Exeter)
1013	1018(?)	1018(?)
Ethelmer	Ðored	Þoryd
Elfgar	Aslac	Aslac
Odda	Tobi	Tobi
Ethelric	*Ælfgar*	*Ælfgar*
Elfgar	*Odda*	*Odda*
Ælfgar	Ordgar	*Ælfgar*

[107] Bolton, *Empire*, pp. 22–35, with part of this material expanded to form my *Conquest and Controversy*.

[108] S. 931b.

[109] S. 933, 934, 951 and 953. On the variant witness-lists attached to the last two see Bolton, *Empire*, pp. 25–6, n. 59.

Here on occasions either side of the conquest an Ælfgar or Elfgar witnesses immediately before Odda, and another Ælfgar or Elfgar closely following them after an intermediate figure (either *Ethelric* or Ordgar). The geographical distance between Barking and Exeter makes it unlikely that any cross-contamination of the documents could have occurred, and moreover the association of these men in such sources can be shown to have endured throughout the next decades of the eleventh century. By tracing their continuing careers through the following years it is possible to identify this Odda as an important politician who held the estate of Deerhurst in Gloucestershire, where he built a surviving chapel in honour of his brother.[110] In 1051 he was elevated to the office of earl of Western Wessex. The Ordgar here also commonly witnesses documents amongst this group of associates, and in fact in Cnut's reign Ordgar features only once where he is not immediately associated with Odda.[111] Like Odda, his later charter attestations allow us to identify Ordgar as the royal minister of that name to whom Edward the Confessor granted land at Littleham in 1042.[112] Through this grant it is possible to deduce that Ordgar was the head of an influential aristocratic family based on the Devonshire and Cornwall border.[113] The appearance of both Odda and Ordgar alongside their respective brothers in a Devonshire document from the mid-1040s demonstrates that Ordgar had a brother named Ælfgar, who is perhaps one of the two men by that name here.[114]

The second group of associates discernible in Cnut's charters focuses on the name of the second Ælfgar in the 1018 witness-lists from Exeter, who can be shown to be the same Ælfgar, son of Æthelweard mæw (also known independently as Ælfgar mæw), whom John of Worcester places

---

[110] See Williams, *Land, Power and Politics*, for details of Odda's later career and family connections.

[111] S. 976, a spurious grant supposedly from 1035, which includes only four ministers.

[112] S. 998.

[113] See Finberg, 'The House of Ordgar', and his *Lucerna*, pp. 186–202, for discussion of his family and landholdings on the Cornish border.

[114] S. 1474.

amongst the English turncoats at the Battle of Sherston. The longer version of the 1018 Exeter witness-list reads:[115]

Þoryd
Aslac
Tobi
Ælfgar
Odda
Ordgar
Ælfgar
Ælfmær
Ælfged
Byrihtric

The names here immediately following the second Ælfgar – Ælfmær (corrected to Æthelmær), *Ælfged* (Ælfget), and *Byrihtric* (Beorhtric) – attest together on a large number of documents from Cnut's reign in positions of great prominence.[116] Looking backwards into Æthelred's charters, we note that there was only one prominent minister named Ælfgar in the last years of his reign, and he is named in a grant dated 999 as Ælfgar mæw.[117] Furthermore, in the charters from Æthelred's last years this Ælfgar mæw nearly always attests with an Æthelmær and his father Æthelwold.[118] Æthelwold's name does not appear after 1007 and he perhaps died then, but Æthelmær may have continued to witness in conjunction with Ælfgar mæw in a charter of 1007; and more probably alongside Ælfgar and a *Brihtric* who may be Ælfgar's son, Beorhtric

---

[115] That appended to S. 953 (Exeter).

[116] While it is evident that the names Ælfmær and Æthelmær are distinct from each other, they are often confused in the sources. See Keynes, *Diplomas*, p. 235, n. 15, for discussion of the phenomenon. This is the only witness to a minister with the name Ælfmær during the reigns of Cnut and Harthacnut, and four other charters (S. 896, 953, 955, 961 and 969) have an Æthelmær in this context. The emphasis in italics in this list of names is mine.

[117] S. 896. His attestations in these years have been traced by Keynes, *Diplomas*, p. 209.

[118] All are named together in S. 896.

mæw, in another of 1009.[119] Confirmation of this identification can be found by tracing their careers forward. The attestations of both Ælfgar and Æthelmær cease during the 1030s, and they probably did not live beyond that decade; however, the last name here, Beorhtric, endures into the 1040s, 1050s and 1060s, being accorded the titles *nobilis* in 1050 (the same title as Odda in that document), and *consiliarius* (perhaps translated as 'royal advisor') in 1061.[120] Beorhtric is none other than the wealthiest non-noble landowner below the rank of earl recorded in Domesday Book, which identifies him in 1065 under the name of Beorhtric son of Ælfgar as holding a vast property empire based in Gloucestershire and Worcestershire.[121] The estates of Cranborne and Dewlish listed amongst his possessions there allow us to see that he is the same man described in the late medieval chronicle of Tewkesbury Abbey, which also names his father *Algar meaw* (Ælfgar mæw) and grand-father *Haylwardus meaw* (more correctly Æthelweard mæw) with their distinctive byname.[122] This epithet *mæw* (pronounced similarly to modern English 'mew') is an Anglo-Saxon onomatopoeic name for 'seagull'. The Tewkesbury Chronicle, while not fully understanding this outdated word and swapping it for 'snew' (meaning 'snow'), relates the perhaps true story that members of the family suffered from an albino-like skin condition that left them with large white patches on their faces.

These two groups of men seen to have given their support to Cnut during the invasion of 1015–16 – and they thrived as a result. At least one of the crucial members, Ælfgar mæw, is recorded amongst the turncoats at the Battle of Sherston. As the two groups were immediate

---

[119] S. 915 and 921.

[120] S. 1021, 1033 and 1034. See Keynes, 'Regenbald the Chancellor', pp. 200–1, for discussion of the first of these.

[121] See Clarke, *English Nobility*, pp. 260–2, for an assessment of his vast estates, and Williams, 'A West Country Magnate', for an account of his later career.

[122] The main body of the Tewkesbury Chronicle was edited in Dugdale, *Monasticon Anglicanum*, II, pp. 59–65. However, the relevant sections of his exemplar were corrupt at some of the points relevant to the 'mæw' family. These sections can be restored by use of London, British Library, Additional MS. 36985 and Oxford Bodleian, MS. Top. Glouc. D.2. Domesday Book, Dorset 1,16 and 25,1 (Thorn, Thorn and Newman). See Williams, 'A West Country Magnate', p. 48. On the witnesses to this part of the Tewkesbury Chronicle, see Bolton, *Empire*, p. 33, n. 99.

neighbours – with Odda's estates apparently focused on Deerhurst in Gloucestershire (at least later in the century) and Ælfgar mæw's family holding the large adjacent estate of Tewkesbury – it is highly unlikely that they acted independently of each other. With the shadow of the Second World War still hanging over us, some find certain terms for such behaviour uncomfortable, but I have been unable to find any better one to describe them. These men were collaborators.

What is perhaps most shocking about these individual collaborators is that many were related to Edmund Ironside: Odda was certainly related to one of Æthelred's other sons, Edward the Confessor, to whom some of his property passed after his death; Ordgar was the grandson of a namesake whose daughter Ælfthryth married Edgar, Æthelred's father, in 964; and the Tewkesbury Chronicle records that Ælfgar mæw was 'descended from the illustrious line of King Edward the Elder', Æthelred's great-grandfather.[123] Treachery such as this was not by any means morally acceptable in eleventh-century England. During the period of invasion, Archbishop Wulfstan of York preached against men turning on their rightful lord in tones aimed at acts such as this.[124]

Cnut's Christianity must have considerably increased his appeal in the eyes of the English. Without doubt many of the Scandinavians who followed him to England in his armies were not Christian. The Norwegian dynasty of the Jarls of Hlaðir were passionate pagans, who had used their religious affiliations to assert themselves against their Christianizing rivals for power in Norway.[125] Many others must have added the Christian god to a pantheon of pagan deities, or undergone halfway ceremonies such as the 'primsigning' discussed above, and one suspects that Thorkell the Tall fell into this category.[126] However,

---

[123] See Bolton, *Empire*, pp. 30–1 and 34–5.

[124] Wulfstan, *Sermo Lupi ad Anglos* (Whitelock, p. 31).

[125] See Ström, 'Poetry as an Instrument'.

[126] For such ceremonies, see p. 38 above. Thorkell certainly did act as a Christian when in England. He was remembered at Bury St Edmunds, in a marginal reference in the Easter Tables of a Psalter once owned by the community there, as involved in the reform of that community (see Keynes, 'Cnut's Earls', p. 56, n. 65).

Cnut as the head of this structure was uncompromisingly Christian, and thus the English could feel reassured that if he was to be the future king of England then he at least shared their religious values.

Let us now return to the war of 1015–16. Perhaps fearing the potential effect of the London garrison in future battles, Cnut returned again to that city. Edmund travelled farther into Wessex to raise more troops, returning with these to London to relieve the siege. This assault drove sections of the invading forces to their ships and they fought at Brentford.[127] Fear of the London garrison evidently gripped Cnut, and as soon as Edmund returned to Wessex, Cnut again besieged the city, before travelling up the River Orwell to raid. Edmund led a charge against them in Kent and the war may have seemed to have turned in his favour; certainly, the untrustworthy Eadric streona rejoined the English forces. Cnut and his allies, both old and new, threw everything into a single battle, sailing with the fleet to Essex, where they drew Edmund into a fierce conflict at a hillsite named Ashingdon or *Assandun*.[128] Negotiations before this, or just fear inspired by the scale of the invading armies, caused Eadric streona to desert Edmund again for Cnut. This was the decisive battle, and the roll-call of the dead included 'the flower' of the English nobility, with the E text of the Anglo-Saxon Chronicle declaring that 'Cnut had the victory and won himself all England.'[129] The obituary lists of Ely show that many of the landed aristocracy of that region also fought and died for Edmund at Ashingdon/*Assandun*, and they are unlikely to have been alone in this.[130] It is important for how we view Cnut's religious beliefs that the *Liber Eliensis* states that the monks of Ely who were present carried the relics

---

[127] The fighting at Brentford is also recorded by Óttarr svarti's *Knútsdrápa*, verse 7 (Whaley, p. 775), as a sacking of the town.

[128] The battle of Ashingdon, or *Assandun*, is also recorded by Óttarr svarti's *Knútsdrápa*, verse 10 (Whaley, p. 779), as a 'great feat of battle'.

[129] ASC 1016 E (Irvine, p. 74).

[130] Ely Calendar in Cambridge, Trinity College, MS. O. 2, I (Dickens, p. 21).

of St Wendreda of March into the battle.[131] The account tersely notes that they were seized by Cnut (presumably on the battlefield of Ashingdon/*Assandun* after victory) and later deposited in Canterbury. Crucially, rather than break up the ornamental reliquary for its valuable precious metal and gemstone components into more easily transportable treasure that could be divided amongst his followers, Cnut kept the reliquary and its contents in one piece for some months (and perhaps until 1018), until he was in a position to present it to Canterbury.[132] He had no fixed centre for his armies at this stage, and thus nowhere to deposit treasure, and so the reliquary and its component parts must have been carried with him and his forces. It is tempting to speculate that, just as the monks of Ely had borne them into battle, Cnut carried the relics at the head of his forces, as was common on contemporary battlefields in mainland Europe, or at least displayed them amongst his own possessions while on campaign.[133] The fame of St Wendreda probably did not extend much further than Ely, but she was English, and that she appeared to allow her relics to be taken by the invaders, and carried by them, must have implied much to both the English and Scandinavian Christians about divine support for Cnut's candidacy.

Edmund appears to have wanted to fight on, but his support base seems to have been quickly draining away. Skaldic verse suggests that in the aftermath of Ashingdon/*Assandun* a single further battle occurred on the northern side of a great forest named *Danaskógar* in Old Norse, most probably to be identified with the Forest of Dean on the western side of the River Severn.[134] The verse claims that there was a massacre of English forces, and following it messengers must have been sent by

---

[131] *Liber Eliensis*, II:79 (Blake, p. 148). St Wendreda was a local saint, about whom little is now known. She had founded a nunnery at March in Cambridgeshire, at an unknown point in English history, and her relics were subsequently translated to Ely in the tenth century, where they were placed in a gold shrine set with jewels. See ibid., II:76 (pp. 145–6).

[132] See below at pp. 108–9.

[133] See Erdmann, *The Origin of the Idea*, p. 24.

[134] Óttarr svarti's *Knútsdrápa*, verse 10 (Whaley, p. 779); see Poole, 'Skaldic Verse', pp. 275–6 for discussion of this.

Edmund to Cnut to arrange peace talks. They met at nearby Deerhurst in Gloucestershire, a site most probably owned by the collaborator Odda (it was certainly his some decades later). The two commanders arranged their forces on opposing sides of the River Severn to avoid random clashes, and the leaders were rowed out in fishing boats to meet on a small island named *Olanege/Olanige* (meaning 'the island of Ola', and now no longer a separate entity but reclaimed and part of fields some 300 metres to the west of the standing structure of Odda's chapel).[135] There Cnut, Edmund and their respective advisors reached an agreement, dividing up the southern and Midland parts of the kingdom, with Edmund receiving Wessex and Cnut receiving Mercia (in which lay Deerhurst and Tewkesbury, and thus the main interests of his collaborators). The north was left in the hands of Cnut's ally, Eiríkr, perhaps because it lay somewhat outside of the English king's direct grasp and Edmund lacked the power even to attempt to take it back.

Just as in 1013, this arrangement was short lived, and Edmund died on 30 November in the same year, most probably in London. Two Anglo-Norman historians, Gaimar and Henry of Huntingdon, claim that he was murdered in an ignominious manner, either stabbed with a spear or shot with a crossbow bolt from below while sitting on a toilet, but it is equally possible that he died from wounds sustained during the long campaigns of 1015–16 or from subsequent infections.[136] The earliest sources to note his death, including the Anglo-Saxon Chronicle and the *Encomium*, do little more than record it, the latter suggesting that it was God's will in order to avoid the division of the kingdom.[137] Following this, Cnut called a *witenagemot* at London, which elected him king of the whole country.

[135] It has most convincingly been identified by Harris as an area of land of approximately 6 acres immediately between Deerhurst and the Severn and separated by a brook (in fact a much silted-up and once larger watercourse), named in the seventeenth century and later as the Naight (a contraction of Middle English 'atten ait', i.e. 'an island') and mapped at the same time. See Harris, 'The Site of Alney' for discussion and maps.
[136] Henry of Huntingdon, *Historia Anglorum*, VI: 13 (Greenway, pp. 360–2), and Gaimar, *Lestorie des Engles*, ll. 4396–4496 (Bell, pp. 140–1).
[137] *Encomium Emmae Reginae*, II:14–15 (Campbell, p. 30).

The accounts of 1016 do not appear to describe an unstoppable invasion. Edmund had success at Penselwood, at Otford, and in the stalwart and continued defence of London, and Cnut seems to have feared the London garrison throughout the conflict. The multiple changes of sides by Eadric streona appear to be a good indicator of the shifting successes of each side in the invasion. Ultimately, the fate of the war seems to have rested on the mood of the English aristocracy. They were exhausted and defeated before Cnut began, and the tone of the Anglo-Saxon Chronicle rises to its most indignant shriek when narrating Edmund and Uhtred's ravaging of the English counties unwilling to send them troops. Cnut had been wise to wait for a crisis in the English leadership, but sheer luck brought him windfalls in Æthelred's sickness and death during this conflict. Support for Edmund appears to have been lukewarm in some quarters, and the loss of his father probably forced more nobles into a neutral position to wait for a victor before offering support. The competition between Cnut and Edmund for the crown seems to have been that of a cunning and intelligent man versus a more straightforward warrior, with Cnut using more underhand methods such as securing the support of a core of English collaborators to tip the balance in his favour, whereas Edmund repeatedly tried to raise more troops. One suspects that any stability, no matter who ended up on the throne, was welcomed with open arms by the English, perhaps even more so if that came with the promise of an end to Scandinavian raiding.

Chapter 3

THE EARLY YEARS OF RULE IN ENGLAND

THE YEARS OF SURVIVAL: THE INITIAL TWO YEARS OF RULE IN ENGLAND

Peace had finally come to the English, and many in the country must have agreed with the *Encomium*'s interpretation of recent events, that God 'took away from the body the prince' (Edmund) so that 'at his decease free ingress might be open to Cnut, and that with the conclusion of peace the two peoples might have for a time an opportunity to recover'.[1] However, the view was different from the top, and Cnut must have felt drawn in two opposing directions. He was a young man surrounded by mature and powerful allies, and he had as much to prove to his newly conquered people as he did to his Scandinavian followers, each with large armies now at rest in England. He was the de facto ruler of a vast country, made up of a number of regions. At the heart of this stood Wessex with a highly organized central nervous system of national and regional government focused on the person of the king and his regular meetings. Cnut may have known of some of this before, but now he had to embrace it and become part of it. His only right to rule other than that of conquest was as a son of a would-be king who had not even survived long enough to attend his own formal election. The English were war-weary and hungry for peace, while the invading Scandinavians doubtless expected substantial spoils of conquest, and

---

[1] *Encomium Emmae Reginae*, II:7 (Campbell, p. 23).

THE EARLY YEARS OF RULE IN ENGLAND 93

Cnut had to satisfy them both. Between these two clearly defined groups was a third made up of those whose interests lay partly with both groups. Amongst them were English noblemen who threw in their lot with the Danes and thus expected rewards, as well as Scandinavians who had settled in England before Cnut's invasion and identified more with the interests of the English landowning populace. It must have been a mare's nest of conflicting wants, exacerbated by several decades of mutual hate and distrust. As the dust settled in the aftermath of Edmund's death, it was probably clear to Cnut that the rag-bag and part-time nature of his forces meant that he could not rule by force for very long, and in the long run he had as much to fear from elements of his own armies as he did from any of the English who might oppose him. He had to appease the English and show himself to be a calm and moderate ruler, while rewarding his Scandinavian followers with the orgy of seized wealth and lands that they expected.

The strains of these opposing forces and perhaps also his inexperience showed in the first couple of years. These were ones of apparent knee-jerk reactions to keep Cnut in power. Firstly he had to deal with other potential claimants to Æthelred and Edmund's throne. In the aftermath of Edmund's death, Cnut called a national assembly at London. John of Worcester states that at this assembly he questioned the nobles about their agreement with Edmund concerning inheritance of the kingdom, and the council agreed that Edmund himself had not entrusted any part to his brothers in life or death, and that he had wished, rather surprisingly, for Cnut to act as a guardian to his children in the event of his untimely demise. The first part of this agreement is not entirely unlikely; however, it beggars belief that Edmund's potential heirs should be safe under Cnut, and if John's witness is accurate here then in 1016 this clause was probably the creation of Cnut or those seeking to appease him. The meeting ended with the taking of oaths to Cnut and his formal election as king.

However, it was not all one-sided, and here we see Cnut's first attempts to reassure the English and to assume the mantle of his predecessors.

Cnut's lawcode of 1018 has been solidly attributed to the drafting hand of Archbishop Wulfstan of York and its promulgation placed at the national meeting at Oxford in that year.[2] However, Pauline Stafford has rightly noted that a section of it stands apart from the main body and clearly pre-existed the full code.[3] The section now known rather dryly as II Cnut, chs. 69–83, does not draw on the same sources as the rest of the code that now encompasses it; it uses terminology not found anywhere else in the canon (for example, the collocation 'lagu teacan' in II Cnut 75.2); it uses typically non-Wulfstanian vocabulary (for example, 'bunda' for husband in II Cnut 76.1b); and it is completely innovatory in its topic (the abuses of lordship from the king downwards, heriots or death duties owed to the crown, what should happen to widows, and the protection of a man's landholdings from rapacious seizures).[4] Yet it has internal coherence, beginning with an address in the first person ('Now this is the mitigation by which I wish to protect all of the people from what they were hitherto oppressed . . .'), like the opening of several other lawcodes (in II Cnut it appears elsewhere only in the prologue and opening chapter), and ending with a lengthy homiletic addition by Wulfstan urging the people to love God and follow the law (II Cnut 84). Stafford sought to see a coronation charter in this lawcode, and in the sense of a brief lawcode probably promulgated immediately on Cnut's coming to full power I am in agreement with her. Clearly it pre-dates the 1018 code, and was written without the intervention of Wulfstan. It may have been drafted for promulgation to Cnut's Mercian subjects in 1016, or more probably the whole nation in 1017.

The focus of this short lawcode on the condemnation of the abuses of lordship and other abuses of power, such as the protection of a man's landholdings from seizures and what should happen to widows, is telling. Concerns such as these were doubtless widespread throughout a country that had seen several decades of invasion and raiding, which

[2] Whitelock, 'Wulfstan and the Laws' and 'Wulfstan's Authorship'.
[3] Stafford, 'The Laws of Cnut'.
[4] Ibid. and Pons-Sans, *Norse-Derived Vocabulary*, pp. 159–62.

created further injustices in their own wake and drew the attention of the agents of the law away from the immediate needs of the populace. Eadric streona had made a name for himself by exploiting his position of power under Æthelred's government to rapaciously build up his landholdings at the expense of others, and he was unlikely to have been completely alone in this. Moreover, with the wholesale slaughter of a significant part of the male English population, the issue of unjust marrying of widows in order to control the estates and rights they inherited must also have been one of great topical importance. This early lawcode offered placatory words from an incoming conqueror, and its clauses were aimed at the whole uppermost stratum of society, from the lord to the lowest landowning class. This earliest lawcode and its reassurances that Cnut was interested in a return to the quiet rule of law may stand behind John of Worcester's statement that in 1017 Cnut 'then concluded a treaty with the nobles and the whole people, and they with him, and they confirmed a firm friendship between them with oaths, and laid aside, and set at rest all their own animosities'.[5]

Cnut now turned his attention to the political map of England and appeasing the most powerful of his Scandinavian followers. The southern English elites may have been angered at his father's plan to move the centre of power northwards, and he was not about to make that mistake again. His rule was to be focused on the south, and he would only adapt the status quo rather than attempt to replace it. The Anglo-Saxon Chronicle states that in 1017 he 'succeeded to the whole kingdom of England, and divided it in four: Wessex for himself, East Anglia for Thorkell, and Mercia for Eadric streona, and Northumbria for Eiríkr'.[6] What is meant by this short entry is not entirely clear. Thorkell and Eiríkr were given their regions as earldoms, and the latter had most likely remained in his since partway through the invasion. These were politically sound acts, according these powerful

---

[5] John of Worcester, *Chronicon*, s.a. 1017 (Darlington and McGurk, p. 502).
[6] ASC 1017 CDE (O'Brien O'Keeffe, p. 103). Note Molyneaux, *Formation of the English Kingdom*, p. 1, on the use of the term *Angelcynnes ryce* here.

Scandinavian lords significant respect in the division of spoils, while putting some distance between them and the hub that was Wessex. Western Mercia remained in the hands of Eadric streona, as he was most probably already its de facto ruler and would have been a wily and difficult figure to uproot. Cnut took the old rump of royal power, but the region already had at least one living ealdorman who would remain in control, and we are left to speculate that in fact this region fell under the special control of Cnut. Few of his predecessors from the West Saxon line had made many forays out of Wessex, and so if all that was meant was that Cnut focused his attentions there, then the chronicler's words would appear redundant. It is possible that what is being suggested here is that despite more than half a century of the drawing together of all England south of the Tees through legal and coinage reforms and the imposition of royal agents, Cnut effected a substantial break between these regions.[7] The machinery of West Saxon government stood, but each of the three nobles mentioned here may have been given greater autonomy over their regions.

For western Mercia this arrangement did not last long, and at Christmas 1017, Eadric streona was tricked into appearing at the court in London away from his own estates and supporters, and summarily executed.[8] In the long run this act seems to have drawn more praise than criticism, and while Eadric streona must have had supporters in western Mercia (most of whom presumably fell from power soon after him), he made his way to the top by treading on other's necks, and his enemies must have been legion. The resulting political vacuum presented Cnut with an opportunity to settle more of his powerful Scandinavian followers in that region, and he implanted Hákon, son of

---

[7] See Molyneaux, *Formation of the English Kingdom*, for an excellent study of the unifying influences from the mid-tenth century onwards. For Cnut's apparent division of the kingdom, and the focus of his activities and patronage on Wessex, see Bolton, *Empire*, pp. 60–2, 68–72, 86–7, 104–6 and 109–19 (but note I argue he took a greater role in East Anglia after Thorkell's expulsion in 1021).

[8] ASC 1017 CDEF (O'Brien O'Keeffe, p. 103), with the late F text adding 'very justly' to the notice of his execution. John of Worcester adds that his body was thrown over the city walls and left unburied (*Chronicon*, s.a. 1017 [Darlington and McGurk, p. 504]).

his ally Eiríkr, into the top of the administration of Worcestershire, evidently alongside the pre-existing ealdorman, Leofwine.[9] In the account of Hemming from later in the eleventh century, the arrival of Hákon is placed immediately after the invasion and laying waste of Worcestershire, which presumably was part of the invasion campaign of 1015–16, and so it is possible that Hákon had held some role there since then, which was later formalized and extended after Eadric streona's execution.[10] Another Scandinavian, Eilaf, was placed into an earldom centred on Eadric streona's stronghold of Gloucestershire, appearing in royal charters from 1018 onwards.[11] Finally, the area that had followed Eadric streona into the battle of *Assandun* in 1016, the *Magonsætan* (comprising the populations of Herefordshire north of the River Wye and southern Shropshire), received by Cnut's order a Scandinavian named Hrani as its earl, again dated by Hemming to the autumn of 1016.[12] Hemming records that Hákon and Hrani were accompanied by a band of followers who also took part in the abstraction of estates from Worcester Abbey, and it seems likely that Eilaf also brought other Scandinavians to the region.[13]

Local records suggest that a number of Scandinavians were settled in other areas, notably the south-east, apparently without formal offices. They were of sufficiently high social status for English scribes to record them with aggrandized titles, but when it is possible to check, they do not appear to have fulfilled the duties normally associated with the titles. A Halfdan is named 'princeps regis' in a document purporting to record Cnut's confirmation of the privileges of Christ Church, Canterbury, in 1018, and he must also be the *Haldene scearpa* again

[9] See Williams, ' "Cockles amongst the Wheat" ', pp. 6–8, and the same author's 'The Spoilation of Worcester' in general on the settlement of Scandinavians in this region.

[10] Hemming, *Chartularium* (Hearne, I, p. 251).

[11] See the variant forms of the witness-list appended to S. 951 and 953 as examples. Hemming in his *Chartularium* (Hearne, I, p. 280) records Eadric's connection to this region. As Eilaf's name is not recorded in an East Norse version in any runic inscription, I have used the English spelling here as it is a close approximation to what one might expect from the Old Danish version of his name, and was probably written phonetically by the scribe.

[12] Hemming, *Chartularium* (Hearne, I, p. 274).

[13] Ibid., pp. 274 and 251. See also Williams, 'The Spoliation of Worcester', p. 385.

described as one of Cnut's 'principes' who was remembered in the obituary lists of the community as the donor of estates at Hythe and Saltwood.[14] He may also be the man of the same name recorded amongst the earls in a charter granted by Cnut to Abbot Æthelwold and the brethren of St Mary's, Exeter, in 1019, but he is otherwise unrecorded as an earl and is unlikely to have held a proper earldom.[15] Another such figure is to be found in the Thored who appears in the Christ Church, Canterbury, confraternity entry alongside Cnut and two other Scandinavians (Kartoca and Thuri, each named as 'our brother' by the community).[16] He was probably the 'optimatus regis' recorded in a land sale of 1020×1023, which 'was confirmed in London in the presence of King Cnut', and the man who donated an estate at East Horsley, Surrey, to Christ Church, as well as two Gospel Books decorated with gold and silver.[17]

Something now had to be done with the potential heirs: Edmund Ironside's brother Eadwig, and his sons Edward and Edmund. The former was outlawed, with the C text of the Anglo-Saxon Chronicle noting that he was killed on Cnut's orders, and the latter two were sent away to 'the king of Sweden' (Cnut's half-brother and sometime ally, and in fact probably ruler of just the area around Lake Mälaren and its vicinity) to be killed, but instead he sent them on to Hungary.[18] The Anglo-Norman Gaimar has them sail from Porchester directly to Denmark, and alludes to a later plot to restore them to power, and he may be in possession of other parts of the same story not known to John

[14] S. 952. See the edition of the obituary-lists by Fleming, 'Christchurch's Sisters', p. 130, and on Halfdan, see Keynes, 'Cnut's Earls', p. 62.

[15] S. 954.

[16] London, British Library, Royal MS. I. D. ix, fol. 43v. Reproduced in this volume.

[17] S. 1463 and 1222. See Fleming, 'Christchurch's Sisters' for the various versions of the obituary-list, and see also Bolton, *Empire*, p. 17, n. 22.

[18] ASC 1017 CD (O'Brien O'Keeffe, p. 103), and John of Worcester, *Chronicon*, s.a. 1017 (Darlington and McGurk, pp. 502–4), who claims that the sending away of the royal heirs to be killed was done on the advice of Eadric streona. John notes that Edmund died some time later, but Edward married and his children were Margaret, Queen of Scots, a nun named Christina and Edgar, who returned as an abortive royal candidate in the later eleventh century. On these figures see Hooper, 'Edgar the Ætheling', and Williams, *The English and the Norman Conquest*, pp. 7, 32, 99 *passim*.

of Worcester here.[19] Another figure who may have been part of the royal family is now known only as Eadwig 'king of the ceorls' (*ceorl* = free man of lowest class), and he was perhaps also expelled at this time.[20] However, the purge could not stop there, and the Anglo-Saxon Chronicle lists a series of Englishmen who presumably had shown their opposition to Cnut openly and were now put to death.[21] They included Æthelweard, son of Æthelmær stout, the ealdorman of the western provinces who had submitted to Swen at Bath in 1013, and Beorhtric, son of Ælfheah, the governor of Devon (with John of Worcester adding 'although blameless' to this).[22] Cnut's union with Ælfgifu of Northampton, and the bonds between him and the northern aristocracy and the obligations that these brought, now seems to have been an inconvenient hangover from his father's abortive plans. The son of Ealdorman Leofwine of Mercia, Northmann, who had played his part in these northern alliances, was also killed.[23]

These acts may have been necessary for Cnut to remain in power, but few can have been popular with the English. Reassurances of peace and continuity with the previous regime were brought about by other means. The political currency of his union with Ælfgifu of Northampton most probably died along with Swen, and she must have been set aside sometime after that and before 1017. This allowed another figure of fundamental importance to Cnut's life to enter the stage, and in July

[19] Gaimar, *Lestorie des Engles*, lines 4548–60 (Bell, pp. 144–5).

[20] The Anglo-Saxon Chronicle presents us with a problem regarding this character. Setting aside the question of who he was, and what his strange appellation is meant to mean, the fact is that the main core of the Chronicle (ASC 1017 DE [Cubbin, p. 63, Irvine, p. 74]) at this stage reports his expulsion in 1017, immediately after Eadwig, Edmund Ironside's brother, whereas the C text moves the note of his expulsion to 1020 associating it with the outlawing of Ealdorman Æthelweard (ASC 1020 C [O'Brien O'Keeffe, p. 104]). This might be scribal error on the C copyist's part, but his addition of a notice of the death of the preceding Eadwig on Cnut's orders shows that he had some facts relevant here that were not known to his peers. Alternatively the note on this Eadwig 'king of the ceorls' may have been misplaced in the D and E texts, next to the name of the other Eadwig who was Edmund's brother. This is now incapable of resolution, and readers may choose whichever solution suits them best.

[21] ASC 1017 CDE (O'Brien O'Keeffe, p. 103).

[22] John of Worcester, *Chronicon*, s.a. 1017 (Darlington and McGurk, p. 504).

[23] ASC 1017 CDE (O'Brien O'Keeffe, p. 103).

1017 he ordered Emma, the wife of the deceased Æthelred and the daughter of Duke Richard II of Normandy, to be brought to him, and he married her with full Christian rites.[24] She was most probably brought from Normandy, where she had fled.[25] The *Encomium* notes the sending of emissaries by Cnut to the Norman court, and the *Inventio et Miracula Sancti Vulfranni*, written in the Norman abbey of St Wandrille in the early 1050s, claims that Duke Richard gave his assent to the union.[26]

Emma seems to have been a formidable political figure in her own right, and was especially well positioned to exploit the situation to its full. Her mother was a Danish noblewoman named Gunnor, and her family had been unashamedly proud of their Danish origins.[27] She must have spoken Cnut's own language, probably had contacts with members of the Danish aristocracy, and understood the fragile nature of Scandinavian elite marital unions. It may have been her insistence that Cnut and she were married fully in the Christian (and thus non-Scandinavian) tradition, forming a more permanent link between them.[28] She had been Æthelred's wife since 1002, and within England she brought Cnut continuity and was a close personal contact who knew the court and its key players. The *Encomium* is probably quite accurate when it notes that their marriage contributed greatly to laying 'the disturbances of war to rest'.[29] Beyond England's borders Emma

---

[24] Stafford, *Queen Emma*, pp. 220–4.

[25] Thus I set aside the theory of Poole that skaldic verse suggests she was in London ('Skaldic Verse and Anglo-Saxon History', pp. 290–2). He constructs an argument based on a reference within the skaldic verse *Liðsmannaflokkr* to a widow who lives within stone (perhaps the stone walls of London), namely, that she was trapped in London. However, his only other sources for this are the less than reliable Thietmar of Merseburg and William of Jumièges, and comparison with the skaldic corpus suggests that this appeal to a woman is a rare poetic device rather than denoting an actual historical figure.

[26] *Encomium Emmae Reginae*, II:16–17 (Campbell, p. 32), and see van Houts, 'Historiography and Hagiography', p. 251. Note that elsewhere van Houts interprets the Latin poem *Semiramis* as a satire on this marriage ('Note on Jezebel and Semiramis'). There is also much useful comment on these diplomatic relations in the same author's 'The Political Relations'.

[27] Stafford, *Queen Emma*, pp. 209–10 and 212–14.

[28] See Bolton, 'Ælfgifu of Northampton', pp. 253–8, on these Scandinavian elite unions.

[29] *Encomium Emmae Reginae*, II:16 (Campbell, p. 32).

brought even greater security, as Normandy could be expected not to now aid any proposed military incursions to reinstate Æthelred's children, Alfred and Edward (later 'the Confessor'), who remained in exile in the Norman ducal court.

In addition, much stability must have been ensured by Cnut's English collaborators. The sparse records of this brief period include very few mentions of them, but the appearance of a fully fledged court hierarchy in the witness-lists from 1018 onwards suggests that it was in this formative period that Cnut began to organize around himself the circle of men who would later sit at the top of the national government. This involved ealdormen and earls, both from Æthelred's administration and new Scandinavian appointments like Eiríkr and Thorkell and new Englishmen such as the famous Godwine, who appears first in the witness-lists of charters as an earl in 1018.[30] Odda, Ælfgar mæw and their followers are also prominent in this circle of government ministers, just below a thin layer of Scandinavian officials such as Thored, father of Azor. Thored's name appears at the head of ministers or in a prominently high position in eleven of the twenty-seven of Cnut's charters that contain any witnesses of this social rank; he figured at the head of this group in the Exeter witness-lists of 1018, and likewise in grants from 1023 and 1024.[31] His career continued until 1045, and crucially he received a grant of land in Ditchampton from Edward the Confessor in 1045×1046.[32] Ditchampton is less than two miles from Wilton, and a Thored (here *Toret*), who must be the same man, appears in Domesday Book as the giver of land at Laverstock, Wiltshire, to Wilton Abbey, providing that his two daughters were subsequently clothed by the community.[33] After his death Thored was succeeded by

[30] Keynes, 'Cnut's Earls', pp. 70–4 and 84–7. For his dynasty see also Raraty, 'Earl Godwine of Wessex', Williams, 'Land and Power in the Eleventh Century', Mason, *The House of Godwin*, and Barlow, *The Godwins*.

[31] S. 951 and 953, 959, 961, 960, 964, 967, 962 and 975. Thored's influence at court has been discussed in Bolton, *Empire*, pp. 15–19, and by Lewis, 'Danish Landowners in Wessex', p. 180.

[32] S. 1010.

[33] Domesday Book, Wiltshire, 13, 20 (Thorn and Thorn).

his son Azor Thoredsson, who was until recently thought to be a wealthy landowner in Wiltshire.[34] However, recent identifications of him else- where in Domesday Book, made possible by the development of the Prosopography in Anglo-Saxon England project, have enabled us to see that his landholdings were over four times as large (in wealth) as previ- ously thought, with holdings in twelve counties placing him amongst the very wealthiest landowners of his day beneath the level of the king and the earls.[35] Odda, Ælfgar mæw and their associates, accompanied by a handful of implanted Scandinavians, brought continuity to Cnut's court, and knowledge of the innermost workings of national and local government that must have been invaluable. What is certain is that they did not disappear, and they and their offspring appear at the head of the national and relevant local government as important and influential statesmen throughout Cnut's reign, that of his sons and Edward the Confessor – and in the case of Beorhtric mæw, up to the Norman Conquest.[36] It is quite incapable of proof, but I have wondered whether Cnut spent parts of the months in 1016 while lord of Mercia, and parts of 1017 as full-king in occasional intensive studies of English infrastruc- ture under the tutelage of these Englishmen.

A general observation may be made about the numbers of Cnut's charters surviving for each year of his reign. To argue anything from the absence of evidence is always a dangerous exercise, and we must agree with M. K. Lawson that for charters Cnut's reign 'is the least well- represented of any between those of Æthelstan and Edward the Confessor', but it is notable that the number of surviving charters issued by the royal court almost drops away to nothing in these early years.[37] The numbers for Æthelred's last years are few but quite stable, and under Cnut are usually regular if not stable.

---

[34] See Clarke, *English Nobility*, p. 32, for details of his wealth.

[35] See Lewis, 'Danish Landowners in Wessex', pp. 180–2, with particular note to n. 76 that lists the PASE identification as 'forthcoming'. The PASE project has been published online at: http://www.pase.ac.uk/index.html

[36] See Williams, 'A West-Country Magnate'.

[37] Lawson, *Cnut*, p. 66.

ROYAL CHARTERS ISSUED BETWEEN 1011 AND 1035[38]

Date	Number of charters
1011	2
1012	5
1013	3
1014	2
1015	1
1016	2
1017	0
1018	2
1019	2
1020	1
1021	0
1022	1
1023	2
1024	1
1025	0
1026	1
1027	0
1028	0
1029	0
1030	0
1031	2
1032	3
1033	5
1034	1
1035	4

[38] Owing to questions of authenticity and proposed datings that are not confined to a single year, it is impossible to produce a complete tabulation of the royal charters issued in this period. What is given here is an approximation only, intended to illustrate trends in production. Note that here I have given the maximum possible allowance for authenticity, and admitted charters that may have suspect features, but that may plausibly contain an accurate record or have authentic witness-lists that would indicate access to a now-lost authentic record. Where there is doubt about the date of the charter within a close range of years, the datings or use of the charter in Keynes, 'Cnut's Earls', has been followed. I have had to set aside charters with the wide date ranges over a large number of years, as with S. 949 (1017×1035), 979 (c. 1023×1032, but probably early 1030s), 979 (1023×1032), 982 (1028×1035) and 992 (1033×1035).

For Æthelred's last years between two and five charters survive for each year, from various archives. The year 1013 was the last one inside this range with three charters, with drops thereafter in 1014–16 to one or two, most probably because the normal business of government was disturbed by the various raids and archives were burnt by invading armies. Only two charters (issued by Æthelred and Edmund Ironside respectively) survive for 1016, and then there is nothing until 1018. Of the other gaps in Cnut's charters the largest reflects his absence from the country: that of 1027–30 when he was in Rome and then in Scandinavia. The years 1025 and perhaps 1021 are also vacant, and Cnut was almost certainly in England for some of these years at least, but these are perhaps the exceptions that prove the general rule. As noted above, a small number of charters have date ranges that are too wide to allow easy tabulation here, and these should be noted as potentially falling into such gaps. However, even if these were issued in the years 1017, 1025 or 1027–30, they would only slightly alter, rather than change, our entire impression of these trends.

What are we to make of this? It is possible that the charters for these early years were all destroyed by chance, but not really probable. The dwindling numbers of Æthelred's last years suggest that this dearth in Cnut's early years is instead part of a trend, and perhaps there were fewer or even no charters granted by Cnut's royal court in 1016–17, and in these years some of the normal functioning of government, at least that which produced written charters, was put on hold.[39] This can only have been because, as in Æthelred's last years, the fight to stay in control required enormous effort.

[39] This also noted in passing by Keynes, 'Church Councils', p. 128.

STABLE KINGSHIP: 1018 AND SUBSEQUENT RULE IN ENGLAND

By 1018 Cnut was more secure, had managed to appease the English somewhat, dispose of troublesome figures such as Eadric streona, and reward his most powerful Scandinavian followers without too much risk to his own control over Wessex. His survival of this period clearly gave him confidence and he seems to have found his feet as a ruler. What we can see of the instruments of royal government appear to have returned to functioning in a regular and orderly fashion. Cnut now had breathing space to concentrate on dispensing with the rank and file of the Scandinavian forces, and consolidating the impression of himself as a fair and moderate ruler in the eyes of the English.

In 1018 what the Anglo-Saxon Chronicle calls 'the tribute' (*gafol*) of £72,000 was rendered all over England, with London forced to pay an extra £10,500 doubtless due to its wealth and long-standing support of Æthelred and Edmund Ironside.[40] This was entirely in accordance with Scandinavian practice, and seems to be a common form of tax claimed by an invader or incoming king at the outset of his reign, perhaps in order to allow him to pay off the debts incurred during coming to power. Harthacnut did the same on his invitation to the English throne in 1040, immediately exacting a 'very severe tax' from the population. A similar practice would appear to be recorded by Robert of Torigny in the mid-twelfth century, in which he notes that the Norse king of Sodor and Man owed tribute to the Norwegian ruler, paying ten marks of gold when each king succeeded to rule, and then 'does nothing else for him in his whole life, unless another king succeeds'.[41] A substantial part of these monies must have been used to reward those who had joined the

---

[40] ASC 1018 CDE (O'Brien O'Keeffe, p. 104). The size and veracity of this tribute has inspired a lengthy debate amongst modern historians. See Lawson, 'The Collection of Danegeld and Heregeld', '"Those Stories Look True"' and 'Danegeld and Heregeld Once More', and Gillingham, '"The Most Precious Jewel"', 'Chronicles and Coins', as well as Metcalf, 'Can We Believe'.

[41] ASC 1040 CDE (O'Brien O'Keeffe, p. 107), and Robert of Torigni's *Chronica*, edited in *Chronicles of the Reigns of Stephen, Henry II and Richard I* (Howlett, IV, p. 229).

campaign with a promise of a share of the booty or to pay off more
formal mercenaries hired to bolster these forces. As a result of this
the Anglo-Saxon Chronicle records that many of Cnut's forces were
sent back to Denmark in 1018, leaving him with just forty ships.[42] The
collection of these funds was made rapidly, and with significant risk of
upsetting the status quo and startling the English. Many ecclesiastical
institutions must have lost substantial treasures at this time, and other
sources show that estates could be confiscated and forcibly sold to anyone
who could immediately pay the tax due on them. In doing so Cnut
managed to demobilize the majority of his forces back in Scandinavia,
safely away from his new English realm, and could demonstrate to the
English populace that while it had cost them another Danegeld, he could
achieve what no English ruler had managed to do, namely, successfully
order the raiding parties to leave permanently. Despite the immediate
cost, for the English this must have seemed like an answer to their prayers.

Cnut's attention returned immediately to reassuring his new English
subjects. It has been argued, quite convincingly, that the *witenagemot*
called in Oxford in 1018 was presented with a brief lawcode that was an
adapted version of Æthelred's Enham code of 1008, and which now
survives in a single manuscript: Cambridge, Corpus Christi MS. 201.[43]
The preamble of this code talks of the establishment there of the peace
(*frið*) and friendship (*freondscip*) between the Danes and the English, and
with a literary flourish promises to observe the laws of Edgar, that is to
return to the perceived golden days of Æthelred's father. The preamble
finishes with the statement that the *witan* would 'with God's help
investigate further at leisure what was necessary for the nation'. This

[42] ASC 1018 CDE (O'Brien O'Keeffe, p. 104). Amongst the demobilized men were members
of a kin-group who left runestones in the vicinity of Orkesta, north-east of Stockholm. U344
records that an Ulf took geld (payment) in England three times, the first with Tosti, the second
with Thorkell (probably 'the Tall'), and the third with Cnut. Approximately thirty such
'England runestones' survive, scattered across Sweden and Denmark, and recording those
who had returned from England or who had died and been buried there (see Sm101, which
records the death of a Gunnar who was buried in a stone coffin in Bath). On these see
Nilsson, 'Vikings Deceased in England', and Syrett, *The Vikings in England*.
[43] Kennedy, 'Cnut's Law', pp. 72–3. The text has since been published online as part of
the *Early English Laws* project: http://www.earlyenglishlaws.ac.uk/laws/texts/cn-1018

investigation of 'what was necessary for the nation' most probably led to Cnut's more extensive lawcodes: those known as I Cnut (a religious and church lawcode) and II Cnut (a secular lawcode), both probably issued in 1020.[44] This 1018 Oxford code is in Wulfstan's idiom and survives in a manuscript associated with him, but the spirit of this code and the public ceremony surrounding it accords with Cnut's other conciliatory acts and is probably that of him and his immediate circle.[45]

The drawing of a line under past grievances between the Danes and the English, and publicly opening inquiries into further injustices that might be corrected, was political theatre at the outset of Cnut's reign, offering the English reassurance and portraying him as a ruler who cared about the ills that beset them and who would commit time and resources to addressing them. This was a politician emerging, replacing the young invader as the bulk of his fleet disappeared over the horizon.

From 1018 at least he was working hard on winning over key members of the Church. His Christianity has been noted above, and this must have gone some way to reassuring the English clergy.[46] Clearly Wulfstan had already committed himself to Cnut's cause by the time of the Oxford meeting, perhaps drafting the lawcode for Cnut at that time. His words here indicate unequivocally his personal support for Cnut and his rule in England, with the admonition that 'foremost' the people must hold to a single Christian faith and 'love King Cnut with due loyalty'. This was sharpened in the 1018 brief code with the addition of the phrase 'as is correct' (*mid rihtan*), stressing the legitimacy of the new regime.[47] Moreover, the exhortation in this early code to 'zealously observe the laws of Edgar' was also a politically loaded endorsement of Cnut with sharply defined connotations. In Wulfstan's compositions from the final years of Æthelred's reign, the reign of Edgar was

---

[44] Edited by Liebermann, *Die Gesetze*, I, pp. 278–307 and 308–71.
[45] See Whitelock, 'Wulfstan and the Laws' and 'Wulfstan's Authorship', and Wormald, *The Making of English Law*, pp. 347–8.
[46] See pp. 36–7 above.
[47] Kennedy, 'Cnut's Law', pp. 72–3.

nostalgically portrayed as a golden age.[48] Connecting Cnut to this both conveniently hopped over the reign of Edgar's son, Æthelred, and signalled to a contemporary audience a return to peace and prosperity. We cannot know whether the form of Cnut's letter to the English of 1019–20 is as he issued it, but its survival amongst homilies in a series of leaves of a manuscript evidently used for preaching by the archbishop, and perhaps annotated in Cnut's own hand, does indicate that Wulfstan took an active role in the endorsement of Cnut's rule.[49]

Similarly, Cnut's initial interactions with the archbishopric of Canterbury smack of a desire to win support there and perhaps demonstrate his devotion. Two of the earliest records of his reign are a writ, dating approximately to 1017×1019 and formally endorsing the archbishop's liberties and privileges, and a grant of 1018 recording a royal gift of woodland in Ticehurst, Sussex, directly to Archbishop Lyfing.[50] The former notes that Cnut made a royal visit to Canterbury to lay a written version of that document on the altar of the cathedral before a public assembly. Further traces of this royal visit can perhaps be found in the addition of the names of Cnut and three of his Danish followers in a Gospel Book from that house, evidently recording their entry into confraternity with the community of Christ Church.[51] There Cnut is lauded in elevated terms as 'our beloved worldly lord, and our spiritual brother in heaven', and interestingly David Pratt suggests that the Gospel Book itself was a gift from Cnut to the community.[52] Furthermore, the *Liber Eliensis* states that the relics of St Wendreda in Ely were seized by Cnut immediately after the battle of *Assandun* and were later

---

[48] Whitelock, 'Wulfstan and the Laws', pp. 442–3, discusses the occurrences of Edgar's name in Wulfstan's writings.

[49] On this source and its limitations see the sources section above, at pp. &&&. The text is published in *Die Gesetze* (Liebermann, I, pp. 273–5), and the manuscript has been published in facsimile as Barker, *York Gospels*, fols. 158r–160v. See Ker, 'Handwriting', especially pp. 330–1 for the potential identification of Wulfstan's own hand.

[50] S. 950 and 985.

[51] London, British Library, Royal MS. I. D, ix, fol. 43v. Reproduced in this volume.

[52] Pratt, 'Kings and Books', pp. 335–8. Note also his discussion of the fact that the addition appears to be in the hand of the scribe Eadwig Basan.

deposited in Canterbury.[53] This public ceremony might have been the most advantageous for relics of an Anglo-Saxon saint, taken by an invader and returned to an English cathedral.

The little we can detect of Cnut's interaction with the bishoprics of Wessex, the rump of support for the previous regime, was in the same conciliatory vein. On two occasions in the early 1020s he seems to have attempted to influence the succession of a bishop, in trying to get his own candidate elected, but when challenged on this he let matters run their own course rather than push through his wishes by force. Goscelin's *Vita Sancti Wlsini* indicates that when Bishop Brihtwine of Sherborne was expelled from his see in unknown circumstances c. 1023, Cnut imposed a preferred candidate, Abbot Ælfmær of St Augustine's, Canterbury.[54] However, William Thorne in his *Chronica* reveals that Ælfmær went blind soon after and had to return to Canterbury, at which point Cnut was unable or unwilling to impose another favoured candidate and after a few years Brihtwine returned to office (and certainly had returned by 1030).[55] Similarly, William of Malmesbury, in his *Gesta Pontificum Anglorum*, states that Bishop Æthelwine of Wells was forcibly replaced by another Brihtwine early in Cnut's reign.[56] Again this probably occurred c. 1023, and the Anglo-Saxon Chronicle's record of this Brihtwine as one of the three members of clergy involved in the translation of the relics of St Ælfheah identifies him as an associate of Cnut.[57] However, William of Malmesbury makes it clear that Æthelwine returned soon after to expel Brihtwine from office, and eventually

[53] *Liber Eliensis*, II:79 (Blake, p. 148).

[54] *De Vita Sancti Wlsini*, ch. 16 (Talbot, 'The Life of Saint Wulsin', p. 82). The dating is established by Ælfmær's final attestation in S. 959. See Bolton, *Empire*, p. 99.

[55] William Thorne, *Chronica*, ch. 4 (ed. Twysden, *Historiae Anglicanae*, col. 1782); see Bolton, *Empire*, p. 99.

[56] William of Malmesbury, *Gesta Pontificum Anglorum*, ch. 90 (Winterbottom and Thomson, p. 304). Note that Lawson, *Cnut*, p. 150, n. 143, suggested that these two events are conflated versions of a single series of acts, but records of the bishops of Wells indicate otherwise. See Bolton, *Empire*, pp. 99–101, for fuller discussion.

[57] ASC 1023 D (Cubbin, p. 64).

Brihtwine re-expelled Æthelwine and held on to the bishopric. This last act may have been with royal support, but the toing and froing here of the candidates hardly indicates Cnut's firm influence.

However, these attempts to win favour (or at least not to merit scorn) with the archbishops and the bishops of Wessex seem to have masked other rapid manoeuvres to reduce the power of Cnut's enemies and plant his followers in important ecclesiastical and secular posts. London and East Anglia had held staunchly to the cause of Æthelred and Edmund Ironside, and they were the most probable sites for resistance to his regime. London had become the economic powerhouse of southern England during the later tenth century, and was of crucial importance. Thus it was placed under permanent military occupation, with a resident fleet of Scandinavians garrisoned nearby, perhaps on the adjacent southern bank of the Thames.[58] These were the 'lithsmenn in London' who chose Harold Harefoot as king after Cnut's death, and the taxes measured by rowlock recorded in that same source for 1035 and 1040 are probably those collected to pay for this fleet.[59] *Liðsmannaflokkr* identifies 'pleasant London' as the site where the warband who recite the verse will settle down, and it was clearly a point of safety for Cnut early in his reign where he could seize and execute Eadric streona in 1017 and set out on the assault on St Paul's to seize the relics of St Ælfheah in 1023.[60] The traces of this garrison are also felt in the Old Norse loanword *husting* for London's urban assembly, and Pamela Nightingale concluded that this name was introduced in the early eleventh century due to the Scandinavian domination of this assembly.[61] Certainly by the time of the Norman Conquest, the city's administration was firmly in the hands of a figure of Scandinavian

[58] On London's position in the economy, see Hill, 'Trends in the Development' and 'An Urban Policy'.

[59] ASC 1035 E (Irvine, p. 76) and 1041 CDE (O'Brien O'Keeffe, p. 107). See also Hooper, 'Military Developments', p. 98, and references there.

[60] *Liðsmannaflokkr*, verse 10 (Whaley, p. 1028); ASC 1017 CDE (O'Brien O'Keeffe, p. 103); and Osbern, *Translatio Sancti Ælfegi* (Rumble, pp. 300–8).

[61] See Nightingale, 'Origin of the Court', pp. 562–4.

descent, who is named Esgar by the *Carmen de Hastingae Proelio*, and identified by the Waltham Chronicle as the grandson of a Danish immigrant and senior political figure during Cnut's reign, Tovi pruða.[62] Linguistically, the influence of their long-term residence there can be detected in the dedication of St Olave's, Southwark, to a Scandinavian saint, and the naming of the adjacent Tooley Street, which, as Bruce Dickins noted, is derived from a garbled version of the Latin of the saint's name. A substantial ethnically Scandinavian population was still discernible there in the early twelfth century, when a parish dedicated to a St Magnus, most probably the Scandinavian Jarl of the Orkneys (d. 1116), was founded on the opposite bank of the Thames, at the foot of a fording point leading from Southwark to the city proper.[63] The archaeology closely mirrors this, most obviously in the presence of a large stone in the cemetery of St Paul's with a carved beast in the Scandinavian Ringerike style, featuring a runic inscription naming the men who raised the stone as Ginna and Toki.[64]

The ecclesiastical elites of this region had been powerful supporters of the previous regime, and could not have expected to be left alone for long. However, unlike Cnut's dealings with secular lords who had displeased him, he could not merely trap and execute a bishop or abbot without great scandal and the ensuing condemnation of the Church. He seems instead to have concentrated his efforts on reducing their financial power and thereby eroding any potential threat. London, at the southernmost tip of this eastern coastal region, acted as its centre for trade. It had supported Æthelred and Edmund Ironside throughout Cnut's invasion, and its bishop, Ælfhun, had escorted Æthelred's children to safety in Normandy in 1013. Ælfhun did not return from there

---

[62] *Carmen de Hastingae Proelio*, ll. 679–752 (ed. Barlow, pp. 40–4). Waltham Chronicle, ch. 14 (ed. Watkiss and Chibnall, p. 24). He came to be a substantial landholder, see Lewis, 'Danish Landowners in Wessex', pp. 185–6.

[63] Dickins, 'The Cult', p. 67.

[64] Vince, *Saxon London*, p. 57. On the runestone, see Wilson and Klindt-Jensen, *Viking Art*, pp. 135–6, Fuglesang, *Some Aspects*, p. 189, Roesdahl et al., *The Vikings in England*, pp. 136 and 163, Barnes, 'Towards an Edition', p. 33, and Graham-Campbell, *Viking Art*, pp. 130–1. It is reproduced in this volume.

but his successor, Ælfwig, was presumably the cleric who played the greatest part in the election of Edmund Ironside to the kingship in 1016. It was perhaps to be expected that London's bishop would fare badly during Cnut's initial years. The punitive tax of 1018 on the whole city of London has been mentioned above, and in addition Domesday Book records another large exaction by Cnut from the bishopric, the vast thirty-hide manor of Southminster, Essex, which was not returned until after 1066.[65] Susan Kelly has argued that a list of naval dues owed by the bishop of London and the community at St Paul's, which is preserved in a charter from that archive, is a record of the entire landholdings of those institutions c. 1000.[66] If this is correct then we should note that of the fifteen identifiable estates held by the community at this time, six were in private hands by 1066 with all but two remaining so (one of which, the estate of Tollington, was held by a man of the king); and of the eleven identifiable estates held by the bishop c. 1000, two were in private hands by 1066 and remained so, and another had been reclaimed from private ownership. Cnut was also responsible for removing a source of income from the monastery of St Paul's in London. This was the resting place of the relics of St Ælfheah, the archbishop murdered by Scandinavians in 1009, whose cult grew quickly after his death. Both the Anglo-Saxon Chronicle and Osbern's *Translatio Sancti Ælfegi Cantuariensis* record Cnut's involvement in the removal of the saint's body from London to Christ Church, Canterbury, in 1023.[67] The latter presents it almost as a heist with the king's *huscarls* (immediate Scandinavian retinue) feigning an attack on the gates of the city. Meanwhile Cnut, the archbishop of Canterbury and a small number of men stole in, broke open the tomb with a candelabrum, and carried off the body to a waiting armed longship, which Cnut personally steered along the opposing bank to avoid possible attacks from inhabitants of

---

[65] Domesday Book, Essex, 3, 9 (Morris).
[66] Kelly, *Charters of St Paul's*, p. 98.
[67] On this see also Marafioti, *The King's Body*, pp. 192–5.

the city.[68] Pilgrimage routes must have been re-established after peace returned in 1016, and the loss of the relics of a popular and topical saint would have reduced the finances of St Paul's considerably. Moreover, while the main part of the saint's body was carried to Canterbury, a fifteenth-century chronicler of Westminster Abbey, John Flete, stated that Cnut had donated a series of relics to them including a finger of St Ælfheah.[69] This community, a few miles upriver from London and significantly outside the city walls, was small during the years that preceded Cnut's reign but grew under his patronage and that of later Anglo-Saxon kings; and Flete also suggests that Cnut intervened in monastic affairs there to guarantee the election of his preferred candidate, Wulfnoth, as abbot in 1023.[70] If correct, then such an act would have diverted many potential future pilgrimages, and the revenue they brought, to Ælfheah's relics away from the non-corporal relics in St Paul's to nearby Westminster, and under the control of Cnut's preferred candidate there.

As noted above, Ely lost the relics of St Wendreda during the invasion, and it is notable that the abbots of Ely, Thorney and Ramsey, who had mostly held consistent positions of prominence in Æthelred's charters and courts, all but disappear from Cnut's, with the exception of documents for which they were crucial local witnesses.[71] Only the abbot of Peterborough bucked this trend, and that may be more to do with his close association with Emma, Cnut's new wife (having accompanied her into exile and returned with her in 1017), than the geographical placing of his see.[72]

At the same time Cnut was implanting his followers into the secular institutions of Wessex. In the decades before he came to power, Wessex had been divided into two distinct areas of influence: the

[68] ASC 1023 CE (O'Brien O'Keeffe, p. 104). D is fuller (Cubbin, p. 64), and see also Osbern's *Translatio Sancti Ælfegi* (Rumble, pp. 300–8).

[69] John Flete, *History of Westminster Abbey*, ch. 14 (Armitage Robinson, p. 70).

[70] Ibid., ch. 18 (Armitage Robinson, p. 81).

[71] Bolton, *Empire*, pp. 90–1.

[72] Ibid., p. 91.

eastern counties of Hampshire and Berkshire, perhaps with authority extending into Sussex and the areas around London, and the 'Western Provinces' of Wiltshire, Somerset, Dorset, Devon and Cornwall. The office of the earl of the crucial eastern part, whose areas of influence faced and perhaps bordered London, was vacant in 1017, and into this Cnut put the young and probably ambitious and aggressive politician, Godwine.[73] Godwine's father seems to have been dispossessed by Æthelred and perhaps exiled, but kept the support of that king's sons. He appears to have thrown in his lot with Cnut as another disgruntled member of the English aristocracy. Godwine was serving in this office by 1018, and Cnut seems to have subsequently raised him up and tied him into the Danish royal family after a campaign in Scandinavia that can be dated to 1022.[74] In the words of the *Vita Ædwardi regis*, at this point Godwine was made *dux et baiulus* (earl and office-bearer) of 'almost all the kingdom' and married to Gytha, the sister of Jarl Ulf of Denmark, who himself married Cnut's sister, Estrith, as part of this complex dynastic knot.[75]

The earldom of the 'Western Provinces' appears to have been held by an Ealdorman Æthelweard from either 1015–16 or 1017–18 to 1020.[76] He was most probably a member of an aristocratic family who held authority there for a number of generations, and it has been suggested that he may be identified with the son-in-law of Ealdorman Æthelmær (who himself held a prominent position at Æthelred's court in the 990s and opening years of the eleventh century, founded Eynsham Abbey and retired there around 1005, lastly coming back out of retirement to act as ealdorman of the 'Western Provinces' at the end of Æthelred's reign).[77]

[73] Keynes, 'Cnut's Earls', pp. 70–1. General studies of this character are listed above in n. 101.
[74] Ibid., pp. 71–3, and Bolton, *Empire*, pp. 47 and 213.
[75] *Vita Ædwardi regis*, ch. 1 (Barlow, p. 6).
[76] See Keynes, 'Cnut's Earls', p. 68, for discussion of the date on which Æthelweard took up the office of ealdorman.
[77] Both suggested by Keynes, 'Cnut's Earls', p. 68.

One county under Ealdorman Æthelweard's jurisdiction, Dorset, has more evidence for the settlement of Cnut's secular followers than any other. Much of this comes from charters. Through the chance survival of the cartularies of Sherborne and Shaftesbury, and strong antiquarian interest in the now-lost Abbotsbury cartulary, we have a greater than usual number of grants (or records of them) surviving for Dorset.[78] As early as 1019, Cnut granted land at Cheselbourne to a man with the Scandinavian name Agemund, while another Scandinavian named Bovi, who was certainly a landholder in the region a few years later, appears in the witness-list of this document and was perhaps also resident in the region at the time.[79] In 1024 a grant of land at Portisham was made to a minister of Cnut with the strange name of Urk. This name was so incongruous even to English contemporaries that the draftsman of a later charter concerning him explains that this figure 'after the fashion of his own people was known since infancy by the name'.[80] In 1033, Cnut granted further estates in Horton to the Bovi of the 1019 witness-list, naming him 'his faithful minister' there.[81] In addition, seventeenth-century transcripts survive of fragments of records once contained in cartulary of Abbotsbury.[82] Both the antiquaries John Leland and Clement

[78] Keynes, 'Lost Cartulary'.
[79] S. 955. We must be careful when claiming that Cnut granted these men their estates. An additional clause in Old English in S. 969 shows that in 1033 Bovi obtained the estate of Horton through the payment of the tax owed on this forfeited estate (see p. 106 above). However, whether they were given the lands or bought them, their obtaining of royal documents to ratify this suggests Cnut's acquiescence, if not his hand, in this. Bovi's unusual name is that recorded elsewhere on runestones in the East Norse form 'Bosi' or 'Bose' (see Peterson, *Nordiskt Runnamnslexikon*, p. 47).
[80] S. 961. The contemporary note on his name is in S. 1004. The translation from the Latin here is by Ann Williams; see 'A Place in the Country', p. 158. In the same work she tentatively suggests that the name might mark him as Orcadian in origin (p. 166, n. 3, based on the observation by Gillian Fellows-Jenson made in 1994 that outside of a handful of English records it occurs only in a patronymic in an Orcadian runic inscription, with Williams postulating an unlikely Pictish origin for it). She lists the variants 'Orcy' and 'Urki' from charters, as well as 'Orecy' in the guild-statutes of Abbotsbury (see ibid., pp. 158 and 166, n.1), and thus I would prefer to see it as a variant of *Orikkia (Old Swedish) or *Óroekia (Early West Norse), with elision of the second vowel, which is recorded on runestones in the close forms 'urika' (nom., U539A and U350) and 'uruku' (acc., DR83). See Peterson, *Nordiskt Runnamnslexikon*, p. 175.
[81] S. 969.
[82] See Keynes, 'Lost Cartulary', for details of these transcripts.

Reyner connected the foundation of a monastic house at Abbotsbury to Urk, and him to Cnut.[83] Reyner dated this monastic foundation to 1026. Another antiquarian, Thomas Gerard, noted that Cnut granted the estate used for the foundation to Urk, and an undated extract from this charter survives in the transcripts of another antiquary, Henry Spelman.[84] Furthermore, Gerard's account records another estate named Hilton that Cnut gave to Urk, as well as the fact that lands at nearby Tolpuddle were owned by Urk's wife, and thus may also have been a royal gift.[85] Finally, a manuscript of Spelman's account records a single phrase from the body of an undated grant to Bovi, evidently from another, otherwise unknown, grant to him.[86] The charters suggest that these men operated as a co-ordinated local group, witnessing royal grants as local figures of importance. Bovi appears amongst the ministers of both Agemund's grant of 1019 (fifth of thirteen ministers there) and Urk's grant of 1024 (in third place in the second column of ministers). Similarly, Agemund appears in Urk's grant of 1024 (second in the first column of ministers), and Urk appears in Bovi's grant of 1033 (fourth of twenty ministers). Spelman's record of a lost charter concerning Bovi in the Abbotsbury cartulary also indicates links between these two as the cartulary was associated primarily with Urk as the founder of the community. The inclusion of one of Bovi's grants in this archive suggests, as Simon Keynes says, that they 'had dealings of some kind with each other'.[87] As local witnesses, Bovi and Urk represented the area in the royal court together, witnessing a grant of Cnut to Sherborne Abbey of sixteen hides at Corscombe, an estate within their sphere of influence in Dorset.[88]

---

[83] *Collectanea* (Hearne, IV, p. 149), and Reyner, *Apostulatus*, p. 132. See Keynes, 'Lost Cartulary', pp. 221–3, for discussion of these.

[84] See Keynes, 'Lost Cartulary', pp. 220–32, for the texts of both Gerard's and Spelman's records.

[85] Keynes, 'Lost Cartulary', pp. 222–3. On Urk's later career see Williams, 'A Place in the Country'.

[86] The nine-word Latin phrase occurs only in the Harvard manuscript of Spelman's tract. See Keynes, 'Lost Cartulary', p. 232, for this.

[87] Keynes, 'Lost Cartulary', p. 232.

[88] S. 975.

Clearly these men arrived from Denmark with Cnut. None of these names occurred in any documents from Æthelred's reign, and Urk and Bovi are named in documents as royal *huscarl*, a title that at this early date most probably indicates membership of a Scandinavian ruler's private retinue.[89] That is certainly its meaning in the *Translatio Sancti Ælfegi*, where the term is explained as 'the soldiers of his [Cnut's] household, who are called *huscarles* in the language of the Danes'.[90] A fragment of evidence from the Domesday Book for Dorset also suggests that such officials were heavily involved in the local administration in this region, in that Dorchester, Wareham, Shaftesbury and Bridport paid one mark of silver for each ten hides in the borough 'for the use of the royal *huscarls*' (*ad opus huscarlium regis*).[91] This type of reference occurs nowhere else in Domesday Book and has defied simple explanation.[92] The tax must have been calculated from the relative prosperity of these towns. (Dorchester paid tax to the king for ten hides, and thus one silver mark for the *huscarls*, while Bridport paid tax for five hides and half a mark to the *huscarls*, and Shaftesbury paid tax for twenty hides and two silver marks to the *huscarls*.) This appears to be more than a simple case of demobilized soldiers, and begins to look like a conscious attempt by Cnut to insert members of his immediate retinue into the Dorset landscape and provide for their ongoing lives there.

It is when we try to reach outside of Dorset that we encounter problems. We can scour the records of moneyers and the rather late records of Domesday Book for the south-western counties looking for

[89] Urk in Gerard's text (see Keynes, 'Lost Cartulary', p. 222) and an extant writ of 1044 (ed. Harmer, *Anglo-Saxon Writs*, no. 1, pp. 120 and 425–6), and Bovi in the rubric of S. 969. While there has been some debate about this title, with the suggestion that it might just be the Scandinavian equivalent of a landowning man (see Hooper, 'Housecarls', pp. 172–5), the majority of the sources for this view come from the late eleventh century. We are in different territory when dealing with men who most probably came with Cnut from Scandinavia, and who knew the term at first hand from its use in Scandinavia, rather than as a loanword. See Bolton, *Empire*, pp. 54–5.

[90] *Translatio Sancti Ælfegi* (Rumble, p. 302).

[91] Domesday Book, Dorset, B (Morris and Newman). The entry for Dorchester says only 'ad opus huscarlium', the remaining three add 'regis'.

[92] See Williams, 'A Place in the Country', p. 159, for the most recent comment.

Scandinavian names and concluding that these were similar implants into the landscape there.[93] However, the only solid identification of a potential candidate is that of a moneyer named Viking who worked at Lydford and Exeter from c. 1029 to 1035 and c. 1059 to 1062.[94] My previous use of this approach, albeit tentatively and speculatively, has attracted criticism (probably quite rightly) from C. P. Lewis, who took a wider approach and extended his survey of likely Scandinavian settlers across the whole of Wessex.[95] He is right to point out that 'the circumstances in which the [Dorset] charters have survived make it unsafe to read anything more into their small numbers and restricted geographical distribution', and it is a sobering thought that neither Agemund, Urk or Bovi definitely appears in any source outside the records of the Abbotsbury cartulary.[96] A fundamental notion that separates my approach from that of Lewis is the position of Godwine after Æthelweard's outlawry. I suggested that whereas Godwine was clearly the earl of eastern Wessex from Cnut's earliest years, he may not have been responsible for the western part until late in the reign, thus leaving an administrative vacuum for Cnut's Scandinavian followers to fill; Lewis prefers to see Godwine as earl of both parts immediately after Æthelweard's downfall, thus leaving no vacuum.[97] There is no solid evidence either way, and we must content ourselves with only suggestions. We might decide that the statements of the *Vita Ædwardi regis* that Godwine accompanied Cnut on a campaign in Scandinavia (otherwise datable to 1022), entered into a marriage alliance, and was appointed *dux et baiulus* of 'almost all the kingdom' by Cnut, should be read as a

---

[93] As I did in my *Cnut*, pp. 55–9, with emphasis on the hypothetical nature of such an interpretation.

[94] Bolton, *Empire*, pp. 57–60, 311.

[95] Lewis, 'Danish Landowners in Wessex', in particular p. 206, n. 69.

[96] Ibid., p. 178. Urk and Bovi appear nowhere else. An Agemund appears in the suspect S. 959 and 981 from Christ Church, Canterbury, and Keynes has identified him as the same one who received Cheselbourne from Cnut (Keynes, 'Lost Cartulary', pp. 230–1). However, I have argued elsewhere that he is probably a separate Kentish individual: see Bolton, *Empire*, pp. 18–19.

[97] Bolton, *Empire*, pp. 47–51, and Lewis, 'Danish Landowners in Wessex', p. 177.

sequence of actions that occurred one after another.[98] This allows us to identify 1023 as the year in which Godwine began to witness Cnut's charters as the primary earl, and connect that to his appointment as *dux et baiulus*. The first two statements can be shown through other sources to have occurred together, but the last sounds like a laudatory flourish to me, and the text was written over four decades after 1022. Alternatively, we could see that as occurring later in the 1030s, when he and Leofwine become the sole earls included in the majority of charter witness-lists, but always with Godwine first.[99]

In addition, Lewis and I are asking slightly different questions. He, quite convincingly, charts some eighty-one possible Scandinavian settlers to Wessex who are recorded in Domesday Book as alive during the reign of Edward the Confessor (1042–66). He shows that they may have arrived during Cnut's reign or been the children of such immigrants, and are spread across the entire landowning social scale and the whole of Wessex. However, as he himself notes, this is unlikely to have been the result of a single influx of Scandinavians. It must instead be the product of Cnut's settlement of his followers throughout his reign, Godwine's grants to others, and perhaps with the more successful of them, some fifty years of building up landed empires within the region. On the other hand, what I find quite remarkable about the Dorset group, if we can call them that, is that they are recorded in the landscape so early in Cnut's reign (Agemund and perhaps Bovi in 1019; Urk in 1024). Moreover, even if we had no surviving record of the Abbotsbury cartulary, then the strange references to the silver marks due to the *huscarls* in Dorset would mark this county off as something special. I was probably wrong to theorize, however tentatively, that this settlement elsewhere in Devon and across the Somerset border could be connected to Cnut's early years. On reflection, Dorset does seem to be a unique case. However, it is this case that bears witness to Cnut's

[98] *Vita Ædwardi regis*, ch. 1 (Barlow, p. 6). This is the basis of Keynes' dating of Godwine's coming to power there: Keynes, 'Cnut's Earls', p. 73.

[99] Keynes, 'Cnut's Earls', pp. 53 and 84–7.

implanting of his close followers into the English landscape and the continuing contact between those men and his royal court.

Such insertions into Dorset, at least, may have angered Ealdorman Æthelweard, and caused him to act. His career came to a dramatic end in the early part of 1020 when Cnut outlawed him at Easter.[100] What his crime was we can only speculate, but it was clearly a great scandal and followed a period in which Cnut had been in Denmark, perhaps to accept the kingship there. If we can place the addition to the C text of the Anglo-Saxon Chronicle about the outlawing of Eadwig 'king of the ceorls' also in this Easter assembly, then we might read into this that Æthelweard played an instrumental part in a revolt against Cnut.[101] We can, however, be surer of the effects of this sentence. As an outlaw Æthelweard was outside the protection of law, and could be harmed or killed with impunity. Most probably he followed the path of many other outlaws and went into exile. He does not appear in our sources again.

The outlawry of such a grand figure as an ealdorman, the head of the regional administration and almost certainly a key member of an established English local elite, was sure to stir up unrest, and Cnut appears to have returned to his conciliatory mode. Although undated, his visits to Glastonbury Abbey to honour the tomb of Edmund Ironside by offering prayers and laying a cloak embroidered with peacock feathers upon his sarcophagus, and his donation of a gold shrine for the relics of St Edith (a sister of Æthelred) at Wilton, were probably made at this time.[102] The construction of a stone church at the battle site of *Assandun* to commemorate the dead (albeit in neighbouring Essex and not Wessex proper), and its consecration in 1020 by Cnut, Thorkell the Tall, Archbishop Wulfstan and other bishops, abbots and ecclesiastics, was probably also part of this public appeasement.[103]

[100] ASE 1020 CDE (O'Brien O'Keeffe, p. 104).
[101] See p. 99 above on this, as well as Keynes, 'Cnut's Earls', pp. 69–70, and Bolton, *Empire*, pp. 45–6.
[102] William of Malmesbury, *Antiquitate*, ch. 64 (Scott, pp. 132–3), and the same author's *Gesta Regum*, II:184 (Mynors et al., pp. 330–1). Goscelin, *Vita S. Edithe*, II:13 (Wilmart, pp. 280–1). On this see also Marafioti, *The King's Body*, pp. 195–6.
[103] ASC 1020 CDEF (O'Brien O'Keeffe, p. 104).

In addition, the death of Archbishop Lyfing in early 1020 presented Cnut with another opportunity to reassure the elites of western Wessex of his support. In November 1020, Cnut appointed Æthelnoth, previously dean and prior of Christ Church, Canterbury, to the archbishopric. An aside in Osbern's *Translatio Sancti Ælfegi Cantuariensis* states that Cnut and Æthelnoth's intimacy originated in the fact that Æthelnoth had 'anointed him', perhaps indicating that he had presided over a ceremony of confirmation at Cnut's election in Southampton in 1016, as suggested by Edward Freeman, or alternatively either the peace settlement of 1016 or at Oxford in 1018.[104] Æthelnoth was presumably present at Cnut's entry into confraternity with the community of Christ Church alongside three Scandinavian followers in 1018.[105] Most importantly, he appears to have been a member of Ealdorman Æthelweard's immediate family and his appointment occurred only six months after the outlawry of the ealdorman. John of Worcester recorded that Æthelnoth was 'the son of the nobleman Æthelmær', who can be identified with Ealdorman Æthelmær of the Western Shires, the probable predecessor of Æthelweard in the office and perhaps his father-in-law.[106] Thus, Æthelnoth may have been equal in status within his family to the ealdorman, and of approximately the same age. He may even have stood closer to the core of the kin-group as a natural son of Æthelmær, rather than a son-in-law.

If Cnut had been supportive of the archbishopric of Canterbury before, now he offered them virtual *carte blanche* within Kent. As soon as Æthelnoth was invested, Cnut extended the liberties he had endorsed for Lyfing, including in this new document the rights of *griðbryce*, *hamsocn*, *forstal* and *flymenafyrmðe*, the same liberties that were reserved in II Cnut 12 exclusively for the king unless he wished to 'show especial

---

[104] *Translatio Sancti Ælfegi* (Rumble, p. 300). Freeman, *Norman Conquest*, I, p. 692.
[105] See pp. 98 and 108.
[106] John of Worcester, *Chronicon*, s.a. 1020 (Darlington and McGurk, p. 506). See also Keynes, 'Cnut's Earls', pp. 67–8, Brooks and Kelly, *Charters of Christ Church*, p. 219, and Bolton, *Empire*, pp. 81–2.

honour to anyone'.[107] Elsewhere Cnut granted to Æthelnoth extensive judicial and financial rights over 'as many thegns as I have granted to him'.[108] These rights excluded all other authorities, and have little precedent in Anglo-Saxon royal grants.[109] As a part of this, the archbishop also seems to have been granted the 'third penny of the shire' (*tertium denarium de comitatus*), which was the third of the revenues of justice that was to be kept by the local ealdorman or earl as payment for ensuring the local peace.[110]

Outside of the southernmost counties of England, and after the depredation of some ecclesiastical institutions in East Anglia and London, Cnut's role in the period from 1018 to mid-1021 was that of a nominal king or absent overlord, who seems to have left the running of East Anglia, western Mercia and the north to his appointed earls, ealdormen and jarls, appearing in a single recorded instance of a large meeting at Thorney Abbey perhaps in 1020 or early 1021.[111] Similarly, he appears to have taken almost no interest in Scotland, Wales and Ireland in this period, beyond that of perhaps acting as a distant overlord on a single occasion to King Rhydderch ap Iestyn of Morgannwg.[112]

[107] II Cnut, 12, *Die Gesetze* (Liebermann, I, p. 316). This originally noted by Brooks, *Early History*, p. 290.

[108] The document edited by Harmer in *Anglo-Saxon Writs*, no. 28, pp. 183 and 449–50.

[109] See discussion in ibid., pp. 79–82 and 449–50.

[110] The account survives as in a late eleventh-century copy, now London, British Library, Cotton MS. Augustus ii. 36. The text has been edited by Douglas, 'Odo', pp. 51–2, and for relevant discussion on the point here see Bolton, *Empire*, p. 73.

[111] See Gerchow, *Gedenküberlieferung*, pp. 195 and 326, Keats-Rohan, 'The Prosopography', pp. 223–4, and my comments here at pp. 135–7.

[112] Bolton, *Empire*, pp. 126–32. The sole sources for evidence for his claims to overlordship of these regions are the *Encomium Emmae Reginae*, II:19 (Campbell, p. 34), which lists Wales and Scotland amongst his other rulerships, and a *lausavisa* (a skaldic verse recorded without a title and hence with more potential for forgery) attributed to Sigvatr Þórðarson (Whaley, p. 714), which claims that 'The most outstanding lords have presented their heads to Cnut from the north out of mid Fife; it was the price of peace.' The first may be a rhetorical flourish with the history of English domination of Wales and Scotland in mind; the second is more confusing and would seem to relate to a specific lost incident. It appears in the verse as a counterfoil to the next statement, that Óláfr Haraldsson 'never surrendered his skull thus to anyone in this world', and whatever the event was it may have been blown out of all proportion here for literary effect.

The year after Æthelweard's outlawry, Cnut faced another ostensible challenge to his rule, but this time from a more familiar opponent, Thorkell the Tall. Keynes has shown that Thorkell's subscriptions to royal charters identify him as the most important nobleman in England up to this point, and this impression is upheld by the address of Cnut's letter to the English of 1019–20 directly to Thorkell as his principal royal agent in the country.[113] Similarly to Æthelweard, all we have is a few brief words concerning his outlawry. The Anglo-Saxon Chronicle records that on 11 November 1021 Cnut outlawed the earl, with John of Worcester adding that Thorkell's wife, Edith, was outlawed alongside him, perhaps implying her involvement in some way in whatever caused the fall from favour.[114] Freeman suggested that Thorkell had made a bid for the English throne, and considering what we can deduce of his prior interaction with Cnut and his family this does seem likely, or at the least that Thorkell's actions immediately before November 1021 led Cnut to conclude that such a coup d'état was imminent.[115] Freeman noted that the late Scandinavian account of Thorkell's dynasty known as the 'Supplement to the *Jómsvíkinga saga*' states that Thorkell married a daughter of King Æthelred who had previously been the wife of Ulfcetyl of East Anglia.[116] No other source claims that Ulfcetyl was married to a daughter of Æthelred, but it is not improbable. Freeman also noted that a daughter of Æthelred named Edith did in fact marry Eadric streona, and thus was a widow after 1017. However, there is clear garbling in the name given to this woman in the 'Supplement', Ulfhildr, which is suspiciously Old Norse in origin and literary in that the first element of it all too neatly echoes the first element in Ulfcetyl's name. That much is Freeman's theory, and it has recently received

[113] Keynes, 'Cnut's Earls', pp. 82–4. Cnut's letter is edited by Liebermann as *Die Gesetze*, I, pp. 273–5.
[114] John of Worcester, *Chronicon*, s.a. 1021 (Darlington and McGurk, p. 506).
[115] See Freeman, *Norman Conquest*, I, pp. 666–70, and the same material handled more sceptically by Campbell in his *Encomium Emmae Reginae*, pp. 87–91.
[116] Freeman, *Norman Conquest*, I, p. 670.

strong criticism from Ann Williams.[117] She is correct to point out the weaknesses in Freeman's theory, but this does not mean we must strike off the whole affair as unknowable beyond the bald fact of Thorkell's outlawry.[118] It is remarkable, and demands our attention at least, that a late Scandinavian source does state that Thorkell was married to a daughter of Æthelred. Even without this Scandinavian source, we would still be left to draw some conclusion about John of Worcester's apparently pointed reference to the exile of Thorkell's English wife alongside him. It is incapable of proof, but his possible revolt against Cnut or a bid for power in England is the most reasonable explanation for his sudden fall from Cnut's favour, and entirely in keeping with what we can discern elsewhere of their tense relationship.

The matter could not end with Thorkell's outlawry and probable exile. Like the Scandinavians in western Mercia, Thorkell had most probably settled many of his closest followers on estates throughout East Anglia. Threats may still have lurked there, or at least Cnut seems to have been concerned about the potential for this, and he went on a royal visit to the region a few months later in 1022. A visit to Ely is recorded in the *Liber Eliensis*, and can be dated by a land exchange between Cnut and the abbot of Ely, almost certainly ratified during this visit.[119] This exchange was made in 1022 on an auspicious date perhaps suggesting a public ceremony: the festival of St Æthelthryth (23 June), the saint credited with founding the house. Elsewhere in the region, Cnut's influence left traces in grants of land at Horning in Norfolk to the abbey of St Benet of Holme, which date to c. 1022.[120] In addition, this may well have been the point when Emma was given responsibility

[117] Williams, 'Thorkell the Tall', p. 152.
[118] I played out and discussed much of Freeman's theory in Bolton, *Empire*, pp. 211–12, and for the reasons stated here in my sources section I believe I was right to do so, rather than strike off the principal Scandinavian source for this with the line 'the less said the better', as Williams does ('Thorkell the Tall', p. 152).
[119] *Liber Eliensis*, I:85 (Blake, pp. 153–4); S. 958.
[120] S. 984; dated by Keynes, 'Cnut's Earls', p. 49, n. 39, after Thorkell's expulsion in November 1021 and before Æthelnoth's departure for Rome in the autumn of 1022.

for eight and a half hundreds of land in west Suffolk.[121] Lucy Marten suggests that this involvement of Emma in the region may have been intended by Cnut to partially fill the vacuum left by Thorkell's exile.[122]

The evidence is more sporadic and anecdotal than for Dorset, but it remains a possibility that Cnut also settled some of his trusted Scandinavian followers in this region, presumably to fill the power vacuum and keep an eye on Thorkell's remaining followers. Traces of these men are found in a number of local records. The Ramsey Chronicle states that Cnut alienated the estates of Englishmen in the region of the monastery and gave them to his 'comrades in arms', and names one of these as a Thorkell, who held the estate of West Elsworth, Cambridgeshire.[123] The same text then records that many such Danes fled in the late eleventh century, enabling Abbot Æthelric to buy or cheat their lands (proudly relating that one such transaction occurred when the Dane was drunk, and presumably thus agreeable to a less competitive price).[124] A document copied into the body of the same text gives the will of a woman called Thurgunt, who gave land at Sawtry to the abbey.[125] Her husband, Thorkell of Harringworth, enforced the will, and he was without doubt a Danish immigrant and was named *Turkil Danus* by the entries of Domesday Book for Huntingdonshire.[126] The Red Book of Thorney reports that after the Norman Conquest 'he abandoned his estates, and gave his support to the Danes who were his kinsmen', presumably during Swen Estrithsson's invasion of 1069–71.[127] The twelfth-century foundation charter of Sawtry Abbey links Thorkell of Harringworth to Cnut. It states that the king caused him to settle in the

[121] See Sharpe, 'The Use of Writs', Stafford, *Queen Emma*, p. 133, and Marten, 'The Shiring of East Anglia', especially p. 22, n. 105, for further references.

[122] Marten, 'The Shiring of East Anglia', pp. 21–7.

[123] *Chronicon Abbatiae Rameseiensis* (Macray, p. 129). It is highly unlikely that this was Thorkell the Tall.

[124] Ibid., pp. 140, 143 and 135.

[125] Ibid., pp. 175–6.

[126] Domesday Book, Huntingdonshire, 2.8 (Morris and Harvey).

[127] Red Book of Thorney, ed. Caley, Ellis and Bandinel in *Monasticon*, II, p. 604. Also noted by Whitelock, 'Scandinavian Personal Names', p. 140, and Hart, *Early Charters of Eastern England*, p. 237.

area of Northamptonshire and Huntingdonshire, and records his involvement in the local administration on Cnut's behalf, reapportioning the fen to the south and east of Whittlesey Mere.[128] Thorkell of Harringworth and his wife Thurgunt are most probably the *Turkil* and *Turgund* in the Thorney *Liber Vitae*, amongst the lists of names of local landowners who made donations or entered confraternities with the abbey in the first half of the eleventh century.[129] A few entries above these two are the names of *Turkyl Hoge* and his anonymous wife. This Thorkell hoga was recorded in the chronicle of Hugh Candidus as a wealthy benefactor of Peterborough Abbey, and appears to have been a landholder based in Cambridgeshire.[130] He was of some significance in the local administration, in that amongst the estates he left to Peterborough Abbey was a record of his ownership of a *monetarius* in Stamford, perhaps part of the revenues of the mint there.[131] In addition, we can establish a connection here to Cnut, in that Thorkell hoga prominently attested a charter of Cnut dated 1024 amongst names of men who were some of the king's closest advisors.[132] Moreover, the charter was the one granting Portisham to Urk, a region on the opposite side of England where Thorkell hoga cannot have been present as a local witness but instead seems to have figured as an important Scandinavian who probably knew some, if not all, of the men settled in Dorset. This charter of 1024 for Urk also includes two further Scandinavian names that appear in local East Anglian records, those of Brothir and Thorsten, who must be the *Browter* and *Turstan steallare*, who appear together after Thorkell hoga's

---

[128] *Cartularium Monasterii de Rameseia* (Hart and Lyons, I, pp. 163–4), and see Hart, *Early Charters of Eastern England*, pp. 236–8, for the connection.

[129] Gerchow, *Gedenküberlieferung*, p. 327, von Feilitzen and Insley, 'The Onomasticon', pp. 206–7, and Keats-Rohan, 'The Prosopography', pp. 245–6. See Whitelock, 'Scandinavian Personal Names', p. 140, for the connection.

[130] Hugh Candidus, *Chronica* (Mellows, p. 70). Here his name is recorded as *Turkilus Hoche*, and he is recorded as donating several estates and a mint to the house.

[131] Grierson, 'Domesday Book', especially p. 88, argues that it was normal for individuals or ecclesiastical institutions to own part of the proceeds of a mint in the eleventh century.

[132] S. 961. He attests this as the fifth of twenty *ministri*, amongst names otherwise connected to Cnut's court.

name in the Thorney *Liber Vitae*.[133] The 'staller' is another Scandinavian office, like that of *huscarl*, which was introduced with Cnut's men, but seems to have been confined to the Eastern Danelaw and eastern coast-line.[134] It was a title denoting high rank and a court position.

The reader must permit me an aside here on Danish matters even though this chapter focuses mainly on England, as matters in England now forced Cnut to turn his attention to Denmark. Thorkell the Tall had shown himself able to raise armies in Scandinavia quickly and effi-ciently, and less than a decade before he had worked for Æthelred against Cnut and his father without any qualms. The *Translatio Sancti Ælfegi* states that on Thorkell's exile to Denmark by Cnut with only six ships, he 'was suspected by the leaders of the Danes, lest he should foment internecine strife'.[135] Similarly, the late eleventh-century *Vita Edwardi regis* would appear to be talking about this threat when it states that in Denmark 'some unbridled men, putting off his [Cnut's] authority from their necks, had prepared to rebel'. That source places this event within a series of others that led up to its hero, Earl Godwine, accom-panying Cnut on a military expedition to Denmark in 1022×1023, the year(s) immediately following Thorkell's exile.[136] The C text of the Anglo-Saxon Chronicle records that in 1023 he and Cnut were recon-ciled, and it adds that the two exchanged sons, while Cnut 'entrusted Denmark' to his own son and Thorkell.[137] Evidently the implication here is that Cnut lacked the power to oust this influential opponent, but could force him to come to terms. More will be said about this arrange-ment in a subsequent chapter.[138] The *Translatio Sancti Ælfegi* ends its comment on Thorkell with his pursuit through all the districts of Denmark, and death at the hands of 'an ignorant mob and being

---

[133] Elsewhere Thorsten only witnesses the authentic S. 958 for Ely, and Brothir's name appears only in the witness-list appended to the spurious S. 980 for Bury St Edmunds.

[134] Mack, 'The Stallers'.

[135] *Translatio Sancti Ælfegi* (Rumble, p. 298).

[136] *Vita Edwardi regis*, ch. 1 (Barlow, p. 5). On the dating of this campaign see Bolton, *Empire*, p. 213.

[137] ASC 1023 C (O'Brien O'Keeffe, p. 104).

[138] See below at p. 133.

thrown ignominiously to the wild beasts and the birds'.[139] Death at the
hands of a mob was a common end for Scandinavian rulers, and Cnut
may not have played a direct part in this.[140]

Cnut had been fortunate with this second uprising. Thorkell was
clearly a more viable threat than Æthelweard, but the threat had been
contained quickly and sent back to Scandinavia. Indeed, with the passing
of time and some hindsight it may have appeared to Cnut to have been
a blessing in disguise, as this affair had brought the apparently simmering
tension between Thorkell and him to a head, and ended in Thorkell's
downfall. In addition, Cnut appears to have avoided any major factioning
of the Scandinavians still in England over this issue, and by driving
Thorkell out and then chasing the battles to Denmark and the Baltic,
these armed conflicts had not been felt on English soil, and in English
eyes therefore Cnut would still be the man who brought them the much
longed-for peace. Interestingly, Henry of Huntingdon notes an English
contingent in these forces, and the *Vita Edwardi regis* makes it clear that
Godwine proved himself to Cnut in these battles. In this, the English
forces may have had their first taste of victory in several decades, and
that against a Scandinavian enemy on their own home soil. Even though
they served alongside other Scandinavian allies, it must have seemed like
a role reversal of Æthelred's last years, with the English as the slaugh-
tering raiders. Again, Cnut was all things to all men. For the Scandinavians
he was the ideal powerful and benevolent ruler of skaldic verse, who
could prevail against any opponent and gain support through redistrib-
uting booty, while for the English he was a guarantor of peace, who had
turned their fortunes around.

---

[139] *Translatio Sancti Ælfegi* (Rumble, p. 298).
[140] Both Eiríkr Hákonarson's father, and Knut 'the Holy', who ruled Denmark from 1080
to 1086, certainly died at the hands of a mob, and we might see the death of Óláfr
Haraldsson of Norway in battle with a band of Norwegian nobles in the same light.

Chapter 4

THE RISE TO DOMINANCE OVER SCANDINAVIA

The actions of Cnut following the sudden death of his elder brother, Harald, around 1019, speak volumes about Cnut's feelings towards his homeland. Many modern English historians have preferred to see him as a convert to English culture, and because the wealth of his English realm far exceeded that of contemporary Denmark it must have seemed a very attractive prize.[1] Moreover, Cnut's dynasty were only recent arrivals in Denmark and his main opportunities for advancement until his brother's death had been in England. However, on the death of Harald, Cnut readily accepted the hornet's nest that was rule of a Scandinavian country, and both defended this realm and used English resources to extend his grasp over it. It is perhaps worth contemplating that he could have focused on his acquisition, and left Denmark to its own fate. England may have been of crucial importance to him, but he seems to have remained at heart a Scandinavian.

Before moving on to Cnut, we should say a few words about Harald. Like many members of an important dynasty who die young, Harald is a shadowy figure of whom few, if any, facts are known with certainty. We are therefore forced to trace what little is known of his life from a brief range of sources, none of which gives an impartial picture. We know from the *Encomium* that he remained in control of Denmark when Cnut left to reinvade England in 1015.[2] Harald was certainly alive in

[1] See my comments on this above, at pp. 3–4.
[2] *Encomium Emmae Reginae*, I:3 (Campbell, p. 12); Thietmar of Merseburg places him at the siege of London in 1016 alongside Cnut (*Chronicon*, VII:40 [Holtzmann, p. 446]), but this goes against the grain of all other sources, and is probably a mistake by Thietmar.

1017×1019 when his name was entered after Cnut's in a note of confraternity in a Christ Church, Canterbury, Gospel Book, but this does not mean he was in England and Harald may just have been included as the only other senior living male member of Cnut's dynasty.[3] The mid-thirteenth-century Danish *Annales Ryenses* relates a complex story which claims that Harald was deposed for being 'effeminate' (*effeminatus*) *and* completely dedicated to lusts or pleasures in favour of Cnut, then Cnut was rejected due to his absence in England, and finally restored after Harald's death.[4] Campbell calls this 'absurd'.[5] However, it is our only source, and it is not so incredible that Harald suffered a period of unpopularity during Cnut's time in England (either in 1013–14 or more credibly 1015–20).[6] Here the term effeminacy may not indicate anything about Harald's gender orientation or sexual persuasion. It is used in the sense of a homosexual in the Vulgate Bible, but appears in other contexts in the Middle Ages, most commonly to describe a failure to hold oneself in check, or to maintain control.[7]

It has long been surmised, probably quite rightly, that when the Anglo-Saxon Chronicle notes that in 1019 Cnut went to Denmark 'with nine ships and dwelt there all winter', it was to receive the royal title there following his brother's recent death.[8] Cnut's letter to the English of 1019–20 states that he had travelled to Denmark 'from where the most harm came to you; and then with God's help have taken a stand, so that from now on, no hostility shall ever come to you from there, as long as you are justly ruled by me, and as long as my life lasts', without mentioning the kingship. However, the record of the Anglo-Saxon

---

[3] London, British Library, Royal MS. I. D. ix, fol. 43v. A reproduction of the inscription is given in this volume.

[4] See *Annales Ryenses*, ch. 91, ed. Kroman in *Danmarks Middelalderlige Annaler*, p. 161.

[5] Campbell, *Encomium Emmae Reginae*, pp. lv–lviii, at lvii, n. 5.

[6] In discussing this period Lawson (*Cnut*, pp. 90–1) tentatively attempted to connect the Scandinavian immigrant Halfdan/Haldan with a Haldanus in a garbled story in the Roskilde Chronicle, an individual who was killed by one of Swen's sons (unfortunately identified as Gorm and Harthacnut in the narrative). This is too garbled for me to make sense of, and is probably a false identification.

[7] See Herter, 'Effeminatus'.

[8] ASC 1019 CDE (O'Brien O'Keeffe, p. 104).

Chronicle that Cnut took only nine ships of followers and troops (significantly fewer than the forty-five ships retained by Thorkell the Tall
when he remained in England in the service of Æthelred in 1013)
strongly suggests that Cnut did not feel threatened on this voyage. His
lack of significant force may indicate that he had been invited by the
ruling part of the Danish elites to take up the crown.

Harald's death must have had a profound effect on Cnut. In England
in 1018 he cannot have expected that Harald would be dead within
a few months, and indeed as his brother must have been in his twenties
or very early thirties, it was unlikely.[9] The emotional toll may have
been great. The brothers seem to have been close, and the record
of the *Encomium* that after their father's death the two brothers
went together into *Slavia*, most probably Poland, to fetch their mother,
is suggestive of a strong bond between them.[10] If, as seems likely,
Harald's name was added to the confraternity entry in the Christ
Church, Canterbury, Gospel Book without his presence in England,
then it was most probably Cnut who ordered his name to be placed
here at the end of a short paragraph noting the worldly guardianship
and heavenly 'brother' status that the role of king of England brought.
Their father had died only about six years earlier, and so in 1019
Cnut had only his sister Estrith and perhaps their mother (if she
was still alive) as immediate family. He was only in his twenties
himself. Doubtless he had male associates and retinue members
whom he had known since childhood, but the loss of his father and
elder brother, perhaps his strongest male influences, so close together
must have been an isolating experience at an early and crucial point in
his life.[11]

Unfortunately, the lack of evidence for the composition of the court
in Denmark, as well as the fact that Cnut's father had already begun to

[9] No source records Harald's age, but he is unlikely to have been many years older than
Cnut, who at this stage must have been in his twenties.

[10] *Encomium Emmae Reginae*, II:2 (Campbell, p. 18).

[11] On the predominantly male retinue or *hirð* that surrounded Scandinavian rulers in this
period, see below at pp. 179–82.

build up urban centres and secular and ecclesiastical infrastructure to centralize authority in his hands and draw it away from local elites, ensures that we can only speculate about how this affected Cnut. Most probably the youth who knew he had to make his own successes now evolved into a young man who knew he had to make further gains on his own. In a society as unstable as eleventh-century Denmark, threats doubtless lurked everywhere, and if we can believe the *Annales Ryenses*, Cnut's brother had been briefly deposed only months before. Thus, we perhaps see a suspicious and even mistrustful Cnut ascending the throne in Denmark, and placing close family members or perhaps members of his court into positions of power. Moreover, his father's centralization of power was to be reinvigorated.

Above all other practical problems Harald's death robbed Cnut of a trusted Danish ally who might rule that country while Cnut was in England, forcing him to search for an alternative figurehead to run the administration in Denmark. The *Annales Ryenses* claim that when Cnut was considered for the kingship there, he was rejected for being too long in England, and there may be a kernel of truth in this narrative.[12] Denmark was not politically stable enough to cope with long absences of its ruler, and England would demand much of Cnut's time in the next decade.[13] He could hope, perhaps, to be little more than an occasional visitor to Denmark in the immediate years to come. Harald had served as regent for their father, but Cnut appears to have had no surviving adult male relative to whom he could now entrust this role.

We know nothing of arrangements to fill this political vacuum from his departure for England in the spring of 1020 until 1023, when Cnut was forced to settle his grievances with Thorkell and recognize that

---

[12] *Annales Ryenses*, ch. 91, ed. Kroman in *Danmarks Middelalderlige Annaler*, p. 161.

[13] Much the same dilemma was faced by Harthacnut in the early 1040s, when he could not effectively compete with his half-brother for the English crown for fear of losing his Danish rule even during a brief absence. See below at p. 198 for details.

figure's partial authority there.[14] Most probably he had to rely on a
series of royal advisors, very likely drawn from his own retinue or from
supporters of his father and brother. As noted earlier, the C text of the
Anglo-Saxon Chronicle states that in 1023 Cnut and Thorkell were
reconciled, exchanged sons, and Cnut 'entrusted Denmark' to his own
son and Thorkell.[15] That Harthacnut was only a small child (no more
than five years old) at the time, and that he can be shown to have been
in England in 1023, are two facts that have spawned numerous theories
as to which child of Cnut was involved in this exchange of hostages.[16]
However, later sources agree that Harthacnut arrived in Denmark in
the 1020s, and was firmly in control of that country at the point of his
father's death, so the simplest explanation by far is that soon after this
agreement was made Harthacnut was sent to accept rule there at the
head of a faction of nobles loyal to Cnut. We are left to choose between
the view that the Anglo-Saxon Chronicle has slightly misrepresented
this (and perhaps Cnut's taking of hostages from Thorkell's family) as
an exchange of hostages between equals; or that Harthacnut was
initially amongst such hostages while having a crucial role in Denmark,
but was released from this arrangement when Thorkell was killed soon
afterwards. I should probably append here a few words for any reader
who might be startled at this notion of sending away a young child to
be the nominal head of a foreign government. The debate on the
nature of medieval childhood has raged back and forth in the past half
century, but what is certain is that rulers of the Middle Ages commonly
employed their children in this way.[17]

[14] On this episode involving Thorkell, his expulsion from England and return to Denmark,
see pp. 127–8 above.
[15] ASC 1023 C (O'Brien O'Keeffe, p. 104).
[16] Harthacnut's birth cannot have preceded his parents' marriage in 1017. For examples
of theories that these sparse facts have created see Williams, 'Thorkell the Tall', p. 155,
n. 52, and the highly inventive Howard, *Swein Forkbeard's Invasions*, p. 143, n. 101, which
proposes that the Anglo-Saxon Chronicle conflated the details of Cnut and Thorkell's
peace settlement with Ulf's later appointment as the governor of Denmark.
[17] See the articles in Classen, *Childhood in the Middle Ages*, for a survey of this debate.

The late Scandinavian sources, with two centuries of hindsight, pass over this short period of joint rule that ended with Thorkell's death to the joint rule of Harthacnut and a Danish nobleman named Jarl Ulf.[18] Jarl Ulf and Thorkell were most probably closely associated, and Ulf may have been Thorkell's replacement in the region.[19] Immediately after Cnut's military campaign into the Baltic and perhaps also eastern Denmark in 1023, Cnut initiated a complicated knot of political marriages, which would bind Jarl Ulf to him, and place his sister Estrith at the heart of Ulf's court, while drawing Ulf's own sister into the English court of Cnut's principal earl, Godwine. Thus, Jarl Ulf was tied to Cnut's dynasty by a marriage to Cnut's sister Estrith, while Ulf's sister Gytha was married to Cnut's loyal English supporter, Earl Godwine. This arrangement both stabilized the political balance of Denmark, and tipped the scales in Cnut and Harthacnut's favour. They were all now, in medieval eyes at least, members of the immediate royal family. While this brought prestige to Ulf as well as the reassurance that his sister would be at the centre of Cnut's court through her husband Godwine, it also stationed Cnut sister as a watchful pair of eyes in Ulf's court, and added another member of Cnut's immediate family to the ruling elite in Denmark.

Jarl Ulf would turn up sporadically in English records in one short period in c. 1022, perhaps as part of a single diplomatic visit to Cnut's court there to attempt to settle the problems between Cnut and Thorkell, or to cement the new alliances and undertake these marriage ceremonies. Ulf attested a royal charter for St Benet of Holme, issued c. 1022 (crucially not including Thorkell and so most probably after his outlawry in November 1021), and is mentioned in a spurious charter from Christ Church, Canterbury, showing that tradition at least connected him with that site in the mid-eleventh century.[20] He also appears at the end

[18] Snorri Sturluson, *Heimskringla*, ch. 134 (Bjarni Aðalbjarnarson, II, p. 235). On this Jarl Ulf, see Balle, 'Ulf Jarl', Gallén, 'Vem var Ulf Jarl', and Arup, 'Kong Svend 2.s Biografi'. However, none of these is free from errors, some glaring.

[19] Bolton, *Empire*, pp. 232–7.

[20] Keynes, 'Cnut's Earls', p. 63, and S. 980 and 981.

of a group of earls in the lists of names in the Thorney *Liber Vitae*. Such lists contain the names of men and woman who appear to have entered confraternity with the monastery, and were to be remembered by its inmates.[21] Such lists were added to on numerous occasions, with pages often containing regular columns, which when full were encased within later names added in the margins and interlineally. Such was clearly the case with the Thorney *Liber Vitae*, in which a block of names added across the late tenth and eleventh centuries was copied up by a single hand around 1100. Within those names fossilized in its columns is a substantial list of Scandinavian names, which since Dorothy Whitelock's study have been associated with those of Cnut and a number of his earls found in the previous column.[22]

The inclusion of Thorkell the Tall amongst the earls has been taken to mean that the royal meeting at Thorney during which these names seem to have been recorded was before his exile in November 1021. This dating has been accepted by the most recent monograph on this source, but I think it unlikely that Ulf made two trips to England, one before and one after Thorkell's outlawry and departure for Denmark, or that he remained in England for the whole period of 1021–2. On closer inspection the relevant entries in the Thorney *Liber Vitae* look to be more complex than previously supposed. While I do not dispute that some of the names here are most probably those of a Scandinavian retinue of either Cnut, his Scandinavian earls based in England, or Ulf himself, the whole list of names survives in a single copy from c. 1100 (between 1093/4 and 1112/13) which has suffered some rearrangement and apparent 'flattening' into a single and almost

[21] On this type of source see Gerchow, *Die Gedenküberlieferung*, Keynes, *Liber Vitae of the New Minster*, and Rollason, *Thorney Liber Vitae*.

[22] See Whitelock, 'Scandinavian Personal Names', but note that her decision not to edit the text there, and her discussion of all the Scandinavian names in that section of the manuscript, over-represents the number of Scandinavian names that appear in a single block. Editions of the text can be found in Gerchow, *Gedenküberlieferung*, item c., and Rollason, *Thorney Liber Vitae*; the latter with photographs of the relevant pages of the manuscript.

uniform list.[23] The placement of the names of Earl Waltheof (earl of Northamptonshire, Huntingdonshire and perhaps also Cambridgeshire and Bedfordshire c. 1065–76), his unnamed wife (in fact, Judith, a niece of William the Conqueror) and Earl Siward (earl of Northumbria 1032/3–55) above the head of the column of secular officials that begins with the earls is crucial. This strongly suggests that the document which stands behind this later clean copy added their names in the mid- or late eleventh century to a pre-existing column of officials, or as Richard Gameson suggests in the recent monograph, that they were added to the list soon after the main document was written by the original copyist.[24] It would also have been possible to add names interlineally to the original list and these would most probably then have been copied within the main sequence by the later scribe. In fact, Dorothy Whitelock suggested that this might have happened with the name 'Ælfgifu' which follows 'Emma regina', with the second name once being potentially an interlinear gloss on Emma's English name.[25] Further chronological problems are hinted at by the fact that Cnut and his sons, if they all attended a meeting together in 1020–1, would not all have been given the title 'rex' as they are here. Harold Harefoot's inclusion here may well relate to another visit to Thorney, 'flattened' by the later copyist into the document we now see.[26] For our purposes here, what is most worrying is the fact that the names Osgot clapa and Tovi (pruða) occur nine entries down the column of secular officials, but crucially at the head of the secular ministers. These men do not otherwise definitively appear in our records until 1026.[27] The earlier exemplar of this list may

[23] For most recent dating of the document see Gameson, 'Planning, Production and Paleography', p. 116.

[24] Ibid., p. 117

[25] Whitelock, 'Dealings', p. 131.

[26] Bolton, 'Ælfgifu of Northampton', pp. 262–3. I have attempted there to explain this potentially fraught meeting of Cnut, his first and second wives and their offspring who went on to rule England, as forced by the need to bring together as many of the elites of England and Denmark as possible, but on reflection we might just as well conclude that multiple visits augmented the main Thorney list.

[27] First occuring in S. 962. See Bolton, *Empire*, pp. 20–1, where I shed doubt on the identification of a 'Tobi minister' with Tovi pruða.

well have had a separate column for these officials, to which the names of these two men were added at its top, just as those of Waltheof, his wife and father were added to the top of the list of earls. The subsequent conflation of these columns would then have brought Osgot clapa and Tovi pruða into the earlier group of Scandinavian names. While this probably changes little about our conclusions drawn from this source, it does mean that we cannot be so precise as to use it to show Ulf was in East Anglia in 1020–1. His name may have been a later addition to the list, perhaps made c. 1022 when we know he was in England, and in East Anglia.

Harthacnut's youth must have ensured that Cnut remained firmly in control of policy decisions throughout the 1020s, and the building up of social infrastructure and new urban sites continued apace. Cnut had clearly known and probably participated in his father's forced abandonment of the German-influenced urban centres and their bishoprics for the newly founded sites under direct royal control, and the access to the wealth and resources of England brought a renewed vigour to the task.

Cnut's ecclesiastical appointments were men loyal to him rather than to the German ecclesiastical missions, and now to definitely fixed urban sees. Adam of Bremen records the appointment of a clergyman named Gerbrand to a see based at Roskilde, another named Reginbert to a see based on Funen, and yet another named Bernhard to a see based in Skåne.[28] Gerbrand's appointment can be dated to before 1022 as he appears amongst the witnesses to an English charter of that year.[29] All apart from the appointment based on the island of Funen were fixed to urban sites, and on Funen, in the absence of an urban site, the bishop may have been based on royal estates instead.[30] Despite attempts by

[28] Adam of Bremen, *Gesta*, II:55 (Schmeidler, p. 115).

[29] S. 958.

[30] See Jeppesen, *Middelalder-Landsbyens Opståen*, pp. 24–6, for the evidence of a pre-urban settlement at Odense (predominantly ceramic evidence). During Harthacnut's rule this site seems to have developed into an urban one, with a mint from the 1040s, and late in the century Adam of Bremen would call it a 'great city' (*Gesta*, IV:4 [Schmeidler, p. 232]).

modern historians to read an implicit power structure into Gerbrand's consecration by Archbishop Æthelnoth, it is most likely that Cnut continued his father's practice of not appointing an archbishop above these bishops.[31] Thus, they were royal officers, whose power was dependent on him.

Adam states that these new bishops were English, but this is hard to make agree with the fact that none has a name of English origin, or even a Scandinavian name that could indicate a Danelaw origin.[32] In fact, all have names with a continental German origin, and thus despite Adam's statement they appear to have been ethnically closer to him than any inhabitant of England. It seems likely to me that these bishops were from areas on the fringes of the Empire, but not formally within its borders, such as Frisia, or were Danes who also had German names. The presence of Danes with what are presumably baptismal Germanized names as well as their original names amongst the Danish clergy is known from the later eleventh century in the figure of Bishop Tymmo/Thietmar of Hildesheim.[33] This individual had served Cnut's family and accompanied his daughter to Germany in the 1030s, and had accepted the bishopric of Hildesheim after her death. Adam records that he was first named Tymmo, a Danish name, and he presumably adopted 'Thietmar' once in Germany for its similar elements.[34] Clearly, they were not Englishmen, but Adam detected something English in them, and his use of this term here may rest partly on his reluctance to mention any missionary activity or clergy in Scandinavia who were not sanctioned by his see of Hamburg-Bremen.

[31] Adam of Bremen, *Gesta*, II:55 (Schmeidler, p. 116). Gelting, 'Elusive Bishops', p. 177, suggests that Cnut sought to organize his Danish Church dependent on Canterbury, while Lund, 'Cnut's Danish Kingdom', p. 42, would see instead that Cnut intended to make Roskilde an archiepiscopal see.

[32] Note that von Felitizen, *Pre-Conquest Personal Names*, pp. 191, 260, 274 and 348, records an exclusively continental German origin for the name-elements: *Ger- Got-, Regin-* and *-brand*. See Larson, *Canute*, p. 190, and Abrams, 'Anglo-Saxons', p. 228, on this same point.

[33] On this figure see pp. 36–7.

[34] Adam of Bremen, *Gesta*, II:79 (Schmeidler, p. 136). Interestingly, this name does not appear in the runic corpus, unless it is a garbled version of Tōmi/Tūmi/Tummi (see Peterson, *Nordiskt Runnamnslexikon*, p. 222).

They may have been partly educated in England. Adam could not have admitted that Cnut's dynasty equipped themselves with court ecclesiastics drawn from centres other than Hamburg-Bremen, as to do so would have opened up many questions about his see's failings in this area in a work intended to glorify its successes. A spell of education in England after 1016 perhaps allowed him to point the finger at that country for their origin.

Whether these men were ethnically English or not, it is obvious from the archaeological evidence that there was an English population introduced onto some Danish elite sites. At Viborg, Roskilde and Lund excavations have unearthed sherds of pottery from domestic vessels of great importance for our purpose. Two sherds of this ware were discovered in the lakeside Søndersø site at Viborg, which was prepared and built on in the first decades of the eleventh century, with these sherds datable to the winter of 1018–19×1025.[35] Approximately thirty further sherds have been found in the large rural estate of Lejre, near Roskilde, specifically in a group of pit-houses close to the main hall, in a context imprecisely dated to the late tenth or early eleventh centuries. The numbers of these finds are dwarfed by the 130 sherds of this material uncovered by successive excavations in Lund.[36] All are from domestic vessels and all are scattered throughout the archaeological layers dating to the late tenth and early eleventh centuries, but perhaps tellingly they are not known from layers datable to the second half of the eleventh century or later. Before the twelfth century, pottery production was extremely rare in Scandinavia, and the use of a potter's wheel is almost unknown until the thirteenth century. Thus, where pottery is found from this period it is almost always imported. These sherds are from wheel-thrown pots identical in style to those produced in late Anglo-Saxon England in the pottery industries of the north-eastern English coast at Stamford and Torksey, and were first assumed to be imports from there. However,

[35] Christensen et al., 'Early Glazed Ware'. See also Roesdahl, 'English Connections' for evidence of these immigrants to Viborg.
[36] Christensen et al., 'Early Glazed Ware'.

petrological analysis shows that their clay is local to the region around
Viborg.[37] Rather than argue the somewhat preposterous notion that
potters in the established industries of eastern England suddenly
decided to import Danish clay to make wares for export back to the site
of the material's origin, it is far easier to conclude that the potters, not
their material, were foreign to Denmark; having arrived there, they
continued to make the pots they needed in the form they knew, but
from local materials. Viborg and Lund we have discussed above. It
should be noted that Lejre is likely to have been an important royal
estate during Cnut's reign, and was named by Thietmar of Merseburg,
in connection with events in 934, as the 'head of the kingdom'. It was
used by a skaldic poet a few decades after Cnut's death when he
described the king of Denmark as 'furious resident of Lejre'.[38]

Further probable traces of an English population and skilled English
builders and artisans can also be detected in church architecture,
namely in the influence on construction techniques and materials
employed. Excavations in the Kongemarken at Roskilde, in the region
of St Jørgensbjerg in the north-west of the present city, have revealed a
churchyard with the remains of a wooden church, loosely datable by
grave-goods to the late tenth and early eleventh century.[39] The name of
the site, while not recorded until the modern period, suggests royal
ownership. The church at St Jørgensbjerg (originally dedicated to St
Clement) was excavated in the 1950s, revealing trenches left by the
foundations of part of an earlier stone-built church (a chancel and
nave) beneath the early twelfth-century fabric of the present church,
foundations that could be dated by a coin hoard found in one of the
trenches to c. 1029.[40] All that appears to remain of this earlier church
now is the northern doorway of the present building, probably reused

---

[37] Hjermind, 'Keramik' and 'Bestemmelse af Proveniens'.

[38] Thietmar, *Chronicon*, I:17 (Holtzmann, pp. 23–4). Steinn Herdísarson, *Nizurvísur*, verse 2
(Gade, p. 361). See also Christensen, 'Lejre Beyond Legend'.

[39] Christensen and Lynnerup, 'Kirkegården i Kongemarken'.

[40] See Olsen, 'St Jørgensbjærg Kirke'. The most recent dating of this hoard is that of
Jensen, 'Møntskatten'.

from the earlier structure. What is utterly remarkable here is the fact that the construction is in stone, and Scandinavia at this time had almost no history of construction in this material. It was, however, common in England, and the surviving doorway, while carved from local stone, finds its closest parallels in late Anglo-Saxon models, particularly that of Barholme in Lincolnshire.[41] As for Lund, Maria Cinthio has deduced that the crypt of the church dedicated to the Holy Trinity there was modelled on the example at Old Minster, Winchester.[42]

Another approach, by Barbara Crawford, has looked at the dedications of churches to St Clement in this region.[43] This protective maritime and missionary saint was very popular in England (with fifty known dedications there), but almost unheard of in Scandinavia outside of eleventh-century Denmark (at least twenty-six dedications in Denmark, six in Norway and none in medieval Sweden). There are crucial dedications in Roskilde and at Lund, where in the case of the latter the construction of the earliest building was recently redated to the early eleventh century.[44]

Traces of English influence or contact are also detectable northwards and southwards from Lund around the coastline, probably indicating that Cnut, and perhaps his father and brother before him, extended their authority there as well through the use of English officials. A stone church excavated in 1958–60 in Helsingborg, northwards up the coastline from Lund and at the eastern side of the shortest crossing point of the Øresund, has been identified as an 'Anglo-Saxon pre-1074 stage', and of notably similar construction to that of St Clement's in Lund.[45] An earlier excavation at Helsingborg uncovered a small wooden church with about twenty associated graves immediately beneath other graves with coin finds dating the graves to the mid-eleventh century.[46]

[41] Olsen, 'St Jørgensbjærg Kirke', pp. 22–8.
[42] Cinthio, 'Trinitatiskyrkan i Lund', p. 113.
[43] Crawford, 'The Cult of Clement'.
[44] Cinthio, 'Trinitatiskyrkan, Gravarna och de förste Lundboarna'.
[45] Weidhagen-Hallerdt, 'St Clemens Kyrka i Helsingborg', p. 143.
[46] Ibid. and Crawford, 'The Cult of Clement', pp. 266–9.

Similarly, a hoard of coins at Stora Slågarp, south from Lund and present-day Malmö, stands out from the others in the region as having a high percentage of English coins (all but five of fifty-three). They are mainly from the reign of Cnut the Great (concentrating in the last issue, Short Cross), but with the latest being a single coin of Harold Harefoot's Jewel Cross type (struck c. 1035–7).[47] Almost all other such hoards in Scandinavia are composed mainly of German and English coins, with the German part forming the lion's share, and a composition such as this is not otherwise recorded outside the British Isles.[48] The un-damaged quality of the coins indicates that they did not circulate much, and were most probably brought directly from England before being hidden in the deposit.

A single artefact stands out from the Lund excavations as worthy of special note in this context. In 1961 a wooden pencase lid was excavated near a well in a position indicating it had been deposited on the slope leading to the well while that structure was still in use, in the period c. 1025–50.[49] The lid is 34 centimetres in length and is made of sycamore wood. One end widens into a carved snarling animal mask, once used as the grip for opening the case, and the rest of the top is carved with acanthus-leaf foliage. Both of these parts are fine examples of English Winchester-style carving, but the object has further links to England on its reverse.[50] The principal part of the main body has a shallow carved-out area once filled with wax and used to take notes with a stylus. The head has a large inscription with the English name 'LEOFÞINE . . .', while a damaged second line that might read 'MY . . . ER' has been interpreted as 'me fecit' ('made me') or the title

---

[47] von Heijne, 'Viking-Age Hoards'.

[48] Ibid., and Jonsson, 'Coinage', pp. 214–15, where he notes that the most likely reason for these high percentages of German coins in such hoards is that most coins in them (including English ones) came in from Germany. The English coins thus attest to their use in trade by the English with Germany, rather than to contact with Scandinavia.

[49] For a good discussion of it in English see Okasha, 'An Inscribed Anglo-Saxon Lid'. Reproductions of both its upper and lower faces are given here in this volume.

[50] Roesdahl et al., *The Vikings in England*, p. 180.

moneyer.[51] The pencase may have been produced in England and exported, or produced on site in Lund by an experienced English carver, but what is certain is that it was a fine practical object produced for record-keeping or note-taking by a literate immigrant, doubtless one of Cnut's Englishmen at the site. As Cinthio notes, a moneyer named Leofwine is recorded for Lund during the reigns of Cnut and then Swen Estrithsson, and it is tempting to connect the object directly with him.[52]

Cnut appears to have used English die-cutters for his earliest Lund coinage, which may date to 1014–15, and his jump-starting of the Danish coinage relied heavily on English influence and personnel.[53] In 1019 a mint at Viborg was producing coins in Cnut's name along with a royal title, a named moneyer and mint-signature. This mint had an impressive output, being linked to eight out of the sixty published die-impressions.[54] Roskilde's mint activity is not easy to date, but was established there before c. 1025.[55] There were also two smaller non-urban mint sites on Sjælland, at Ringsted and Slagelse, which were probably based on royal estates, but are still understudied and imperfectly understood.[56] Lund's mint went from strength to strength after its first issues, and from 1019 onwards had the largest output of any Danish mint during Cnut's reign, with a claim to twenty-three of the sixty published die-impressions.[57] The English influence on these mints is clear. Moneyers with the distinctively English names of Godwine, Ælfwine and Leofwine are found at Lund, and another with the English name *Brihtred* (for Beorhtred) is recorded on coins produced for Cnut at

[51] The name is sometimes given with the 'f' in square brackets, but it is quite clear on the object itself. What is curious about it is the change of script after 'Leof' so that 'wine . . .' is in display capitals. I have no answer for this.

[52] Cinthio, 'Myntverk'

[53] For the early Lund coins see Blackburn, 'Do Cnut the Great's First Coins'.

[54] Hauberg, *Myntforhold*, p. 45.

[55] Jonsson, 'Coinage', p. 226.

[56] See Grinder-Hansen, 'Ringsted', and Arnskov, *Bogen om Slagelse*, pp. 60–3, for the little comment that exists in print.

[57] Hauberg, *Myntforhold*, p. 45.

Slagelse.[58] Rather than local men, the Scandinavian names on these coins may in fact be those of men from the Anglo-Scandinavian Danelaw, and it may have been easier to convince these officials with some understanding of the language and culture of Denmark to leave England for a period of service there.

The proximity of England to Denmark probably allowed Cnut to take a hands-on role in the affairs of the latter, even when away. The distances were not so great between Jutland and the eastern coastline of England (an addition to Adam of Bremen's text states that it was three days' sail with favourable winds), and there was also substantial trade between England and the coastal Low Countries.[59] Bishop Gerbrand of Roskilde was most probably pursuing a route involving this merchant travel along the coastline of what is now the Netherlands, followed by an overland route past Hamburg and Bremen to the Danish border, when he was detained by Archbishop Unwan of Hamburg-Bremen in the 1020s.[60] The movement of merchants probably ensured a relatively constant flow of information between England and Denmark, and if faster or more secure embassies were needed, they could be dispatched from the naval garrison at London.

We now return to our narrative. Cnut may have hoped that with the death of Thorkell and the recognition of Ulf alongside Harthacnut his problems in Denmark had petered out. However, he could not have been more wrong. His steadily increasing power and influence there in the urban sites and English-influenced infrastructure, as well as fear of a Danish overlordship of Scandinavia, appear to have forged a common purpose amongst his enemies. In 1026 Cnut faced the greatest military threat to his rule, and it appears to have come from an alliance of Danish elites with the rulers of Norway and parts of Sweden. This threat, and his response, was the defining moment of his political

---

[58] See Cinthio, 'Myntverk', for some discussion of the names of moneyers from Lund.

[59] Adam of Bremen, *Gesta*, scholion 100(97) (Schmeidler, p. 229), and in the earliest extant manuscript of c. 1100. On the evidence for trade see P. H. Sawyer, *The Wealth of Anglo-Saxon England*, pp. 99–100 and 104–5.

[60] Adam of Bremen, *Gesta*, ii, 55 (Schmeidler, p. 116).

1. Cnut and Emma present a large gold cross to the New Minster, Winchester, and receive a crown and a veil from angels in return. In the New Minster *Liber Vitae*.

2. Detail of the confraternity additions to a Gospel Book from Christ Church, Canterbury, naming Cnut as the 'beloved worldly lord' of the community, as well as their 'spiritual brother before God', written above the name of Cnut's actual brother, Harald, and three Scandinavian magnates who are each dubbed 'our brother'.

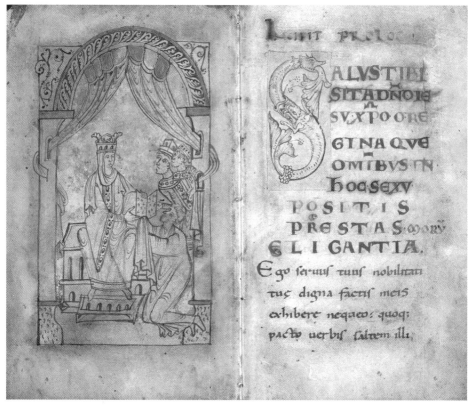

3. Emma crowned and seated on a throne and receiving the *Encomium Emmae Reginae* from the author, while her two sons, Harthacnut and Edward the Confessor, look on. The frontispiece and opening of the prologue to the text.

4. The obverse and reverse of an elaborately carved wooden pencase lid in English style and with the Anglo-Saxon name 'Leofwine' inscribed on the underside of its head. Discovered in Lund in layers dateable to Cnut and Harthacnut's reigns.

seduceret eum fallax uisio · qua seducuntur
quiaplures qui n̄ acquiescunt ueritati cre
dentes m̄dacio · C̄hnut rex angloru̅ huic
mirando spectaculo intererat · et fidele
sit quod obhoc dn̄s eum direxerat · ut
HERIBERTVS p̄dicaret eti̅a p̄ reges · qui
in dieb; suis placens d̄o et inuent̄ iustus fi
deliter obseruauit regissui d̄i leges · Rex
ipse in ueneratione s̄ci humilit̄ conuersus ·
regia dona ingentia & honorifica trans
misit ipsi reuersus · S ic regina saba uenit
a finib; terrę saluo my̅sterio audire sapi
entiam salomonis · sed n̄ habebat ultra sp̄m
uidens gazas aromatu̅ & thesauroru̅ et
infinitate̅ specieru̅ et honoris · hic ergo
in agrippinensi metropoli saluatus · sorori
treueroru̅ metropoli ē destinatus · digitis ·
Redditur manus homini erectis a uola
Non multo post manebat homo in eodem

5. Cnut's appearance as a witness to a miraculous healing of a cripple from Trier, in the eleventh-century *Miracula Heriberti*.

6. The London Ringerike Tombstone, featuring a stocky four-legged beast, its head turned around over its back, surrounded by interlace and lappets from its extremities, which are characteristic of this Scandinavian eleventh-century art-style (oolitic limestone with traces of original bluish-black and red paint).

7. Reproduction and drawing of a gilt bronze mount with Ringerike-style decoration. Excavated in Winchester Cathedral.

8. The Thorney *Liber Vitae*, the page here containing the eleventh-century entries for Cnut, Emma, his sons (head of column 1), English earls and Jarl Ulf of Denmark (head of column 3). The Scandinavian names beneath may have been members of his retinue or of another Scandinavian lord present.

9. A vernacular charter from the archive of Christ Church, Canterbury, in an Anglo-Norman copy, recording a visit of a member of the community named Ælfgar to the royal court of Harold Harefoot at Oxford as the king lay on his deathbed 'very ill, so that he lay despairing of his life' (line 5 here opening 'oxana forde' and describing Harold as 'swype geseocled swa þ[æt] he læg orwene his lifes').

career. Again the contemporary English and later Scandinavian sources tell different versions of the story. The Anglo-Saxon Chronicle names 'Ulf and Eilaf' as Cnut's opponents in this, while the saga sources state that this was a joint invasion by King Óláfr Haraldsson of Norway and King Anund Jakob of Sweden.[61] In increasingly more inventive attempts to resolve this apparent disagreement, it has been argued by various modern scholars that Ulf and Eilaf were the sons of a powerful Swedish jarl, Ragnvald, or that Eilaf was a scribal error for Olaf/Óláfr.[62] However, it is far more likely that this Ulf and Eilaf were the earl named Eilaf who had been placed by Cnut into an area of Mercia and his brother Jarl Ulf, who held some form of overlordship over Denmark.[63] The chronicler's brevity is a mark of his expectation that his readers were already familiar with these men, and an identification with the 'Eglaf duke and his brother Ulf' in the Thorney *Liber Vitae* is most compelling.[64] Simon Keynes observes that this Eglaf/Eilaf frequently witnessed Cnut's royal charters from 1018 onwards, but his attestations cease abruptly in 1024, consistent with his leaving the country to return to Denmark.[65] John of Worcester states that this Ulf was 'the Danish Earl Ulf, son of Spracling, son of Urse' and he identifies him as the father of King Swen Estrithsson of Denmark (Cnut's nephew).[66] 'Spracling' here is easily identified as the byname of a Danish lord named as Thorgisl Sprakalegg in the Danish twelfth-century history written by Saxo Grammaticus.[67] A single late saga source, the 'Supplement to *Jómsvíkinga saga*', states that Ulf and Eilaf

[61] ASC 1026 EF (Irvine, p. 75), and Snorri Sturluson, *Heimskringla*, chs. 132, 134 and 145–52 (Bjarni Aðalbjarnarson, II, pp. 226–7, 234–5 and 269–84).

[62] Moberg, 'Battle of Helgeå', p. 11; Freeman, *Norman Conquest*, I, p. 765, and Campbell, *Encomium Emmae Reginae*, p. 86.

[63] See Keynes, 'Cnut's Earls', pp. 58–60 and 62–4.

[64] Gerchow, *Gedenküberlieferung*, p. 327, and Rollason, *Thorney Liber Vitae*, p. 102.

[65] See Keynes, *Atlas of Attestations*, table lxix.

[66] John of Worcester, *Chronicon*, s.a. 1049 (Darlington and McGurk, p. 548).

[67] In modern literature he elsewhere commonly appears with his name in a West Norse form as Þórgils/Thorgils Sprakalegg. See my discussion of these family traditions in 'Was the Family'.

were brothers and notes their father as one Thorgisl.[68] The different perspectives of the other types of source most easily explain the various versions of the story. The Anglo-Saxon Chronicle's focus was primarily that of English events and figures, whereas, conversely, the saga sources mostly concern themselves with Norwegian and Swedish affairs.

Eilaf appears to have withdrawn from Cnut's service in England soon after 1024 and returned to Denmark, where he and Ulf made common cause with the Norwegians and Swedes, who seem to have been in an alliance with each other from c. 1019 onwards when Anund Jakob's sister married Óláfr Haraldsson.[69] The Swedes appear to have already opened up diplomatic relations with the see of Hamburg-Bremen under Archbishop Unwan, and Sigvatr Þórðarson's *Austrfararvísur* records that its author was sent on a diplomatic mission to Jarl Ragnvald of Sweden c. 1019.[70] Cnut's external enemies look to have been trying to form collective bonds since his accession to the Danish throne, and now Cnut's internal enemies seem to have joined this power-bloc.

Some brief comment must be made here on King Óláfr Haraldsson of Norway and King Anund Jakob of Sweden and their reasons for entering this conflict. Far too much has been made of attempts by later saga traditions to link Óláfr Haraldsson and Cnut as allies or relatives, and these are evident literary fabrications.[71] What they do reflect, which is most probably real, is that even in the thirteenth century it was clear that Óláfr Haraldsson had set Norway on a similar course to that on which Cnut's dynasty set Denmark, and that he was Cnut's great rival

[68] Campbell, *Encomium Emmae Reginae*, p. 92.

[69] This marriage alliance is recorded by a fragment of a poem of Sigvatr Þórðarson (ed. Finnur Jonsson, *Den Norsk-Islandske Skjaldedigtning*, A I, p. 248; B I, p. 231), and in the historical narratives of Theodericus Monachus, *Historia*, ch. 16 (Storm, p. 29), and *Ágrip*, ch. 25 (Driscoll, pp. 36–8).

[70] *Austrfararvísur* (Whaley, pp. 578–614).

[71] On this ruler see Sigvatr Þórðarson, *Víkingarvísur, Nesjavísur, Austrfararvísur, Óláfsdrápa, Vestrfararvísur* and *Erfidrápa Óláfs helga* (Whaley, pp. 532–615 and 663–98), as well as Astås, 'Óláfr, St.', and Henriksson, *St. Olav of Norway*.

for overlordship of the whole of Scandinavia.[72] Much here is based solely on late Scandinavian sources, but I think we can agree on the basic elements of Óláfr's life. He appears to have been the descendant of King Haraldr Hárfagr, through Haraldr Grenske, king of Vestfold. After being baptized in Rouen, Óláfr returned to Norway and ousted the Jarls of Hlaðir, with the support of five petty-kings of the Uppland region. He went on to subjugate the petty-rulers of much of southern Norway, and looks to have begun to centralize authority in his own hands and introduce missionary bishops. This extension of power, however, was not performed as efficiently as in Denmark and does not see in to have included large-scale urban building projects, or the introduction of more than token examples of coinage. Moreover, Óláfr had much to fear from a more organized Denmark with vast reserves of English wealth and military forces.

Anund Jakob likewise was involved in the centralization of power in the region he ruled, most probably that of the area around Lake Mälar in eastern Sweden and its overlordships.[73] He was the son of the reforming Christian king, Olof skotkonung, who had claims to nominal overlordship of large parts of Sweden, a significant military presence in the east of Scandinavia, and some form of alliance with Swen 'Forkbeard' and Cnut before the latter's accession to the Danish throne. During Swen's reign this alliance was probably formed to control the ambitions of the Norwegian king, Óláfr Tryggvason, with the two weaker parties in the Scandinavian triumvirate allying together in order to try to limit the power of the stronger.[74] A subsequent alliance of

[72] See Astås, 'Óláfr, St.', and Andersen, *Samlingen av Norge*, pp. 109–42, and references there.

[73] On Anund Jakob, and his father, Olof skotkonung, see P. H. Sawyer, *The Making of Sweden*, and the same author's 'Cnut's Scandinavian Empire', pp. 14–15 and 18, as well as Ros, *Sigtuna*, pp. 15–32, and Lindqvist, 'Social and Political Power'. His military prowess in the east is attested by Óttarr svarti's verses composed on him, the *Óláfsdrápa sænska* (this not yet published by the Skaldic editing project, and available in Finnur Jónsson, *Skjaldedigtning*, AI, pp. 289–90, and BI, p. 267); and his alliance with Swen, while recorded only in late saga sources, is implied by Cnut's sending of the sons of Edmund Ironside to him (see p. 98 above).

[74] At least Olof's part in a collective military attack on Óláfr Tryggvason is attested by the verse of Óttarr svarti (see previous note for reference).

Sweden with Norway against Cnut once he rose to prominence was probably part of the same pattern, with Cnut in ascendance, and the other two parties seeking to limit his power and actions.

To return to the conflict in Denmark: Sigvatr Þórðarson's *Knútsdrápa* records the first attack made on Sjælland by Norwegian and Swedish fleets, and that one of these forces then ravaged Skåne.[75] The late saga source, *Heimskringla*, claims that it was a Swedish land army that attacked Skåne during the initial parts of the conflict, while marching towards Sjælland.[76] The plan of the rebels and invaders seems to have hung on the notion that Cnut could not react quickly, and that a lightning-fast attack by them would be followed by months in which they could dig in and fortify their defences. We can date the conflict in Denmark from the death of the exiled Bishop Ekkihard of Hedeby-Schleswig on 2 August 1026. On that day he is recorded as dying during a military campaign in Denmark. As he had been in exile in Germany since 988 at least and seems to have made no previous attempts to re-enter his see, this was most probably an endeavour to seize back the see at the head of an army.[77] It beggars belief that after thirty-eight years in exile his attack should happen to fall by chance in the same year as a major insurrection in Denmark. The bishop most probably gathered his forces and set off for Hedeby-Schleswig after he had heard that the uprising/ invasion had begun. As I shall discuss later, Cnut had been invited to attend the coronation of the new Holy Roman Emperor at Easter 1027, and in late 1026 he must have been almost consumed by preparations for this long and arduous journey for himself and his entourage. His Scandinavian enemies must have assumed that these preparations would pin him down in England, and prevent him from striking back immediately. They appear to have supposed, quite reasonably, that if they struck in sufficient numbers and occupied major sites, then Cnut

---

[75] *Knútsdrápa*, verses 3–6 (Whaley, pp. 653–9).

[76] Snorri Sturluson, *Heimskringla*, ch. 145 (Bjarni Aðalbjarnarson, II, p. 269). The Anglo-Saxon Chronicle records that a land force from Sweden was present at the Battle of Helgeå, and these may have been the same troops.

[77] See Gelting, 'Elusive Bishops', p. 179.

would be forced to watch from afar before leaving for Rome early in 1027, allowing them many months and perhaps even a year to entrench themselves before his return.

They were wrong. Cnut was a gifted strategist, and he saw that one move remained which his opponents had assumed was impossible and thus were unprepared for. He immediately led his fleet, presumably hastily assembled from English and loyal Danish forces, to the Limfjord – a vast inland sea in the north of Jutland, open at its westernmost and easternmost points, and at the time at its northernmost point.[78] This unexpected challenge seems to have startled his opponents, and the Norwegian and Swedish forces appear to have withdrawn eastwards without conflict, around the tip of Skåne and into the southernmost part of the Baltic Sea. Cnut gave chase, and the single battle they fought was a naval one. Both English and Scandinavian sources give it as taking place in a river named Helgeå ('Holy River'), identified variously as in Skåne or in Uppland within modern Sweden.[79] The conflict may also have spilled out onto the surrounding land, and Saxo Grammaticus records a land battle between a force led by Anund Jakob and some Danish troops at an unidentified site he names Stångeberg, close to Helgeå.[80] Neither side gained a decisive victory, with one branch of the Anglo-Saxon Chronicle recording 'heavy losses' amongst Cnut's forces, and that 'the Swedes had control of the battlefield', and similarly skaldic verse recording the battle but without explicitly stating that Cnut was victorious.[81] Sigvatr Þórðarson in his *Knútsdrápa* only describes Cnut's preparations for the conflict and his magnanimity in the aftermath, and the one extant stanza of Þórðr

---

[78] Sigvatr Þórðarson, *Tøgdrápa*, verse 8, records the presence of the fleet in the Limfjord.

[79] See Moberg, 'The Battle of Helgeå', pp. 4–7, and Gräslund, 'Knut den Store', pp. 217–28, for varying identifications of the site.

[80] Saxo Grammaticus, *Gesta Danorum*, X:16 (Christiansen, p. 33). See also Christiansen's comments on pp. 195–6, n. 118, and the discussion of the site by Gräslund, 'Knut den Store', pp. 226–7.

[81] The placename of the battle is recorded in ASC EF 1025 (Irvine, p. 75) in the adapted form 'þam holme æt ea þære halgan'. Moberg, 'The Battle of Helgeå', pp. 12–14, tried to interpret the wording of the Anglo-Saxon Chronicle to indicate a victory not a defeat, but this strains the evidence too far (see P. H. Sawyer, 'Knut, Sweden and Sigtuna', p. 89, for a similar conclusion).

Sáreksson's *Roðudrápa* is as vague as can be, lauding the bravery of both
Cnut and Óláfr Haraldsson.[82] Similarly, Óttarr svarti in his *Knutsdrápa*
notes Cnut's success in a muted way, claiming only that he 'held the territory against two princes, where the raven did not at all go hungry'.[83]

A decisive victory may not have been Cnut's aim, but instead he may
just have wanted to push the invaders eastwards away from open water.
Here we must turn to the more suspect of our Scandinavian sources,
but the events they narrate are plausible and in accordance with what
else we know of the conflict. One of the extant fragments of the
so-called 'Oldest Saga of St Olaf', which was written c. 1200, states that
as Cnut retreated from the battle at Helgeå he used his fleet to block the
Øresund, sealing in the Norwegians and Swedes in the Baltic. This is
supported in saga narratives by a skaldic verse attributed to a Norwegian
eyewitness, Hárekr of Þióttá, which has been thought to be correct.[84]
However, as it survives in the narrative introduced as free speech, not as
a pre-existing source with a separate title, we cannot be sure.[85] That
done, Cnut appears to have left his blockading fleet in place, and
returned to his earlier travel plans, moving with his entourage to Rome.
The fact that no subsequent skaldic verse for Cnut includes any record
of another naval engagement after Helgeå, when almost all other
known battles are recorded there – including some in the English
campaign not noted by the Anglo-Saxon Chronicle – may suggest that
some truth lies behind the account of the 'Oldest Saga' and the verse
attributed to Hárekr of Þióttá.

The effects of this refusal to engage with the Swedish and Norwegian
forces were great. The Swedes were free to return home, but the gravity
of the situation for the Norwegians may have only just dawned on

[82] Sigvatr Þórðarson, *Knútsdrápa*, verses 3–9 (Whaley, pp. 653–61); Þórðr Sáreksson,
Roðudrápa (Whaley, p. 243).

[83] Óttarr svarti, *Knútsdrápa*, verse 11 (Whaley, p. 781).

[84] The details can be found on fragments 4 and 5 of the so-called *Oldest Saga of St. Óláfr*.
These are Norway, Oslo, Norsk Riksarkivet, MS. 52 (ed. Storm, pp. 9–10).

[85] Edited by Whaley, *Poetry from the King's Sagas*, p. 808. Finnur Jónsson, *Den Oldnorske og
Oldislandske Litteraturs*, I, p. 460, thought them authentic.

them. They were trapped in a vast enclosed sea, and had doubtless come prepared only for a late summer or early autumn campaign, with plans to take winter supplies from their new Danish subjects. If they now raided the Swedish coastline for such things, the Norwegians would draw out their former Swedish allies against them, and with every day that passed supplies must have dwindled lower and lower, as the weather became more punishing. Finally, the Norwegians were forced to make the decision to abandon their ships and travel home overland. Winter may have already begun. Few medieval armies went overland during winter, and in Scandinavia it almost never occurred. Whether they aimed for the Oslofjord in the south or for the region around Trondheim in mid-Norway, this was a devastating trek through thick forest and mountainous terrain where there were few roads or trails, and it was probably made by men still in clothing intended for a late summer or early autumn sea voyage. Only one comparable situation presents itself. In the early eighteenth century a poorly equipped and exhausted Swedish army under the command of Carl Gustaf Armfeldt decided to engage on a four-day march back to Sweden from Norway over the Tydal mountain range in Trøndelag.[86] When a blizzard sprang up unexpectedly they unwisely pushed on, losing approximately 3,000 men of a roughly 5,000-strong company on the mountainside, with a further 1,500 dying later from frostbite and another 450 men crippled for life and invalided out of the army. The situation cannot have been very different in 1026–7. However many men stumbled out of the forests in Norway, half frozen and starving, they were unlikely to mount further resistance to Cnut.

Cnut's letter to the English of 1027, sent back from his return voyage from Rome, makes it clear that he was returning to Denmark to 'arrange peace and a firm treaty, with the counsel of all the Danes, with those races and peoples who would have deprived us of life and rule if they

[86] Much has been written about this. For an easily accessible account in English, see Lindqvist, *History of Sweden*, pp. 327–8.

could'. It informed the English that when peace was concluded Cnut would return to England 'as early this summer as I can attend to the equipping of a fleet'.[87] The mid-twelfth-century Roskilde Chronicle states that Ulf was executed in the church in that city, and the assembly may well have been there.[88] Eilaf disappears from the record at this time.[89] Many other members of the Danish aristocracy who had aided the rebellion were probably purged at or after this assembly, but the statement of Sigvatr Þórðarson's *Knútsdrápa*, that Cnut 'would allow little plundering of the land', might suggest that any punitive measures were localized and targeted at treacherous individuals.[90] He remained in Denmark some months, doubtless mopping up opposition and shoring up Harthacnut's government.

Norway had demonstrated the substantial threat it could pose to Cnut, and the matter could not be left at that. In the months after his return to England, Cnut either reached out to senior members of the Norwegian nobility in exile from Óláfr Haraldsson's authority, or began to receive embassies from these men.[91] Many of them were old allies of the Jarls of Hlaðir and presumably still had contact with Hákon, the son of Eiríkr, Cnut's trusted ally, and the last scion of this dynasty. The subject of the discussions must have been Cnut's possible ejection of Óláfr from Norway, and his replacement of the latter's regime with one more friendly to Cnut and the Norwegian exiles.

At the same time, Óláfr's popularity in Norway seems to have taken a nosedive, perhaps as a result of the decimation of the forces returning

---

[87] *Die Gesetze* (Liebermann, I, pp. 276–7).

[88] *Chronicon Roskildense*, ch. 7, ed. Gertz in *Scriptores Historiae Danicae Minores*, I, pp. 20–1, Saxo Grammaticus, *Gesta Danorum*, X, p. 17 (Christiansen, pp. 36–7), and Snorri Sturluson, *Heimskringla*, ch. 153 (Bjarni Aðalbjarnarson, II, p. 285).

[89] It should be noted that the *Brut y Tywysogyon*, s.a. 1035 (Jones, pp. 22–3) states that Eilaf left England after Cnut's death for *Germania* (either Germany or perhaps Norway), while the 'Supplement to *Jómsvíkinga saga*' (Campbell, p. 93) states that he went to Constantinople at some stage during Cnut's early career, where he died. Both are probably in error.

[90] Sigvatr Þórðarson, *Knútsdrápa*, verse 9 (Whaley, p. 660). Here I have changed the word 'little' for the 'minimal' given by the new edition. The variant 'little' is offered by the textual appendix and makes better sense in this use.

[91] See Bolton, *Empire*, pp. 250–9.

from Helgeå and the lack of any booty. Surviving verses from a poem composed by Bjarni Gullbrárskáld for the Norwegian magnate Kálfr Árnason record that Kálfr travelled to Cnut as Óláfr fled into exile in Russia.[92] The two possible rulers are set up in opposition to each other, with Cnut offering Kálfr substantial gifts, including apparent promises of 'land'. This most probably consisted of vast estates in Norway or a promise of some petty-overlordship there if Cnut's rule there could be achieved. Important skalds operated as senior court figures and diplomats as well as poets. Judith Jesch's recent and convincing reading of Sigvatr Þórðarson's *Vestrfaravísur*, as a skaldic apology and explanation of the poet's taking service with Cnut briefly in this period, suggests that even close advisors may have deserted Óláfr in 1027–8.[93] Sigvatr's poem was apparently offered to Óláfr once Sigvatr had re-entered his service, and we might even see these parts of it as a public apology made on behalf of entire sections of Óláfr's court.

In 1028, Cnut took the fleet that was mentioned in his letter of 1027 to Norway. The Anglo-Saxon Chronicle and John of Worcester claim that it numbered 'fifty ships'.[94] Þórarinn loftunga's *Tøgdrápa* records that they first mustered in the Limfjord, before sailing to southern Norway and then westwards around the coastline, with Cnut's ship decked out in gold.[95] The surviving verses of Þórarinn's poem show that the original work traced the various stages of this route for its listener (from Lista off the coast of Vest Agder, past Tjernagel in southern Hordaland and a mountain on the border of Nordmøre and Romsdalen named Stemmet, to Nið, the river on which Trondheim stands), with a focus on

[92] Bjarni Gullbrárskáld, *Kálfsflokkr*, verses 3–4 (Whaley, pp. 882–4).

[93] Sigvatr Þórðarson, *Vestrfaravísur* (Whaley, pp. 615–27; note in particular verse 7 in which the skald is asked by Cnut whether he wishes to serve him as he did Óláfr, and responds in a way intended to please the latter: 'one lord at a time was fitting for me', as well as verse 6 in which the poet asks where a seat might be found for him now in Óláfr's hall. Sigvatr had acted on behalf of Óláfr before (see *Austrfaravísur* [Whaley, pp. 578–614], which records his undertaking a diplomatic mission into Sweden), and was clearly a senior court figure as well as a poet.

[94] ASC 1028 CDE (O'Brien O'Keeffe, p. 105), and John of Worcester, *Chronicon*, s.a. 1028 (Darlington and McGurk, p. 510).

[95] Þórarinn loftunga, *Tøgdrápa* (Whaley, pp. 851–63).

the visual impact of this fleet and the reactions of the various peoples
along their route. When they arrived in southern Norway, Cnut played
a trump card in the person of Hákon Eiríksson. His father Eiríkr
Hákonarson had last witnessed a royal charter in England in 1023, and
most probably died in that year or soon after.[96] His uncle Sveinn had
died c. 1016 while in exile in Sweden, and thus Hákon inherited the
claims of the Jarls of Hlaðir to rule over large parts of Norway. Hákon,
like his father, appears to have been a trusted ally of Cnut as well as
close family (being the son of Cnut's elder half-sister), and he could
offer Cnut a legitimate conquest of Norway, which could be presented
as a return to the political order before Óláfr Haraldsson. Thus, Cnut
and Hákon travelled together with the fleet, and as Þórarinn states:
'Then the bold enjoyer of the glory-Jótar [i.e. Cnut] gave his nephew
the whole of Norway.'[97]

Cnut and Hákon appear to have taken control of the region without
much resistance and concentrated their efforts on presenting themselves as alternative candidates for overlordship to Óláfr Haraldsson,
generously distributing wealth and conceding to demands. Óláfr had
either stayed in exile or fled again.[98] A verse of Sigvatr Þórðarson's
Vestrfaravísur indicates that Óláfr refused to engage Cnut and Hákon's
forces, and kept 'himself in the mountains' (perhaps used to denote a
real geographical place, or as an expression for an inaccessible place).[99]
Cnut and Hákon's propaganda campaign can be discerned in a fragment of skaldic verse composed by Hallvarðr Hárekblesi for Cnut after
the conquest of Norway, which employs imagery for Cnut's control
there that echoes a pagan motif previously used by the poets of the Jarls
of Hlaðir.[100] Cnut and Hákon were being placed together, as part of the

---

[96] S. 959.

[97] Þórarinn loftunga, *Tøgdrápa*, verse 6 (Whaley, pp. 860–1).

[98] Snorri Sturluson, *Heimskringla*, chs. 177–80 (Bjarni Aðalbjarnarson, II, pp. 319–27).
This source claims he fled to Sweden and then Novgorod.

[99] Sigvatr Þórðarson, *Vestrfaravísur*, verse 3 (Whaley, pp. 619–21).

[100] Bolton, *Empire*, pp. 265–9. See also Ström, 'Poetry as an Instrument', for its use by the
Jarls of Hlaðir.

same family and as a solution to Norway's problems. Similarly, the later narrative sources show Cnut and Hákon securing the support of the Norwegian aristocracy through lavish gift-giving and by making good on any earlier promises. These acts framed them in Scandinavian traditions as good and proper overlords, but also implicitly put them at the head of a client-relationship with these men. John of Worcester records that Cnut 'sent to them [the Norwegians] much gold and silver beseeching them . . . to surrender to him, and permit him to reign over them', and similar traditions are documented in the anonymous *Passio Olaui*, Theodericus' *Historia*, and the later saga accounts.[101]

Exiled Norwegian magnates now began to return to Norway, and many must previously have been followers of Sveinn and Eiríkr Hákonarson, who could begin to rekindle dynastic alliances with Hákon. The mighty Norwegian lords Einarr Þambarskelfir and Erlingr Skjálgsson had fled Óláfr Haraldsson's wrath in the aftermath of the Battle of Nesjar c. 1015 in which they supported the Jarls of Hlaðir. The late sources *Heimskringla* and the Legendary Saga state that Einarr went to Sweden and then to Denmark, where he may have lived under Cnut's protection for some time.[102] *Heimskringla* states that eventually Einarr negotiated a reconciliation between himself and Óláfr, and returned to his estates; however, he does not appear to have taken up a governing office again until after 1028.[103] The same source claims that Erlingr Skjálgsson got into a disagreement with one of Óláfr's officials after the Battle of Nesjar and fled the country, eventually ending up in England.[104] In addition, Hárekr of Þiótta was an influential nobleman

---

[101] John of Worcester, *Chronicon*, s.a. 1027 (Darlington and McGurk, p. 510), *Passio Olaui*, ch. 9 (Storm, p. 131), Theodericus Monachus, *Historia*, ch. 16 (Storm, p. 31), and Snorri Sturluson, *Heimskringla*, ch. 130 (Bjarni Aðalbjarnarson, II, p. 222).

[102] Snorri Sturluson, *Heimskringla*, chs. 39, 41, 46 and 51 (Bjarni Aðalbjarnarson, II, pp. 50, 52–3, 58 and 67). The *Legendary Saga*, ch. 25 (Heinrichs, p. 78), also notes that he was in Helsingland for some time, as well as Denmark.

[103] Snorri Sturluson, *Heimskringla*, chs. 115 and 171 (Bjarni Aðalbjarnarson, II, pp. 191–2 and 306–7).

[104] Ibid., chs. 116, 120–1 and 131 (Bjarni Aðalbjarnarson, II, pp. 192–3, 203–6 and 226). See also *Fagrskinna*, ch. 25 (Bjarni Einarsson, p. 27) for some confirmation of his flight to England.

in Hålogaland who is reported to have entered into a disagreement over jurisdiction with one of Óláfr's officials, exacting violent revenge on the official and transferring his allegiance to Cnut.[105] Lastly, Þórir hundr is stated to have become involved in a feud with one of Óláfr's officials, and having been forced to accept Óláfr's justice he fled to Finnmark and eventually to Cnut.[106]

We must pause briefly here to note that no similar actions were taken in Sweden after Helgeå. A small number of coins were minted in Sigtuna in the late 1020s and 1030s with an inscription '*CNUT REX SV*' (perhaps intending *rex Swevorum* or *Swenorum*, or 'king of the Swedes'), and were taken to demonstrate Cnut's authority there. However, these inscriptions are the sole piece of evidence to suggest this, and as they are all from a single die, they have now been discounted as probably crude and clumsy adaptations of English coins by Swedish moneyers.[107] Other scholars have discussed the appearance of the English titles *thegn* or *dreng* on runestones and in place names, and tentatively suggested that followers of Cnut were implanted into the Swedish landscape.[108] However, the overwhelming majority of this material is concentrated in a single region, Västergötland (thirty-four inscriptions from a total of fifty-six) and the adjacent coastline up to south-eastern Norway, suggesting instead a localized use of these terms.[109] The reasons behind Cnut's inactivity in Sweden perhaps lie in the nature of contemporary Swedish society. By the 1020s Norway was well on the way to becoming a centralized society, with political and religious power concentrated in

[105] Snorri Sturluson, *Heimskringla*, chs. 123, 140 and 169 (Bjarni Aðalbjarnarson, II, pp. 211, 253–5 and 305).

[106] Ibid., chs. 123, 133 and 139 (Bjarni Aðalbjarnarson, II, pp. 211–13, 227–34 and 250–3). Note that the *Legendary Saga*, chs. 46 and 62 (Heinrichs, pp. 108 and 152) narrates the same story except that it has Þórir flee northwards to Finnmark, not England, for two years.

[107] Jonsson, 'Coinage', pp. 228–30, responding to P. H. Sawyer, 'Knut' (but note his change of position in his *addendum* on p. 92 there) and perhaps also Löfving, 'Who Ruled'. Note Sawyer's own recanting of his former interpretation in his 'Cnut's Scandinavian Empire', p. 20.

[108] See B. Sawyer, 'Appendix', for the most recent proposal of this argument. Both she and Löfving, 'Who Ruled', p. 154, make cases for this.

[109] Figures taken from B. Sawyer, 'Appendix', pp. 24, n. 2, and 25.

the hands of a single monarch and his ecclesiastics. Sweden had expe-rienced something similar in the region around Lake Mälar, but on a lesser scale, and it may well have gone into reverse after the apparent ejection of the rulers there by the local aristocracy in 1030–5.[110] Sweden appears to have remained a conglomerate of small sub-kingdoms and regional chieftaincies in the first half of the eleventh century. As I noted above, when talking about the similar situation in which Denmark found itself in the tenth century and before, this was an inherently unstable social model, most probably characterized by feuding between petty-rulers. Such a society would have required an enormous amount of effort to seize and subdue, and in the long run probably presented little future threat to Cnut. It could therefore be ignored.

By the end of the 1020s, Cnut was at the head of a political 'family business' that sat proudly atop much of Scandinavia. His young son Harthacnut was in control of Denmark, and his enemies in this region had exposed themselves and been dealt with. Norway was under the control of his nephew Hákon, with the former king there exiled. Cnut could afford to ignore Sweden. He was now the most powerful ruler that Scandinavia had ever known. He had realized the pretensions to rule of his father and grandfather, and extended them. It thus comes as no surprise that when he sent his letter to the English in the wake of Helgeå he styled himself 'king of all England and Denmark and Norway and part of the Swedes'.[111] Certainly, this was not a geographic fact in 1027, and in the case of 'part of the Swedes' would never be, but the wording may be original. Cnut had withstood and turned to his advantage an invasion by precisely the Norwegians and part of the Swedes. The end result saw their downfall – not his.

---

[110] Rasmusson, 'Overlooked Type', p. 380.
[111] *Die Gesetze* (Liebermann, I, p. 276).

Chapter 5

CNUT AND THE FIELD OF EUROPEAN POLITICS

It is in the field of international politics, perhaps more than any other, where we can see that Cnut did not model himself on any of his Anglo-Saxon or Scandinavian forebears, but instead ploughed a novel and quite opportunistic furrow. English kings before Cnut had maintained occasional and sporadic links with continental rulers, while King Athelstan established connections through the marriage of his half-sisters with the French court and the Empire, and these links appear to have been responsible for many of the European influences in his court and in English society in general.[1] Similarly, Æthelred took the sister of Duke Richard II of Normandy as his second wife in 1002, probably as part of an alliance against viking attacks. This alliance had originated through the intercession of Bishop Leo of Trevi, who had been sent in 990 by Pope John XV to secure friendship between the English and Normans.[2] However, this contact was far from common, and this marriage was the first of an English king to a continental bride in a century and a half.[3] Cnut's Scandinavian experience with continental Europe probably amounted to little more than a memory of mid-tenth-century hostility that lingered around the court, as well as the tussle for

[1] Foot, *Athelstan*, pp. 99–110.

[2] See Keynes' introduction to the reprint of the *Encomium Emmae Reginae*, p. [xvi], and Stafford, *Queen Emma*, pp. 215–17.

[3] Stafford, *Queen Emma*, pp. 209–24. At page 209 she notes that the nearest preceding marriage of an English king to a non-English bride was that of Æthelred's 'great-great-great-grandfather, almost a hundred and fifty years before ... Æthelwulf's marriage to Judith, the daughter of Charles the Bald'.

control over Denmark between his dynasty and the archbishops of Hamburg-Bremen.

It is clear that Cnut embraced Europe, and while most existing discussion of this topic does include accounts of his attendance of Conrad II's imperial coronation at Easter 1027 in Rome, there is often little else said about this area of his life. Let us begin with the facts of the imperial coronation. Cnut's attendance there accorded him great honour, with Conrad's contemporary biographer recording that Cnut was one of two rulers chosen to act as witness to the imperial benediction by the Pope, the naming of Conrad as 'Caesar and Augustus by name' and the coronation of the Empress, before leading the new Emperor to 'his chamber in the place of honour between the two kings'.[4] Cnut's letter of 1027 to his English subjects seems to radiate with pride at his participation in the event. It offers the information that he had 'vowed to God to make this journey [presumably as a pilgrimage] long ago', and gives thanks to God who has enabled him to visit 'his holy apostles, Peter and Paul, and every sanctuary which I could find within the city of Rome or outside of it'. The letter describes the ceremony and its legions of nobles from throughout Europe, 'who all received me with honour and honoured me with precious gifts', none more so than the Emperor. Cnut had discussed with both the Emperor and the Pope 'the needs of all the people of my entire realm, both English and Danes', securing concessions on their safety and toll-exactions while on the road to Rome, as well as on the expenses incurred by archbishops travelling from England to Rome to collect their pallium.[5] Conrad arrived in Rome on 21 March and remained there for at least two and a half weeks, and Cnut may have been with him for much of this time.[6]

It is apparent that the majority of references placing Cnut in contact with any site in mainland Europe focus on two principal areas: one

[4] Wipo, *Gesta Chuonradi*, ch. 16 (Bresslau, pp. 36–7).
[5] *Die Gesetze* (Liebermann, I, pp. 276–7).
[6] Wolfram, *Conrad II*, p. 104.

around Cologne and another in western France. The former references most probably relate to his voyage to or from Rome to attend the coronation ceremony.[7] As Michael Hare has noted, there is a cluster of records about Cnut and his munificence around Cologne.[8] Lantbert of Liège was born around 1000 and became a monk initially of St Lawrence's in Liège and then in the abbey at Deutz on the opposite bank of the Rhine to Cologne. He appears to have returned to Liège in 1060–1, before dying in 1069, and while at Deutz he wrote the *Miracula Heriberti*, a series describing the miraculous visions and healings performed at the abbey. A chapter describing the that text gives the account of a cripple of Trier who went to the shrine after a vision, and was healed. Lantbert states that 'Cnut, king of the English, was present at this amazing spectacle, and let it be counted true that on this account the Lord had directed him, so that Heribert might also be proclaimed by kings . . . [Cnut] sent him prodigious and honourable royal gifts on his return [home]'.[9] Cnut can hardly have been a well-known figure in Rhineland hagiography, and the anomaly of his inclusion here suggests this account accurately places him there. William of Malmesbury in his *Vita Wulfstani* records other gifts from Cnut to Cologne.[10] He states that while the subject of his text, Wulfstan, was studying in the abbey of Peterborough, Ervenius, his master there, produced an illuminated sacramentary and a psalter. These passed to Cnut and his wife Emma, and were given by them to an unspecified benefactor or religious community in Cologne. Some years later the same books were presented to Bishop Ealdred of Worcester during his visit to Cologne in 1054–5.

---

[7] Despite the less-than-solid suggestion of the *Translatio Beata Mildrethe*, as Barlow states in 'Two Notes', pp. 650–1, there is 'no reputable evidence that Cnut undertook a second pilgrimage to Rome'. See the discussion there for the arguments for this.

[8] Hare, 'Cnut and Lotharingia', pp. 269–77.

[9] *Miracula Heriberti*, ch. 16 (Holder-Egger, p. 1253). A reproduction of the relevant page of the oldest manuscript of the text (British Library, Additional MS. 26788, fol. 64v), which may have been produced at Deutz under the author's supervision, is given in this volume.

[10] William of Malmesbury, *Vita Wulfstani*, I:1 and 9 (Darlington, pp. 5 and 15–16).

He presumably recognized them or the workmanship, and eventually returned them to Wulfstan, then prior of Worcester.[11]

However, even allowing for the fragmentary nature of our records of travel routes in Europe in the eleventh century, it is hard to place Cologne on the way from Denmark to Rome or vice versa. We can probably set aside the trip to Rome, as the eyewitness nature of the account of Cnut's visit to the northern coastline of France or the Low Countries in the *Encomium* indicates that he visited a monastery in which the author was an inmate (either St Bertin or St Omer), most probably on the way to Rome. The same account goes on to specify that Cnut then travelled through Flanders, Gaul and Italy on his way to the imperial coronation.[12] Records of overland trade and pilgrimage routes in mainland Europe in the eleventh century survive only sporadically, but enough can be deduced to show that Cologne is far off any route Cnut might have taken if he was heading directly to Rome.[13] All travel itineraries narrated or mapped in this period or the centuries immediately before or after took travellers southwards from various points along the northern coastline of Europe to either Beaune in south-central France or Vevey in Switzerland, and from there to a small number of passes through the Alps. No road passes close to Cologne from the Norman-Flemish coastline (see, for example, the routes indicated by the chronicler Matthew Paris in the thirteenth century) or from southern Denmark (as taken by the Icelander Nikolás of Munkaþvera in the twelfth century). Moreover, Cnut's trips both to and from Rome were made under some considerable time pressure, most probably delayed by the military manoeuvres in Denmark leading up to the Battle of Helgeå on the journey out, and, as Cnut's letter of 1027 makes clear, hurrying back on the return journey to settle matters in Denmark. Thus, we are

---

[11] See Heslop, 'The Production of *de luxe* Manuscripts', pp. 151–60 and 182–8, as well as Pratt, 'Kings and Books', Hare, 'Cnut and Lotharingia', p. 275, and Lawson, *Cnut*, pp. 133–8 and 150–60, for further discussion.

[12] Note that Gransden (*Historical Writing*, p. 49) doubts that this is an eyewitness account, and prefers to see it as a literary topos.

[13] See Birch, *Pilgrimage to Rome*, pp. 43–9.

left to conclude that his presence in Cologne was intentional, rather than the casual act of a passing pilgrim.

Cologne and Liège were important imperial and cultural centres in eleventh-century Germany, and were the key towns for learning in the Rhineland.[14] Cologne was a hive of ecclesiastical activity, and Liège housed an early cathedral school as well as five separate church schools that supplied a disproportionately high number of leading ecclesiastics throughout the eleventh century.[15] John of Worcester records that a royal priest of Cnut named Duduc, who witnessed English royal charters in a position of great prominence from 1033 onwards, and received the see of Wells in the same year, was from Lotharingia, the region around Cologne.[16] Thus, we might conclude that Cnut went there to collect such scholars for his court. However, the dates of Duduc's appearance in the English records are against this. Even allowing for Cnut's journey to Denmark in 1027 and his rapid departure from England for Norway in 1028, it is hard to see how Duduc could avoid being recorded by English sources until 1033, and instead he most probably arrived in England around that time.[17]

There was one pressing political need that could have drawn Cnut to Cologne in 1027. After the violent death of Bishop Ekkihard of Schleswig-Hedeby on the Danish border, his successor was one Rudolf, a member of the Cologne clergy.[18] Control over the see of Schleswig-Hedeby appears to have been on Cnut's mind in Rome, and seems to have formed a crucial part of his negotiations with the Emperor, with Adam of Bremen recording that the Emperor gave up control of the region north of the River Eider to Cnut.[19] The numismatic evidence

[14] Ortenberg, *The English Church*, pp. 43–4 and 46–7.
[15] Renardy, 'Les Écoles ligeoises', p. 313.
[16] John of Worcester, *Chronicon*, s.a. 1060 (Darlington and McGurk, p. 586). See also Keynes, 'Giso, Bishop of Wells', pp. 207–8.
[17] Note that in Bolton, *Empire*, p. 103, I put forward a quite different view, namely that Duduc accompanied Cnut from 1027 onwards. I was probably in error there, and the evidence does not support that view.
[18] See Gelting, 'Elusive Bishops', pp. 180–1, and n. 48 there.
[19] Adam of Bremen, *Gesta*, II:56 (Schmeidler, pp. 116–17).

supports this, in that the first coins minted in Cnut's name from Schleswig-Hedeby derive from the period 1026–8.[20] Bishop Rudolf of Schleswig held office from 1026 to 1047, but only nominally, and he does not appear to have asserted any claim to his bishopric. He seems to have remained with the Cologne clergy, periodically appears in the records for that city, and was buried there in the church of St Kunibert.[21] Ekkihard's invasion in 1026 was a warning shot that Cnut could not afford to ignore, and he appears to have negotiated significant territorial concessions from the new Emperor in Rome concerning this region. It probably seemed wise to call in on his successor, Rudolf, on the return journey from the imperial coronation, with appropriately lavish gifts and pomp and circumstance, to win over the new incumbent, sound out his future intentions, and underline the fact that despite his appointment, Rudolf's see now lay firmly inside the Danish border.

It should be noted at this juncture that the background to Cnut's invitation to the imperial coronation has often been ignored in modern scholarship, beyond the observation that in 1027 Cnut was approaching the height of his military and economic power, and was an attractive ally for Conrad. Modern historians (including myself) have usually approached the subject of Cnut's attendance at this event in near isolation, without consideration of any further factors that led up to his special role in these proceedings. The result is that Cnut is usually portrayed as a passive figure, whom Conrad sought out as a potential ally, with Cnut only taking an active role in negotiations after he had arrived. I suspect this is wrong, and Cnut's interactions with western France point to a different dynamic between Cnut and Conrad.

The evidence for contact between Cnut and western France is quite different from that in the region of Cologne. There is no indication that Cnut ever went there, the places concerned were not sites of such special religious significance that he may have wished to be

---

[20] Jonsson, 'Coinage', p. 226.
[21] Gelting, 'Elusive Bishops', pp. 180–1.

remembered by them, or sites to which other Scandinavians travelled for any reason; and yet evidence survives of lavish gift-giving to the region without any record of contact with any other part of France. We can probably set aside the rhetorical question of the *Encomium* that 'what church does not still rejoice in his gifts? . . . Italy blesses his soul every day, Gaul begs that it may enjoy benefits, and Flanders above all, prays that it may rejoice in heaven with Christ.'[22] These are laudatory hyperbole composed by an author writing some years after Cnut's death to glorify his heirs, and no further traces survive to back up these statements.

In the late 1020s the Aquitanian chronicler Adémar of Chabannes wrote his history of his time at the abbey of Saint-Cybard of Angoulême in central Aquitaine. When he discusses the Council of Limoges he notes England in passing, and states in an aside that 'the king of this people recently sent Duke William V of Aquitaine a codex written in golden letters which contains Martial listed along with the blessed Peter and the other apostles', adding that he had seen it himself amongst other volumes from this people.[23] Elsewhere, the same author makes it clear that he means Cnut, claiming that Duke William bound firmly to himself Alphonse, king of Spain, Sancho, king of Navarre, and the king of the English and the Danes named Cnut with the greatest of favours, so that each year when their emissaries brought the most costly of gifts, he reciprocated with more costly ones sent to them.[24] I am not sure how much trust we can place in this last statement about annual gift-giving between Cnut and Duke William, as repeated exchanges across many years would be odd, to say the least, considering the absence of any indications that Cnut made similar gifts to other French nobles. In addition, Cnut is in peculiar company alongside Alphonse of Spain and Sancho of Navarre, both rulers of south-western Europe, and it may well be that his inclusion here is a mistake,

---

[22] *Encomium Emmae Reginae*, II:19 (Campbell, p. 36).

[23] Adémar of Chabannes, *Sermones Tres*, ed. Migne in *Patrologia Latina* III, col. 122. These gifts are also briefly noted by Lawson in his book, *Cnut*, p. 159, and his article, 'Archbishop Wulfstan', pp. 160–1, in the wider context of Cnut's gift-giving.

[24] Adémar of Chabannes, *Chronicon aquitanicum et francicum* (Chavanon, p. 163).

extrapolated from some record of multiple gifts. However, the note of Cnut's gift of a book written in golden letters is much more specific and entirely in keeping with what has been deduced elsewhere of his and Emma's diplomatic gift-giving.[25] In the eleventh century such a book was rare and amongst the very finest products of Anglo-Saxon scriptoria, but was not unheard of. One might compare it to the Benedictional of St Æthelwold, made in 963–84 (formerly owned by the Duke of Devonshire but sold in 1957 to the British Library, now their Additional MS. 49598), and the Gospel Book of the first half of the eleventh century (now Cambridge, Jesus College, MS. C.23, which has titles, headings and lections in gold script).[26]

In addition, there may be a link here between this gift and a substantial donation sent by Cnut to Bishop Fulbert of Chartres, implied in the bishop's letter of response to Cnut.[27] Fulbert was a close associate and *amicus* of Duke William, acting as the intellectual advisor and guide to his court.[28] Famously, Fulbert's letter to Cnut thanks the king warmly for his offering, addressing him as king of Denmark and expressing surprise at his 'astonishing wisdom and religious spirit' since 'we had heard tell [of you] as a pagan king' and yet '[you] show yourself a very Christian and generous benefactor of the churches and servants of God'. A number of possible dates have been assigned to Fulbert's letter, but none is based in any secure facts.[29] We should probably therefore accept the widest possible limits of 8 September 1020, when the cathedral of Chartres burnt down, to 10 April 1028, when Fulbert died.

George Beech has tried to explain these points of contact as evidence for a pre-Norman Conquest interest of Englishmen in the region, but

[25] See Heslop, 'Patronage of *de luxe* Manuscripts', and Pratt, 'Kings and Books', pp. 355–71.

[26] For the Benedictional of St Æthelwold, see F. Wormald, *Benedictional of St. Ethelwold*, as well as the digitized manuscript on the British Library's website, at: http://www.bl.uk/manuscripts/FullDisplay.aspx?ref=add_ms_49598.

[27] For the text of this see *Letters and Poems of Fulberht of Chartres*, no. 37 (Behrends, pp. 66–9), and for discussion see Gelting, 'Un Évêque danois'.

[28] See *Letters and Poems of Fulberht of Chartres*, nos. 114 and 117 (Behrends, pp. 204 and 209).

[29] See discussion in Gelting, 'Un Évêque danois', pp. 64–6.

his evidence is stretched so thin that it fails to convince.[30] There is another, perhaps more compelling solution, which suggests that the significance of the region to Cnut was its ruler and his role in the politics of Europe in the mid-1020s. Only at a single point known to me did Duke William's affairs bring him into Cnut's spheres of political influence. After the death of Emperor Henry II on 13 July 1024 there was no clear succession plan. The Empire was thrown into great upheaval, and some feared for its survival.[31] An assembly to elect the new candidate was convened on 4 September 1024 at Kamba, and the cases of two Conrads were heard: the man who would later be Emperor and a younger relative and namesake, who were both the offspring of collateral lines. Ultimately the matter had to be decided by vote. Dissent continued, and Archbishop Pilgrim of Cologne and Duke Frederick of Lotharingia left the assembly belligerent, without bidding farewell and without participating in the election. Conrad II was subsequently crowned king on 8 September 1024 and began a royal progress throughout his new German lands, stopping at strategic sites to negotiate for the support of key elite individuals and groups. This was not completed until June 1025, and he did not set out for Italy until February 1026. It was this period between the death of the old Emperor and Conrad's arrival in Italy that saw Duke William play a crucial role in proceedings. A flurry of correspondence between the various parties reveals that Ulric Manfred II of Turin, with the support of a group of Lombard magnates, sent an embassy from Italy, firstly to King Robert of France and then to Duke William, asking them to accept the kingship of Italy, and thus implicitly a claim to the imperial office.[32] Robert

---

[30] Beech, 'England and Aquitaine'.

[31] For this and what follows see Wolfram, *Conrad II*, pp. 41–67.

[32] The main narrative here is established by Bresslau, *Jahrbücher des Deutschen Reichs*, pp. 72–81 and 106–9, with frequent citation from the relevant letters. There is a short discussion in English in Previté-Orton, *The Early History*, pp. 174–5, and comment in German in Trillmich, *Kaiser Konrad II*, pp. 178–80. Some of the crucial correspondence is edited and translated in *Letters and Poems of Fulbert of Chartres*, nos. 104 and 111–13 (Behrends, pp. 188 and 196–203). Wolfram, *Conrad II*, notes this on pp. 96–7, but plays down the actual going to Italy so as to make it invisible.

declined the offer on behalf of himself and his son and co-king, Hugh Magnus, but Duke William was more receptive, and set out for Italy to consider the proposal. He withdrew only when the Italian political situation and Conrad II's growing support base there convinced him that it was an untenable office, begging Ulric in a letter to drop the matter or first secure the support of Archbishop Aribert and Bishop Leo of Vercelli if he was to proceed.

Cnut's dynastic origins ensured that he had a great deal to lose from Conrad II's election, and the election of a French Emperor whose territorial base was at nearly the opposite end of Europe from his own may have had significant appeal. Since the mid-tenth century the Piast dynasty of Mieszko I (d. 992) of Poland had been engaged in near-constant squabbling with the German king over border regions.[33] These conflicts reached a peak during the reigns of the aggressive and antagonistic Polish kings, Bolesław I 'Chrobry' and his son, Mieszko II. Even a temporary peace accord settled between Emperor Otto III and Bolesław in 1000 at Gniezno ultimately added to the problems of the Emperor, in giving Bolesław the status of a quasi-royal suzerain who, in theory at least, outranked the German dukes along his border. Bolesław may even have claimed a royal title for himself either at Gniezno or after the death of Emperor Henry II in 1024.[34] Bolesław had annexed Slovakia and Moravia by 999, and temporarily seized Bohemia in 1003. The Emperor attempted to have Bolesław assassinated at Magdeburg in 1002, and border regions were fought over repeatedly until 1018 when a peace was negotiated at Bauzen, during which Henry II was forced to concede Polish sovereignty over several territories. Conrad II may have rejoiced in 1025 when Bolesław died, but the political headache of the Polish question endured (and perhaps even increased) with the accession of Bolesław's son, Mieszko II. Conrad initially appears to have tried to placate Mieszko, allowing (or perhaps arranging) his

[33] See Wolfram, *Conrad II*, pp. 210–16, and Lang, 'The Fall of the Monarchy', for English-language overviews of this.

[34] See Wolfram, *Conrad II*, p. 212, and Lang, 'The Fall of the Monarchy', p. 629.

marriage in 1013 to Rycheza (the niece of Emperor Otto III), the daughter of one of Conrad's allies, Ezzo, the count palatinate of Lotharingia.[35] He was perhaps also behind a gift made by Matilda (Conrad's aunt) to Mieszko of an illuminated manuscript prayer book including a letter addressing him as the 'king of the Poles' and with a miniature depicting him enthroned and receiving the volume.[36] However, Mieszko was not to be controlled or bought off so easily, and he struck immediately at western Pomerania, regaining control of it by 1028 (creating a valuable buffer zone between him and the Germans, and placing all of the Baltic coast from the Oder to the Vistula under his direct control).[37] In 1028–9 he invaded Saxony, and in 1030 he led a second campaign westward towards the Elbe. Conrad's attempts to push back these offensives in 1029 and 1030 failed, and he incurred such substantial losses that the Obodrites and Veletians abandoned their support of him and defected to the Polish side.[38]

As I noted in an earlier chapter, Cnut was also a close member of the ruling Piast dynasty of Poland through his mother, and may have been Bolesław's nephew and Mieszko II's first cousin.[39] Cnut and Mieszko even shared a common family baptismal name of Lambert, a name that was prominent in the Piast dynasty in the eleventh and twelfth centuries.[40] These family ties brought with them obligations and probably some weight in the Piast court. Cnut, or perhaps his elder brother Harald, appears to have interceded in Bolesław's interactions with his neighbours in order to calm down the situation and prevent their relative from entering into open conflict with a powerful opponent. An addition to Adam of Bremen's main text, which is not attested until the

[35] Wolfram, *Conrad II*, p. 215.

[36] The manuscript in question was once the property of the church of St Hedwig in Berlin, and was transferred to Düsseldorf University Library in 1842 (their Cod. C 91). The majority of it is still there, but its crucial miniature has been abstracted, presumably before entering the university library, and is known only from later copies. Kürbis, 'Die Epistola Mathildis', presents a comprehensive study of the manuscript with an edition of the letter.

[37] Lang, 'The Fall of the Monarchy', p. 633.

[38] Ibid., p. 634.

[39] See above at pp. 8 and 32.

[40] Gerchow, 'Prayers', pp. 235–6, and Hare, 'Cnut and Lotharingia', pp. 263–8.

thirteenth century, notes that Cnut's sister Estrith was given by him 'to the son of the king of Russia'.[41] Western European historians have been very unsure what to do with this fragment of information, but some of those of Central and Eastern Europe have set it within the context of a conflict between Bolesław and his immediate eastern neighbour, the Russian Grand Prince, Jaroslav the Wise (d. 1054).[42] Jaroslav's rival for power over the Rus' was his own stepbrother Sviatopolk (d. 1019), who was married to one of Bolesław's daughters, leading Bolesław to attack Jaroslav's territory twice on his stepson's behalf, and managing to occupy Kiev for a short time in 1018. To counterbalance this state of affairs, Jaroslav seems to have sought out a marriage alliance with Cnut's family, and it has been concluded that Estrith was most likely to have been promised to Jaroslav's son, Ilja, the prince of Novgorod.[43] However, Ilja died late in 1019 or early in 1020, and as with Estrith's marriage to a Norman duke, this may have been only a nominal union for diplomatic purposes, dissolved when the crisis was over and perhaps without the parties having even met.[44]

What does this context add to our interpretation of this gift-giving in western France? The evidence of this is only a small scrap, but the fact that Cnut made substantial gifts to another candidate for the imperial throne, probably around the time that Conrad's own campaign was far from certain of success, is suggestive of Cnut's political position and weight during Conrad's rise to power. If this interpretation is correct, then Cnut was far from a passive figure in the run-up to the imperial coronation, and appears to have thrown his weight against Conrad's campaign in favour of a candidate who had not been at daggers drawn with his mother's family for many years. If the Russian who married

[41] Adam of Bremen, *Gesta*, scholion 39(40) (Schmeidler, p. 114).
[42] For the views of Western European historians see Campbell, *Encomium Emmae Reginae*, pp. 85–6, Lawson, *Cnut*, pp. 109–110, and Keynes, 'Cnut's Earls', pp. 62–3 and 73, n. 166. For the Eastern view, see Melinikova, 'The Baltic Policy', p. 75.
[43] On Estrith's series of political marriages, see p. 33.
[44] See my work on such political marriages amongst Scandinavian elites in 'Ælfgifu of Northampton', pp. 253–8.

Cnut's sister was indeed Ilja of Novgorod, then Cnut or his brother Harald had already demonstrated their willingness to enter into direct conflict with the Piasts in order to calm down potential disputes, and Conrad may have reasonably looked to Cnut to do the same in the mid- to late 1020s. Cnut was stuck between the devil and the deep blue sea, and must have seen that Conrad's election would drag him into the Polish question on one side or another, either as a direct supporter of his Polish relatives or again in the role of a stabilizing influence on the side of the Empire.

Ironically, this position, which he appears to have tried to avoid, was the very thing that gave Cnut leverage over Conrad and brought him influence within mainland Europe, once Conrad's election to imperial office became a certainty. It presumably formed part of his discussions with Conrad and perhaps the Pope in Rome in 1027, during which the new Emperor made substantial territorial concessions to Cnut. The timing of the marriage of Cnut's daughter Gunhild to Conrad's son Henry (later, and after her death, Emperor Henry III) shows that this question would remain relevant and important for the Germans at least in the following years and after Cnut's death in 1035. The negotiations leading up to this marriage are often assumed to have been part of the discussion of 1027, but as noted separately by M. K. Lawson and Herwig Wolfram this cannot be correct.[45] Conrad dispatched a delega- tion to Constantinople some six months after his coronation to seek the hand of a Byzantine princess (a daughter of Emperor Constantine VIII, who was without a male heir) as wife for his son Henry, and such an agreement must have stood until the death of her father in November 1028 at least, with the imperial title subsequently shifting away from her line.[46] The marriage between Gunhild and Henry was not announced until 18 May 1035 at Bamberg as part of a pact of friendship between their fathers, and the discussions leading up to this most probably

[45] Lawson, *Cnut*, p. 109 (citing Bresslau, 'Ein Beitrag zur Kenntnis von Konrads II', as his source), and Wolfram, *Conrad II*, p. 104.
[46] Wolfram, *Conrad II*, p. 104.

belong to the period 1029–34, rather than 1027.[47] The couple married at Nijmegen at Pentecost 1036, and Gunhild died of pestilence during Conrad's second expedition to Italy two years later, leaving a daughter named Beatrix, who later held office as the abbess of Quedlinburg (from 1045/6 to 1062). Thus the ongoing political headache of the Poles for Conrad ensured that Cnut would remain in his privileged position as a courted ally throughout his life.

No previous English or Scandinavian king had tried to influence the imperial succession, and this background to the imperial election completely changes how we see Cnut's role in that ceremony. If this is correct, then rather than being a passive individual who was courted by Conrad due to Cnut's growing might and influence in northern Europe, he instead emerges as a ruler prepared to negotiate and steer European politics at its highest levels to get what he wanted and avoid future problems, while Conrad is cast as a figure eager to placate and please this dangerously powerful potential ally.

---

[47] *Die Regesten des Kaiserreiches unter Konrad II*, no. 225c (Appelt, p. 109); noted by Keynes, 'Giso, Bishop of Wells', p. 206.

Chapter 6

THE PERIOD OF MATURE RULE IN ENGLAND AND SCANDINAVIA

When Cnut returned to England from Norway in 1029 he came back to the first period of peace, prosperity and stability he had known in his adult life. He was most probably in his thirties, and had lived through a little over a decade of near-constant activity. He had security in power in both England and Scandinavia that he had never enjoyed before, and had extended the boundaries of rule considerably further than any Scandinavian or English predecessor. Cnut had survived over a decade of rule in England and had apparently suppressed two rebellions there, one from the ranks of the English nobility and another from his most over-mighty Scandinavian ally. Moreover, he was approaching a decade of peaceful rule in Denmark, and appears to have soundly emerged the victor from a co-ordinated civil war and invasion by the Norwegians and Swedes, leaving those last two either crippled or unwilling to engage in further conflict. He had rebuilt his grandfather's somewhat nominal dominion over much of Scandinavia, and controlled it much more effectively. To this clutch he had added England as the jewel in the crown. Cnut had begun to operate on the international stage alongside other European nobles, and had his authority and importance in northern European politics recognized by the new Emperor and the Pope. This peace brought prosperity in the form of renewed trade and commerce, and his consolidation of power across his realms continued without check or hindrance.[1]

---

[1] Little can be said with any certainty about this return to prosperity in England in Cnut's last years, but it is probable that it did occur. See Hill, 'Trends in the Development', for a model of England's infrastructure primarily during Æthelred's reign, and the same author's 'An Urban Policy' on Cnut's reign.

There are no reports of any dissenting voices or groups in either England or Denmark in this period; in England, Cnut ensured the rule of law while placating the population, and in Denmark his towns, bishops and English officials continued to centralize his authority and make his presence felt. In England, the officers he implanted into the governing structures stayed in place and grew in importance, and in Denmark, Harthacnut's government endured.

As Cnut did not leave England in this period and its sources are much fuller, our attention must focus there. At the heart of the ruling elites of England, the royal court, Cnut had successfully created a newly emergent culture – an entirely new Anglo-Scandinavian identity, which was firmly in power. This was the end result of his arrival in England in 1013 intent on conquest and forging something for himself there. The charter witness-lists present us with a glimpse of a less cluttered royal court, with no sudden changes or falls from favour amongst senior political figures.[2] Many of the participants were Anglo-Scandinavian in either their ethnicity or probable outlook, and most owed their careers and wealth directly to Cnut. Where we can find prominent Englishmen in these records, their aims were often entwined with the new Anglo-Scandinavian rule.

Paramount amongst these courtiers was Cnut's queen, Emma. As the former wife of King Æthelred she represented continuity for the English, and as the daughter of a Danish noblewoman she could be expected to uphold Danish interests in the court. As noted above, she had asserted herself after her marriage to Cnut as an important court figure, and as he entered his period of mature rule, so did she. In 1018–19 she was listed after or between the archbishops in Cnut's charters, and twice as his wife, but after that she rose in status to being second only to the king.[3] Winchester charters of 1033 saw her reach a

---

[2] See Keynes, 'Cnut's Earls', pp. 87 and 53, for some comment on the earls in this period, as well as his *Atlas of Attestations*, tables lxvi–lxvii and lxix–lxx, for the raw data regarding the ecclesiastical elites and secular ministers of the court.

[3] Keynes, *Atlas of Attestations*, tables lix and lxv. See also Stafford, *Queen Emma*, pp. 231–2.

zenith of this acclamation of her power, jointly at the head of the decla-
ration with Cnut: 'I Cnut king of the English with my Queen Ælfgyfu
confirm my own gift with royal confirmation.'[4]

The highest eschelons of secular power were dominated by two
wealthy and influential earls, Godwine and Leofric.[5] They represent the
two main types of Englishman to thrive under Cnut: the new man raised
up by Cnut to an earldom and quite dependent on him for power; and
the son of an ealdorman who had served under Æthelred and who most
probably survived Cnut's early years of rule by compliance. In addition,
Godwine had been married into the Danish nobility, and through his
wife Gytha became a member of Cnut's own family. Godwine appears
to have taken this bond seriously, and in Danish elite fashion he named
his first two sons after Cnut's father and grandfather, breaking the
pattern only when to do so would result in the naming of a child by a
variant of Cnut's own name. While twenty men are given the title 'earl'
in Cnut's charters overall, by 1032 only these two of this group were
common witnesses to the documents: Godwine appeared first and
Leofric second in all charters thereafter for Cnut's reign.[6] Godwine
appears to have been the backbone of the English court during this
period. It is here that I would place the claim of the *Vita Ædwardi
regis* that he was appointed '*dux et baiulus* [earl and office-bearer] of
almost all of the kingdom'.[7] Doubtless they jostled with each other

---

[4] S. 970 and 972; Stafford, *Queen Emma*, pp. 231–2. The translation is Stafford's.

[5] See Keynes, 'Cnut's Earls', pp. 53, 70–4, 77–8 and 84–7, and *Atlas of Attestations*, table
lxix. For Godwine and his family see p. 101 above. For Leofric, see Baxter, *The Earls of
Mercia*. Leofric had survived Cnut's early years and the death of his own brother Northmann
in Cnut's purges, holding some office in western Mercia, while his father retained an
ealdormanry there somewhat reduced by Cnut's imposition of Scandinavian earls into the
region. Leofric's father most probably died soon after 1023, but Leofric only emerged as a
significant figure in the royal court in the 1030s, following Eilaf's abandonment of his
Mercian earldom when he returned to Denmark to support the uprising in 1026 and
Hákon's departure from his earldom in 1028 to return to Norway. A final Scandinavian earl
named Hranig seems to have remained in western Mercia and worked with Leofric, being
eclipsed by him in charter witness-lists until he re-emerged in Harthacnut's reign. Leofric
must have used their departures to consolidate his power in the region to build a large
enough base of wealth and influence to assert himself at the royal court.

[6] Keynes, 'Cnut's Earls', pp. 53, 70–4, 77–8 and 84–7, and *Atlas of Attestations*, table lxix.

[7] *Vita Ædwardi regis*, ch. 1 (Barlow, p. 6).

for power, and this rivalry may have been by Cnut's design. Stephen Baxter has noted in his study of Leofric and his family how powerful yet precarious an earldom was, and Cnut perhaps sought to balance the power of these two rivals by allowing them, or even encouraging them, to pit themselves against each other.[8] The memories of the scandal of having had to outlaw two earls in his early years must have stayed with Cnut, and he may have tried his best to avoid being forced to do so again.

Earl Siward of Northumbria is the sole other attestation of an earl in the witness-lists from Cnut's mature years, appearing in a single York charter of 1033 immediately after Godwine and Leofric, and probably as a local witness.[9] Siward had arrived from somewhere in Scandinavia, most probably Denmark, in the 1030s, and may have been a member of Cnut's own family through a collateral line.[10] He was implanted into Eiríkr's old earldom, which appears to have been without a single easily recognizable leader since his death in 1023 or soon after. A further English figure named Ælfwine attests as an earl after Godwine and Leofric in three documents of the 1030s, but he is of uncertain status and may just have been a noble honoured with a title reflecting his local importance rather than a stable earldom of a region.[11]

The small number of Scandinavians implanted at the head of the court, but beneath the level of earl, were still present, with Thored Azor's father witnessing at the head of the list of ministers in charters of 1033 and 1035.[12] In 1026 he was joined by two further figures with Scandinavian names: Osgot clapa and Tovi pruða, who were close associates, and later connected by marriage.[13] Tovi pruða was Danish,

---

[8] See Keynes, 'Cnut's Earls', pp. 77–8, and Baxter, *The Earls of Mercia*.

[9] S. 968.

[10] Bolton, 'Was the Family of Earl Siward'.

[11] S. 969, 968 and 975. Keynes, 'Cnut's Earls', p. 78.

[12] Bolton, *Empire*, pp. 15–18; see also Lewis, 'Danish Landowners in Wessex', pp. 180–2, for the most up-to-date assessment of his son's vast landholdings.

[13] S. 967 and 975. S. 962 (from 1026) shows them in the same pattern.

while Osgot clapa was probably of Danelaw descent.[14] They appear to
have held roles in the local administration of East Anglia, Essex and
London, but also had crucial roles at court, with later sources naming
Osgot clapa as 'master of the palace', and Tovi pruða as a royal
standard-bearer, adding that he 'was guiding the monarch' and 'closest
to the king in his counsels'.[15] In addition, the two groups of Englishmen
who had thrown in their lot with Cnut in 1016 were thriving at the head
of the royal ministers. Both the group around Odda and that around
Ælfgar mæw were attesting charters at the head of their peers
throughout the 1030s.[16]

This was not entirely Cnut's doing. He had raised these men up, but
their own ambitions caused many of them, such as Earl Godwine, Earl
Siward, Earl Leofric, Odda and Ælfgar mæw and their respective associates, to use their influence to consolidate their positions, and they had
become paramount within their social class to the exclusion of
newcomers and rivals. Indeed, away from court, two of them, Thored
Azor's father, and Beorhtric mæw, the son of Ælfgar mæw, used this
influence to build up staggering amounts of landed wealth.[17] Yet their
vested interests were tied up with Cnut's, and together they formed a
strong power bloc at the head of society.

However, the charter witness-lists cannot give us the whole picture.
There are some indications that a substantial body of Scandinavian
elite men remained in attendance at Cnut's court in England throughout
this period. It is, perhaps, not surprising that there is virtually no
trace of this group in the charter witness-lists. Pauline Stafford has
already noted that charter witness-lists do not provide a comprehensive

---

[14] S. 962. John of Worcester, *Chronicon*, s.a. 1042 (Darlington and McGurk, pp. 532–4),
identifies Tovi pruða as Danish. Williams, 'The King's Nephew', pp. 333–6, has argued that
Osgot clapa was descended from an English East Anglian family.

[15] Herman, *Liber de Miraculis*, ch. 21, ed. Arnold in *Memorials of St Edmund's Abbey*, I, p. 54.
Waltham Chronicle, ch. 7 (Watkiss and Chibnall, p. 12).

[16] Bolton, *Empire*, pp. 25–35.

[17] We cannot know Thored's landholding, but some indication of it must be possible
through a consideration of his son's vast landholdings. On these see pp. 101–2 above. On
Beorhtric's landholdings, see pp. 85–6 above.

snapshot of the royal court, but merely of those groups selected by the court that were thought appropriate to stand as witnesses to such transactions.[18] Some groups float in and out of these records. In the tenth century, abbots were not always included, but they become a firm fixture from the last years of that century onwards, and abbesses, while of equal social standing to their male counterparts, appear only briefly as witnesses in the tenth century and then not again. Royal priests appear sporadically on witness-lists in the period, peaking in their recorded presence in Cnut's reign and in those of his immediate successors. The queen and royal children also appear there sporadically, apparently only when their elevated status was relevant to an individual transaction.

Potential absences from the records are drawn into sharp relief when we turn to consider who the audience for skaldic poetry may have been. We have a large surviving corpus of skaldic verse produced for Cnut by Scandinavian praise poets, with extant fragments of works by five separate poets, and another three lost poems recorded in the *Skáldatal*.[19] These numbers set Cnut alongside 'the most prominent of patrons for extant skaldic verse, and without question he is the most important non-Norwegian according to such terms'.[20] In addition, his fame in this circle is heavily weighted towards the period after Helgeå, when he became the most powerful ruler in Scandinavia and attracted poets in search of a grand and benevolent patron. The poems themselves make clear that skalds would usually seek out a patron, and recite a composition in his person in the hope of receiving rewards for this. This is clearly the implication of Sigvatr Þórðarson's *Vestrfararvísur*, in which the poet shifts to the

---

[18] Stafford, *Queen Emma*, pp. 193–9.

[19] These have been most recently discussed in Townend, 'Contextualising'. The lost poems are those of Bersi Torfuson, Steinn Skaptason and one by a strangely named poet, Óðarkeptr/Óðarkeftr/*Óttarr keptr, perhaps also recorded with the variant name Ljóðarkeptr in an addition to the *Þórðarbók* witness to *Landnámabók* as having composed another lost poem for Guðleifr Arason, an associate of Þangbrandr, the missionary to Iceland. See Finnur Jónsson, *Den Oldnorske og Oldislandske Litteraturs*, pp. 564–7, and Almqvist, *Norrön Niddiktning*, p. 59.

[20] Townend, 'Contextualising', p. 146.

first person and states, 'I had to make enquiries from outside the main
door before I got an audience with the ruler of the Jótar [i.e. Cnut],'
noting that 'Cnut, highly renowned for deeds, has adorned both our
arms splendidly, Húnn ['bear-cub', i.e. the poet Bersi Torfuson], when
we met the ruler. To you he, wise in many ways, gave a mark or more of
gold and a sharp sword, and to me half [a mark].'[21] The same relationship can be detected in Þórarinn loftunga's *Hǫfuðlausn* and *Tǫgdrápa*.[22]
The first of these survives only as a single fragmentary refrain of a poem,
which the saga narratives state was composed as a thirty-stanza poem in
a single night to replace an inferior composition which had insulted
Cnut.[23] There is support for this story in verse seven of the second poem,
which notes that for the *Hǫfuðlausn* Þórarinn was given a 'repayment of
fifty marks', an enormous sum that Bjarni Fidjestøl calculated to be the
equivalent of 25 lb of high-quality silver or about 200 cows.[24] The dates
of these compositions are important here, and two of the surviving
poems for Cnut can be shown to date to after Helgeå (Óttarr svarti's
Knútsdrápa; Sigvatr Þórðarson's *Knútsdrápa*), and a further four to after the
conquest of Norway (Þórarinn loftunga's *Hǫfuðlausn* and *Tǫgdrápa*;
Hallvarðr Hárekblesi's *Knútsdrápa*; and perhaps a fragment of a verse by
Arnórr jarlaskáld). The implication of Sigvatr's claim that he and Bersi
met Cnut together and were both rewarded for verses seems to be that
the lost verse of Bersi Torfuson should also be dated to after Helgeå
and perhaps following the conquest of Norway. However, Cnut went to
England immediately after the conquest of Norway in 1028 and did not
return to Scandinavia. As Matthew Townend notes, this ensures that
these verses were recited before him in England.[25] Who, then, was the
intended audience for these verses beyond Cnut? While the marked

[21] Sigvatr Þórðarson, *Vestrfararvísur*, verses 2 and 5 (Whaley, pp. 618 and 622–3). On this
subject see Fidjestøl, ' "Have you heard" '.
[22] Þórarinn loftunga, *Hǫfuðlausn* and *Tǫgdrápa* (Whaley, pp. 849–63).
[23] For the saga narratives see p. 849 of the edition cited in the previous note.
[24] Þórarinn loftunga, *Tǫgdrápa*, verse 7 (Whaley, pp. 861–2). Fidjestøl, ' "Have you heard" ',
pp. 118–19, provides the calculation and awards Cnut the title of the 'king most renowned
for his open-handedness towards skalds'.
[25] Townend, 'Contextualising', pp. 164–6.

influence of Old English on the language of some of the poems is often noted, such complex and intricate puzzle-like verses and cryptic word-plays were probably beyond the comprehension of any listener not fully fluent in Old Norse and the skaldic arts. Thus, are we to believe that Cnut, one or two earls, and a handful of Scandinavian royal officers formed the entire audience for such a poem?

The garrison at London might have formed one setting for such recitals, but another appears in Winchester, the main urban centre of Cnut's Wessex.[26] A large concentration of archaeological finds there – including burials in the New Minster cemetery identified as 'essentially Scandinavian', a fragment of a runestone inscribed in Old Norse which most probably comes from the same cemetery, the hogback-shaped gravestone from east of the Old Minster with the Old English inscription 'HER L[I]Þ G[VN]N[I:] EORLES FEOLAGA' ('Here lies Gunni, the earl's [or Eorl's] comrade'), and the small gilt bronze mount decorated in the Ringerike style with two snakes intertwined, discovered in 1910 beneath the south transept of the present cathedral – all testify to a predominantly male and elite Scandinavian presence there.[27] To these should be added the sculptured block most probably from a narrative frieze, recovered from the demolition of the eastern apse of the cathedral. It shows a mailed warrior walking to the left while a bound man lies on the floor behind him, as a large wolf- or dog-like animal holds down his jaw with its front paw and inserts its tongue into his mouth, most probably showing part of the legend of Sigmund and the wolf, otherwise known from the late *Vǫlsunga saga*.[28] These men were most

[26] Following ibid., pp. 166–73.

[27] Following ibid., pp. 169–71. The last artefact was catalogued in Fuglesang, *Some Aspects*, no. 54, pl. 30, and her drawings of it are reproduced in this volume.

[28] See Biddle and Kjølbye-Biddle, 'Danish Royal Burials', pp. 215–17, for the most recent discussion and a colour reproduction of the stone. The legend claims that Sigmund and his nine brothers were imprisoned in stocks in a forest. For nine nights they were visited by an old and evil-looking she-wolf who killed and ate each brother in turn. When Sigmund was left alone, his twin sister sent her servant to smear honey on his face and put some into his mouth. When the wolf arrived, it licked Sigmund's face and put its tongue into his mouth, whereupon he bit it, and in the tussle that followed, broke free from his stocks and tore out the wolf's tongue.

probably Cnut's *hirð*, his personal retinue of warriors sometimes known as *huscarls*, who in Scandinavia at least acted as his bodyguards and advisors, and with whom he is likely to have formed his strongest social bonds.[29] There is no source giving even a feasible number for this retinue, but I think we may assume that when Cnut became the mightiest ruler in Scandinavia he is unlikely to have reduced the number of these men, and in fact his *hirð* probably grew substantially.[30] It is likely to have consisted of many tens of men in the 1030s.

What is perhaps most startling here is that while archaeology and literary sources clearly indicate these men existed, they are all but invisible in our historical sources, beyond the note of their existence in the *Translatio Sancti Ælfegi*, where they are explained as 'the soldiers of his [Cnut's] household, who are called *huscarles* in the language of the Danes'.[31] There are some Scandinavian names in our charter witness-lists beyond those discussed here as members of the royal court or settled on English estates and thus not permanently in Cnut's attendance. They include a Hastin, Toga and Healden in two charters of 1019; a Thurstan and Thrumm in a charter of 1022; a Thorkell Hoga who also appears as an East Anglian landowner in the Thorkell *Liber Vitae* and the chronicle of Hugh Candidus; a Kartoca who is named in the confraternity entry of Cnut and his brother with Canterbury; a Thurgod and a Thurstan in a charter of 1024; two men named Tokig, one a 'minister' the other a 'miles'; and a Totyg who may be a man with a variant of the same name, as well as an Ulf 'miles', in a charter of 1033.

[29] Note also that Pedersen, 'Anglo-Danish Contact', catalogues numerous finds from early eleventh-century Denmark that are of uncertain English or Danish manufacture, and some such as cloisonné brooches that must have been made in England and exported to Denmark. There may have been English workshops producing material for this resident elite in England as well as for an export market.

[30] The one source to give a number is the late and woefully inaccurate *Lex Castrensis*, which is attached to Sven Aggesen's twelfth-century *Historia Compendiosa*. In chapter 2 of that text the author claims the preposterous number of 3,000 men. Christiansen in his preface to *The Works of Sven Aggesen* calls it rightly 'an irritating shadow on the fringes of Anglo-Saxon history'. Interestingly, John of Worcester, *Chronicon*, s.a. 1065 (Darlington and McGurk, p. 598), claims that when Tostig Godwinesson was attacked by the Northumbrians, they slew two of his named *huscarls* before going on to kill 200 men from his court.

[31] *Translatio Sancti Ælfegi* (Rumble, p. 302).

However, none of these present themselves in sufficient numbers to convince us that they were members of this large Scandinavian group.[32] A few records contain clusters of Scandinavian names in contexts suggesting they may have been members of Cnut's *hirð*. The Thorney *Liber Vitae* is the best known, and as Dorothy Whitelock noted it does contain a large block of consecutive Scandinavian names that most probably date back to a visit to the abbey by Cnut and a number of his followers in the early 1020s.[33] Whitelock identified the thirty-one names that follow those of Osgot clapa and his associate Tovi pruða as potentially those of 'the following of one or more of the Danish magnates who head the column'.[34] She also notes that 'the less common names in it do not occur amongst the signatures to eleventh-century charters, suggesting that at any rate we have not the more important landowners'. She points to the marked East Scandinavian (Danish or Swedish) character of the list, noting that the name 'Einder' here is most probably an East Scandinavian form of the West Norse Eyvindr, which is recorded in later forms as Ønder, and that the names Manni and Epi are recorded only in East Norse sources, while Tovi and Toki are overwhelmingly so.[35] To these we should add two charters with similar lists of Scandinavian names. Cnut's charter of 1019 for Agemund has a large number of Scandinavians amongst the ministers of its witness-list (the first seven ministers out of a total of thirteen, and including the *huscarl* Bovi).[36] Another group of seven such names appears at the end of a garbled witness-list attached to a re-endorsement of grants by Cnut to

---

[32] See S. 955, 956 and 958, as well as Bolton, *Empire*, pp. 67–8, 17 and 74. Also S. 961 and 967.

[33] Whitelock, 'Scandinavian Personal Names', and pp. 135–7 above on the date, and the reproduction of the relevant page of the manuscript (British Library, Additional MS. 40,000) in this volume. There from the tenth line of the fourth column the list runs: 'Ulf. Turkyl. Swegn. Toui. Ðolf. Askyl. Illhuge. Toki. Ulf. Swegn. Eglaf. Manni. Guðmund. Blihswegn. Oþði. Stegn. Scul. Scum. Einder. Arbern. Toky. Barð. Turkyl. Epi. Ererti'. After this the list uses patronymics, gives spouses' names and includes English names, suggesting a break in form. Thus I would cut the list short to twenty-five, of Whitelock's thirty-one.

[34] Ibid., pp. 136–7.

[35] Ibid., pp. 137 and 139.

[36] S. 955, edited in Kelly, *Charters of Shaftesbury*, no. 30: the relevant witnesses are 'Ego [H]acun minister + Ego Hastin minister + Ego Aslac minister + Ego Toga minister + Ego Boui minister + Ego Toui minister + Ego Kaerl minister', followed by six English names.

Fécamp Abbey, made by Harthacnut in 1040–42.[37] In this document
these names appear after that of Harthacnut and other witnesses recog-
nizably from his court, and they are most probably his *huscarls*. They
include in the order followed there: 'Aizor' (Azor); 'Turchil' (Thorkell);
Swen (Swen/Sveinn); 'Theustul' (the extremely rare name Þióstólfr in
an apparent East Norse form, and unrecorded in any East Norse form
in Petersen, *Nordiskt Runnamnslexicon*, and not recorded at all by
Björkmann, *Nordische Personennamen in England*); 'Eusten' (Iosten/Iosteinn);
Tovi and 'Turgil' (probably Thorgisl). Of these, only one or two can be
identified with any certainty in our other sources, and three turn up
nowhere else. On reflection, it is perhaps unsurprising that these men
joined the ranks of those who did not appear in the witness-lists of royal
charters. They may not have held land, and thus had little value as local
witnesses to any grant, and as they followed Cnut whether in England
or Scandinavia they may not have been thought to stand outside English
society despite being in his retinue within the court.

A large body of Scandinavian nobles and warriors at the centre of
the royal court may seem incongruous, but we must make room for it.
We must also concede that the court was bilingual, in part at least, as
Old Norse poems and inscriptions infer that there was an audience who
could understand and read them, all within walking distance of the
enclosures of the Old Minster and New Minster in Winchester. We
might add to this the occasional Slavic visitor or ambassador from the
Polish or imperial courts, and we end up with a quite different image of
Cnut's royal court from that of his English predecessors – as a culturally
diverse and bustling marketplace for northern European cultures and
ideas. Within the context of the very many Englishmen at court, these
foreigners would only ever form a minority, but it is a minority that
radically changes our impression of the court during Cnut's reign.

It is interesting that the only tangible acts which this period of quiet
prosperity produced in England were an outpouring of gift-giving to

[37] S. 982.

the Church. M. K. Lawson suggested in 1993 that many of Cnut's gifts to the Church may have been politically motivated, and I later followed that approach myself.[38] To some degree we were both probably correct, but genuine piety sits at the heart of an array of sources close to him, and Church gift-giving must also have been a powerful force behind this benevolence.[39] Cnut's letter of 1027 states that he had long wished to make the journey to Rome and had visited numerous shrines and churches on this pilgrimage, for which I see no motive of forgery, and they are more probably those of Cnut himself. Such motives accord perfectly with Sigvatr Þórðarson's *Tøgdrápa*, in which Cnut is portrayed as having experienced something like a conversion episode whereby he set aside his fixation on warfare, took up a pilgrim's staff and made his way to Rome. They also accord with the *Encomium*'s description of his visit to the monasteries of St Omer, in which he prays reverently, eyes fixed on the ground and pouring with rivers of tears, before pressing kisses on the pavement and beating his breast 'that the heavenly mercy might not be displeased with him'.[40]

The nature of such records scattered amongst ecclesiastical archives means that few include firm dates or dating features, and some from later witnesses may be exaggerations or in fact attributable to his wife Emma, perhaps given after Cnut's death. However, even with these provisos I think we can place our trust in New Minster's (Winchester) records of: a vast golden cross, described by one of the continuators to John of Worcester's account as 'a great and holy cross, made . . . by the order of King Cnut, and most splendidly enriched by him with gold

---

[38] Lawson, *Cnut*, pp. 117–60, and Bolton, *Empire*, pp. 77–106.

[39] A mix of the two motives is perhaps characteristic of almost all medieval donors.

[40] *Die Gesetze* (Liebermann, I, p. 277), Sigvatr Þórðarson, *Knútsdrápa*, verses 10 and 11 (Whaley, pp. 661–3), and *Encomium Emmae Reginae*, II:20–1 (Campbell, p. 36). Note Treharne's discussion of the theatricality of his activities at St Omer as variants of Carolingian accounts ('Performance of Piety', pp. 349–50). These are convincing literary sources, but there are also practical accounts of the need of the penitent in late Anglo-Saxon England to cry (see Roach, *Kingship and Consent*, pp. 199–200), and such acts may have been performed by Cnut as a public expression of piety.

and silver, with gems and precious stones', containing 500 lb of silver, 30 marks of gold, three diadems, and three footrests of pure Arabian gold;[41] Old Minster's (Winchester) claim that Cnut gave the abbey a decorated reliquary for its relic of St Birinus and a silver candelabrum;[42] a shrine made for the relic of St Vincent and valued at 60 lb of silver, some relics of St Edward, presented to Abingdon Abbey before 1030;[43] and the relic of an arm of St Bartholomew presented to Christ Church, Canterbury.[44]

Less certain are: Evesham's claims to have received the relics of St Wigstan as well as a black *causula* and other ornaments, in that these relics were actually translated from nearby Repton, suggesting that this may in fact be only a record of Cnut acquiescing in Evesham building up its relic collection at the expense of its neighbours.[45] Similarly, St Augustine's, Canterbury, claimed that Cnut had given it the relics of St Mildred, when counter-claims to these existed from a rival Canterbury house, St Gregory's.[46] Finally, we might also doubt the late and perhaps spurious or embellished account of Crowland Abbey, which recalled Cnut donating silk vestments, a silver gilt thurible, and twelve white

[41] John of Worcester, *Chronicon*, s.a. 1141 (ed. Thorpe, ii, pp. 133–6). See also Keynes, *Liber Vitae*, p. 35. Many of these gifts have been listed by Heslop at the end of 'The Patronage of *de luxe* Manuscripts'. In my *Empire*, pp. 77–106, I set these gifts alongside grants of land and privileges to these communities and records of prominence of their leaders in the royal court where available. However, as we are unable to perceive the contexts of such land and privilege grants, and some may have been part of property deals or similar, they are set aside here.

[42] *Annales de Wintonia*, s.a. 1016, in *Annales Monastici* (ed. Luard, ii, p. 16).

[43] *Chronicon Monasterii de Abingdon*, and *De Abbatibus Abbendoniae*, in *Chronicon Monasterii de Abingdon* (ed. Stevenson, i, 433, and ii, 291); ibid. (ed. Stevenson, i, 443, and ii, 157).

[44] Obituary list in London, British Library, Cotton MS. Galba E iii, 2, ff. 32r–34r, and an early twelfth-century addition made to the *Textus Roffensis*, Rochester Cathedral Library MS. A. 3. 5, f. 57v (ed. Hearne, p. 37). P. H. Sawyer, *Textus*, p. 16, dismisses this addition to the manuscript, stating that it is a digest of a copy of a local charter (S. 959); however, the information regarding the relic does not occur in any version of the charter. Note that Eadmer, in his *Historia Nouorum*, ii (ed. Rule, pp. 107–8), places this amongst the gifts of Emma to the community, with Cnut merely assenting to it, contrary to its placement in the obituary lists.

[45] *Chronicon Abbatiae de Evesham*, iii (ed. Dunn Macray, p. 83). The same source claims that its abbot at the time, Ælfweard, was related to Cnut, probably through Emma, who is referred to in S. 1423 as governing the house.

[46] The details of the dispute can be found in Harmer, *Anglo-Saxon Writs*, pp. 191–7, and Rollason, *Mildreth Legend*, pp. 58–68.

bear skins in 1032.[47] I have suggested that the relics of St Wendreda taken on the battlefield at Ashingdon/*Assandun* may have been given to Christ Church, Canterbury, in 1018, but there are no dates in the sole source to record this.[48] Additionally, gifts to Glastonbury, Wilton and Westminster have been explained elsewhere, and fit into the context of events in those places.[49] However, the record is still impressive, and far from complete.

Only in newly conquered Norway did the situation change dramatically in this period. Months after having been placed in command of Norway, Hákon died suddenly. Cnut and his rule there was still in its infancy, and the timing was disastrous. Having spent the previous months urging the Norwegian aristocracy to accept the legitimacy of Hákon's claim as pre-dating Óláfr's, Cnut was left without a candidate to stand at the head of such claims. More worryingly, the marriages of the Jarls of Hlaðir when in power in Norway had intricately tied them into numerous powerful regional Norwegian dynasties. So Cnut's former rhetoric now placed some of these dynasties, such as those of Einarr Þambarskelfir (married to Bergljót, daughter of Jarl Hákon Sigurðsson) and Kálfr Árnason (married to Jarl Sveinn Hákonarson's daughter), closer to the throne than any of Cnut's immediate allies. Óláfr appears to have received word of this sudden shift in Cnut's grasp on power, and he returned to Norway to make a bid for power himself.

However, Óláfr's centralization of power in his own hands seems to have left a very unpleasant taste in the mouth of some of the Norwegian aristocracy. Therefore, in 1030 Óláfr was met at Stiklestad, in Verdal to the north-east of Trondheim, approaching the mountainous border with Sweden, by forces formed from amongst his own people, who defeated him and his followers and executed him on the battlefield.[50] The poet Sigvatr Þórðarson was probably present and much survives of

---

[47] This is only recorded in the late and questionable *Historia Ingulphi* (ed. Gale, i, 61).
[48] See above at pp. 88–9.
[49] See above at pp. 113 and 120.
[50] The earliest to mention this are the *Passio Olaui*, ch. 20 (Storm, p. 144), Theodoricus, *Historia*, ch. 19 (Storm, pp. 39–42), and *Ágrip*, ch. 31 (Driscoll, pp. 42–4).

a touching *erfidrápa* (memorial poem) he composed for his patron Óláfr.[51] He confirms the place of the battle and the fact that the opposing forces were 'farmers', 'the people' or 'men from Trøndelag', and he records that Þórir hundr (splitting up his first name from his epithet, in order to use the latter as an insulting term, 'dog') was there opposing Óláfr. A single verse from Bjarni gullbrárskáld's *Kálfsflokkr* notes the site of the battle as well.[52] It records that Kálfr Árnason was also present, and that he could claim to have 'achieved great deeds at Stiklestad' as he 'kept up the attack . . . until the king had fallen'.

Cnut was in England at this point, but doubtless closely monitoring the troubled situation in Norway. There was probably no male heir left of the dynasty of Hlaðir who could serve as a trusted figurehead, and it cannot have seemed wise to Cnut to try his luck on taking a member of the Norwegian aristocracy under his wing as a replacement. Thus, Cnut's first son, Swen (given the epithet Álfífuson in West Norse saga traditions), was dispatched to Norway along with a retinue including his mother Ælfgifu of Northampton and perhaps also a son of Thorkell the Tall, Harald Thorkelsson, apparently raised in Cnut's court after the death of his father.[53] Swen was a young man of only fifteen or sixteen years of age in 1029, and his government must have arrived with a sizeable military contingent to enforce his rule.

Swen, his mother and their followers seem to have immediately set out to placate powerful elements of the Norwegian elites. This can be seen in the political implications of a lengthy skaldic poem named *Glælognskviða*, composed for Swen by one of Cnut's court skalds,

---

[51] *Erfidrápa Óláfs helga* (Whaley, pp. 663–98).

[52] Bjarni gullbrárskáld, *Kálfsflokkr*, verse 5 (Whaley, pp. 885–6).

[53] The first stanza of *Glælognskviða* mentions an unnamed number of faithful Danes who travelled with Swen to Norway. Snorri, in the prose account in which this verse survives (*Heimskringla*, *Óláfs Saga helga*, ch. 239 [Bjarni Aðalbjarnarson, II, p. 399]) identified one of these as Harald Thorkelsson. This identification has recently been endorsed by Townend ('Knútr and the Cult of St Óláfr', pp. 261–2), and is quite plausible. The record of *Skáldatal* to the existence of poetry about him in the thirteenth century suggests that he did have a significant Scandinavian career. If so, then Harald's marriage to Cnut's niece, Gunhild (see Keynes, 'Cnut's Earls', pp. 66 and 62, n. 97) probably took place at this time.

Þórarinn loftunga.[54] The focus of the verses on both Óláfr and Swen together, placing them side by side in Trondheim, one as spiritual king and the other as temporal king, as well as subtly obfuscating any suggestion of violence from the references to Óláfr's death (he 'departed to the heavenly kingdom' and had 'powerfully taken himself to the heavenly kingdom'), indicates that Swen and his mother began to appropriate the growing cult of St Óláfr for its political benefits. Similar implications arise from the late saga traditions. Adam of Bremen notes that Bishop Grimkell came to Norway under the patronage of Óláfr as a missionary-bishop, and he seems to have been a valued member of Óláfr's court, acting as legate to Hamburg-Bremen.[55] *Heimskringla* states that Grimkell fled Norway alongside Óláfr, and that Cnut and Hákon placed another court-bishop named Sigurðr in his stead.[56] The same source adds that Óláfr then sent Grimkell back to Norway where he took up residence in Oppland, remaining there until Óláfr's death. At that point Grimkell was recalled to the region around Trondheim by the area's inhabitants, took part in the exhumation of Óláfr's relics and became one of the strongest proponents of the cult.[57] If this is correct, then with Swen and his mother in residence there, we must presume their acquiescence at least in this reinstatement of a key member of Óláfr's retinue.

In a country such as medieval Norway, which was large enough to contain several factions of elites at any one time and had such a shallow history of centralized power, it was perhaps inevitable that any foreign government would prove unpopular and be ejected before too long. *Ágrip*, the Legendary Saga and *Heimskringla* all identify a lawcode

---

[54] *Glælognskviða* (Whaley, pp. 863–76). Bolton, *Empire*, pp. 271–4, and more recently Townend, 'Knútr and the Cult of St Óláfr'.

[55] Townend ('Knútr and the Cult of St Óláfr', p. 265) has already commented on Grimkell. The references in Adam of Bremen's account are *Gesta*, II:57 and IV:34 (Schmeidler, pp. 117–18 and 268).

[56] *Heimskringla*, *Óláfs Saga helga*, chs. 243 and 217 (Bjarni Aðalbjarnarson, II, pp. 403 and 370–1).

[57] Ibid., chs. 243–4 (Bjarni Aðalbjarnarson, II, pp. 403–5). See Haki Antonsson, 'The Cult', for further comment on this.

enforced by Swen and his mother's regime in the 1030s as the political flashpoint.[58] The series of legal clauses detail royal rights and demands, restrict the movement of ships out of Norway without royal permission, specify the forfeiture of the property and inheritance of outlaws to the crown, the obligations of the landowners to erect buildings on the royal estates and equip every seventh man for military service, and detail a tax to be paid to the king every Christmas. Much here may have a basis in fact, and while there are no extant legal manuscripts that pre-date c. 1200, the Gulathing and Frostathing regional codes do appear to have been in a written form in the late eleventh century, and certainly by the early twelfth century. They include fragmentary witnesses to some of these legal clauses in amendments ascribed to the Norwegian kings Magnús Óláfsson (1034–47) and his son Hákon (1093–4) for the Gulathing amendments, Sigurðr (1125–30) and his two brothers Eysteinn and Óláfr for the Frostathing amendments.[59] These exactions should probably be seen in the context of Cnut's vast tax on England in 1018, as a one-off Scandinavian levy taken by a conqueror or an incoming ruler at the beginning of his reign.[60] However, that does not alter the fact that these exactions seem to have pushed the Norwegian aristocracy towards breaking point, while successive kings of Norway thereafter felt the need publicly to repeal them, doubtless in the interests of public opinion.

Nature and bad luck may have carried them past this breaking point. *Ágrip* notes the misery of the Norwegian people under their rule and blames 'their tyranny and the bad seasons'.[61] In support of this, this source cites a skaldic verse attributed to Sigvatr Þórðarson that records hardship, starvation and the loss of vital food stocks: 'A young fellow

---

[58] *Ágrip*, chs. 28–9 (Driscoll, pp. 40–2), *Óláfs saga hins helga*, ch. 71 (Heinrichs, pp. 172–4), *Heimskringla, Olafs Saga helga*, ch. 239 (Bjarni Aðalbjarnarson, II, pp. 399–401).

[59] These amendments are edited separately from the main lawcodes in Bagge, Smedsdal and Helle, *Norske Middelalder Dokumenter*, pp. 18–23. Some scholarly discussion can be found in Indrebø, 'Aagrip', pp. 43–5, Taranger, 'De Norske Folkelovbøker (før 1263)', I and II, as well as Eithun, Rindal and Ulset, *Den Eldre Gulatingslova*, p. 10.

[60] Bolton, *Empire*, pp. 275–87.

[61] *Ágrip*, ch. 32 (Driscoll, p. 44).

will long remember the days of Ælfgifu, when we ate cattle fodder indoors, as goats [eat] peeled bark. It was otherwise when Óláfr, the battle-gesturer, ruled the country; everyone then had to praise the rick-dried grain [i.e. had lots of grain stocks].'[62] These problems would appear to have attracted other claimants for the Norwegian throne, and a skaldic verse from a poem named *Tryggvaflokkr*, connected to Sigvatr Þórðarson, as well as another from an anonymous and thus less reliable *flokkr* on Swen, record a sea battle between him and a royal pretender, whom the surrounding saga prose identifies as a son of Óláfr Tryggvason. By 1034 the situation had clearly become too volatile, and an array of skaldic poets who composed for Magnús, the son of St Óláfr, record that Swen and his mother fled Norway with their government, prob-ably to Denmark.[63] We can speculate that Cnut planned to reinvade, but his death in the following year cut any such plans short.

It is in the skaldic verses produced during Cnut's mature years, while he was in England, that we can most easily trace important shifts in Cnut's own understanding of his kingship and the ideology which stood behind his rule. Skaldic verse was composed for recital before the patron and his retinue, and those verses that survive usually contain represen-tations of the ruler which were approved by him and his entourage. These innovations thus must reflect changes in the way that Cnut and his Scandinavian followers at least thought about the nature of his rule, or wished it to be portrayed. As Roberta Frank noted in 1994, three poems composed after Helgeå contain variants of an ideological motif that involves a direct alignment of Cnut and God, and in two cases of their roles. A further fragment of verse clearly preserves another example of the same. The relevant sections are arranged chronologi-cally here:

[62] Edited without title in Whaley, *Skaldic Verse*, pp. 732–3. Note that P. H. Sawyer, 'Cnut's Scandinavian Empire', p. 21, believes this verse might be a later forgery.
[63] See Arnórr jarlaskáld, *Magnúsdrápa*, verses 3–4 (Gade, pp. 211–12), Þjóðólfr Arnórsson, *Magnúsflokkr*, verse 3 (Gade, p. 67). *Ágrip*, ch. 36 (Driscoll, p. 48), claims that Swen died in Denmark.

Sigvatr Þórðarson, *Knútsdrápa* (c. 1027): 'Cnut was under the heavens
. . . the eminent prince.'[64]

Þórarinn loftunga's *Hǫfuðlausn* (c. 1027–8): 'Cnut defends the land as
the guardian of Greece [God] [defends] the heavenly kingdom.'[65]

Þórarinn loftunga, *Tøgdrápa* (c. 1029): 'Cnut is under the sun's . . .'[66]

Hallvarðr Hárekblesi's *Knútsdrápa* (c. 1029): 'Cnut defends the earth as
the lord of all [i.e. God] [defends] the splendid hall of the mountains [i.e. heaven].'[67]

It is clear that Þórarinn loftunga in the fragmentary surviving refrain
from his *Tøgdrápa* is echoing that of Sigvatr Þórðarson in his *Tøgdrápa*,
and that Þórarinn loftunga's *Hǫfuðlausn* contains a near-identical
and probably closely related concept to Hallvarðr Hárekblesi's
Knútsdrápa.

This idea of celebrating the power of a ruler through his alignment
with the Christian God is almost entirely novel in skaldic verse. Usually
the ruler is distinguished from other men by the fact that the gods grant
him divine favour. This is demonstrated by his continuing success in
warfare, and hence the extremes of violence and conquest depicted
there, often with accounts of slaughter and bloodshed that read as
barbaric exaggeration to a modern reader. What we see here is surprisingly peaceful and benevolent, and so alien to skaldic verse that after
Cnut's death this motif is almost absent from the genre until the twelfth
century.[68] Here Cnut is directly compared to God, and elevated above
all other men through this comparison. The fragile ideology of power

[64] Preserved in *Knútsdrápa*, verses 3, 6, 7, 9 and 11 (Whaley, pp. 653–63).

[65] *Hǫfuðlausn* (Whaley, pp. 850–1).

[66] *Tøgdrápa*, verse 1 (Whaley, pp. 852–3).

[67] *Knútsdrápa*, verse 8, to be published by Gade and Marold in the forthcoming *Poetry from Treatises on Poetics* volume in the recent Skaldic Verse project.

[68] Of the six extant examples of this motif, four are in poems composed for Cnut. Furthermore, the last is in Arnórr jarlaskáld's *Hrynhenda*, verse 19 (ed. Whaley, *Poetry of Arnórr*, pp. 118 and 179–80), which was composed for Swen's successor in Norway, Magnús Óláfsson. It seems likely that it occurs there through influence from poetry composed for Cnut.

seen in traditional skaldic verse, in which divine favour can leave a ruler at any time (indicated by the loss of battles), is replaced by a more stable form of authority in which just as the Christian God's power cannot fail him, neither can Cnut's.

Both D. Hoffmann and Frank assumed that the origin of these new political ideas lay in Cnut's lengthy contact with England and English political ideas.[69] That is possible, and certainly one skald appears to have used similar imagery when reportedly composing for Cnut's English predecessor, Æthelred: 'All the host stands in awe of the generous prince of England as of God; the race of the war-swift King and all the race of men bow to Æthelred.'[70] However, what is striking is that these ideas seem to have emerged in skaldic verse composed in the period immediately after Cnut's attendance of the imperial coronation, and that is a plausible alternative source of such ideas. Robert Deshman has shown that the image of rulership cultivated by the Ottonians in the late tenth century was a Christo-centric one, where the image of the Emperor and some of his public ceremonial acts mirrored contemporary representations of Christ.[71]

Sigvatr Þórðarson may well have accompanied Cnut to Rome, and his Knútsdrápa, most probably composed c. 1027 on his return, presents an image of Cnut as incongruous skaldic verse as the refrains listed above. He describes how 'Desire for a journey came upon the ruler bearing a staff, who bore warfare in his heart. The leader, dear to the Emperor, close to Peter, enjoyed some of the glory of Rome. Few ring-distributors [i.e. generous rulers] will have thus measured the route south with their steps.'[72] The central couplet of praise here (kærr keisara, / klúss Pétrúsi, i.e. 'dear to the Emperor, / close to Peter') does so through a peaceful comparison of the Emperor with the Pope rather

---

[69] See Hofmann, Nordisch-Englische Lehnbeziehungen, pp. 96–7, and Frank, 'Cnut', p. 117, for examples.

[70] Edited by Finnur Jónsson, Den Norsk-Islandske Skjaldedigtning, A I, p. 194; B I, p. 184.

[71] Deshman, 'Kingship and Christology', pp. 377–96.

[72] Knútsdrápa, verses 10–11 (Whaley, pp. 661–3). This is also discussed by Frank, 'Cnut', p. 118, by myself (Empire, p. 295), and most recently Treharne, 'Performance of Piety'.

than an enumeration of military successes, and this is framed by a form of conversion-episode in which Cnut undergoes a psychological change from warleader to penitent pilgrim. Frank's excellent discussion of this rightly concentrates on these four words, in which while the alliteration on 'k' focuses our attention on Cnut, the words used are all ones from other European languages, and in two cases recent loanwords (from Old French and Latin, in one case probably via Old English).[73] That they were strange and jarring in the genre is clear from Townend's observation in his commentary to the new edition that these are the first occurrences in skaldic verse of all four words.[74] This couplet is both traditional in format and startlingly new in its philological content, facts that must have been evident to its original audience.

Similarly, novel elements can be detected in the famous picture of Cnut and Emma in the Winchester *Liber Vitae*.[75] This manuscript was produced under the guidance of Abbot Ælfwine of the New Minster, Winchester, who had served Cnut as a royal priest and may have been placed in his abbacy directly by him. As has been discussed many times in modern scholarship, the artist here drew from the image of King Edgar offering his charter to New Minster to Christ.[76] However, where he deviated from this model he did so in ways that echo portraits of Ottonian and Salian rulers. The inclusion of Emma opposite Cnut probably reflects her actual increased influence in the court, but it is strongly reminiscent of the couples found in Ottonian and Salian donation portraits; and the veil or *stola* that she receives from an angel is an uncommon feature elsewhere found in depictions of Agnes of Poitou alongside her husband Emperor Henry III in two Echternach

[73] Frank, 'Cnut', p. 118.

[74] Townend in Whaley, *Skaldic Poetry* I, pp. 662–3.

[75] This is one of the most widely discussed drawings of Anglo-Saxon history, and is reproduced in this volume. See Karkov, *Ruler Portraits*, pp. 121–40, Owen-Crocker, 'Pomp, Piety, and Keeping the Woman', and Treharne, 'Performance of Piety', pp. 350, 354–5, in which she draws on the work of Angenendt ('How Was a Confraternity Made?', p. 216) to show that Emma does not touch the cross as women were not permitted to touch the altar in such ceremonies.

[76] The picture of Edgar is in London, British Library, Cotton MS. Vespasian A. viii, fol. 2v. See also Gerchow, 'Prayers', p. 223.

manuscripts.[77] Most importantly, the crown that Cnut receives from the angel in the Winchester *Liber Vitae* image is of a form unparalleled in late Anglo-Saxon art, and while resembling the English trefoil crown as found in the Quatrefoil coinage of Cnut's early years amongst many other examples, it has a bar added over the top of the ruler's head, which closely resembles that of a ceremonial imperial crown worn by Conrad II.[78] The lower portion of Conrad's crown can be dated stylistically to the 990s, and it was remodelled later adding the decorated bar that bears the legend 'CHUONRADUS DEIGRATIA ROMANORU[M] IMPERATOR AUG[USTUS]' in pearls on gold wire. Other contemporary depictions of Emperors show that this crown, or others like it, were in use in the early eleventh century.[79]

When Cnut went to Rome in 1027 and saw the glory of the Papal Curia and the imperial court for himself, he was at the height of his power, with England securely under his grip, Denmark subdued and his external enemies in Norway and Sweden apparently either fenced in or dispersed. He knew he would return to northern Europe with the acknowledgement of his peers as the paramount Scandinavian ruler, and he could claim to be a 'king of all England and Denmark and the Norwegians and part of the Swedes', as his letter of 1027 to the English phrases it.[80] The area he now controlled was based on the ambitions of his predecessors, but it was greater by far and its size was unprecedented. It was perhaps natural that he should begin to look for new ideologies of rule to underpin his new 'empire', and he and his followers appear to have drawn inspiration from both English and imperial sources.

---

[77] Uppsala, MS. C. 93, fol. 1v and Madrid, Escorial, Codex Aureus, fol. 3r (both reproduced together in Nordenfalk, *Codex Caesareus Upsaliensis*, p. 119). See also Gerchow, 'Prayers', pp. 224–5, Bolton, *Empire*, p. 296, and Karkov, *Ruler Portraits*, pp. 129–31.

[78] The crown is now in the Vienna Schatzkammer, and published in Staats, *Theologie der Reichskrone*.

[79] See Bolton, *Empire*, pp. 296–7, n. 24, for references.

[80] *Die Gesetze* (Liebermann, I, p. 276).

How much further these innovations could have gone, and how much more they could have changed the course of English and Scandinavian history, we cannot know, as on Wednesday 12 November 1035 Cnut died while at Shaftesbury in Dorset. He was doubtless surrounded by his court and *hirð*, and as Shaftesbury was one of the towns that rendered a special tax 'for the use of the royal huscarls', perhaps he was also attended by his countrymen and former retainers who had been settled there: Urk, Bovi and Agemund. Shortly afterwards his body was taken to the Old Minster, Winchester, and interred there.[81] One mid-fifteenth-century chronicler states that his tomb was buried in front of the high altar, but other sites have been plausibly proposed by modern scholars. They include one close to the tomb of St Swithun in the tenth-century westwork of the building, or at its eastern end in a section perhaps decorated with a frieze now surviving only in the single block containing a scene interpreted to be that of the Scandinavian legend of Sigmund and the wolf.[82]

Pious requests in a royal grant to Sherborne Abbey, which beseech the monks there to pray for Cnut and to sing psalms and masses daily for his sins, may indicate that he knew his end was nigh, but he is unlikely to have had much advance warning.[83] His father had died unexpectedly while on campaign in England, and likewise his brother Harald had disappeared abruptly from the record c. 1019 without report of foul play. Cnut's eldest son, Swen, predeceased him in 1034, while his two other sons died just a few years later: Harold Harefoot in

[81] ASC 1035 CD (O'Brien O'Keeffe, p. 105), *Encomium Emmae Reginae*, III:1 (Campbell, p. 38), and John of Worcester, *Chronicon*, s.a. 1035 (Darlington and McGurk, p. 520). For the history of Cnut's tomb see Crook, 'Cnut's Bones', where he discusses the present royal tombs visible on stone screens inserted into the presbytery arcade in 1525, now within seventeenth-century chests with inscriptions naming their inhabitants.

[82] Cambridge, Corpus Christi College, MS. 110, p. 339 (a chronicle of English history from Lucius to Henry VI, from Winchester, copied amongst other sixteenth-century transcripts), noted by Crook, 'Cnut's Bones', p. 171, n. 8. Modern architectural and archaeological interpretations of the site of Cnut's burial can be found in Crook, '"A Worthy Antiquity"', pp. 173–6, and Biddle and Kjølbye-Biddle, 'Danish Royal Burials', pp. 212–17. The original building was demolished and rebuilt in the 1090s.

[83] S. 975. The suggestion is that of Lawson, *Cnut*, p. 113.

1040 and Harthacnut in 1042. None of these men was elderly, and most of them had likely not even reached middle age: Cnut was most likely in his late thirties or early forties, while his brother and sons cannot have even been out of their twenties. Contemporaries may have thought this was God's judgement on the members of this dynasty, but with the knowledge provided by modern medical science we should perhaps speculate instead that the men in this line shared a congenital defect, perhaps resulting in strokes or cerebral aneurysms.[84] Ultimately, it was this that cut short Cnut's reign, and within a few short years his remaining two sons would join him, triggering the collapse of his Anglo-Scandinavian realm.

[84] The specification of strokes or cerebral aneurysms comes from the accurate accounts of Harthacnut's death. See below at pp. 203–3.

Chapter 7

THE AFTERMATH OF CNUT'S DEATH

Cnut's sudden death left no clear plan of succession, and two heirs by different mothers, both of whom had spent considerably more time in Denmark than in England. Initial events were framed by circumstance, in that Harthacnut appears to have had no deputy he could trust to hold Denmark in his stead, and so was forced to remain there after his father's death. This left the way open for Harold Harefoot and his mother, Ælfgifu of Northampton, to return from obscurity to English politics. Following the expulsion of Ælfgifu and her eldest son, Swen, from Norway c. 1034, and Swen's subsequent death some months later, she and her second son may even have been in England when Cnut died. Harthacnut's mother, Emma, was also in England, but without a resident royal heir to promote amongst the English elites she was powerless.

At this time, Harold Harefoot was in his prime at twenty to twenty-two years old, and his mother had lost none of her political acumen in her dotage.[1] In either July or August 1036 one Immo, a priest in the retinue of Conrad II, wrote to Bishop Azeko of Worms relating events he had heard from English messengers who had just arrived at the German court.[2] He records that an unnamed 'wretched and wicked step-mother'

---

[1] The presumed age of Harold in 1037 is based on the fact that if he was born as Cnut's second son, this cannot have been before April 1015 (c. August 1013 + 9 months + 1 month + another 9 months). Thus, in 1037 he was twenty-two (+2?).

[2] See Stevenson, 'An Alleged Son', p. 116, and Keynes' introduction to the reprint of the edition of the *Encomium Emmae Reginae*, p. xxxii, for an easily accessible edition and translation of the relevant section of the letter, with some discussion.

of Cnut's daughter Gunhild, who must be Ælfgifu of Northampton, was endeavouring to deprive Harthacnut of the throne in England, and had arranged a great party for the leading men of England at which she attempted to secure their support by entreaties and bribes. The political structures of England during Cnut's last years were dependent on the alliances built by two great politicians, Earl Godwine of Wessex and Earl Leofric of western Mercia, and under this pressure the country split again along the fault line of the Thames, with their followers either side of this natural boundary offering their patronage to one or other of the two potential heirs. As the Anglo-Saxon Chronicle reports immediately after Cnut's death, 'Earl Leofric and almost all the thegns north of the Thames and the shipmen in London chose Harold to the regency of all England . . . And then Earl Godwine and all the chief men in Wessex opposed it as long as they could, but they could not contrive anything against it.'[3] Emma seems to have remained the principal thorn in their side, and Harold quickly moved to reduce her influence, sending what John of Worcester calls his 'personal attendants' (most probably *huscarls*) to Winchester to seize from her 'all the best treasures which King Cnut had possessed'.[4]

The *Encomium* notes that Archbishop Æthelnoth of Canterbury refused to surrender the royal sceptre and crown to Harold Harefoot, or to consecrate him as king, and forbade any other English bishop from doing so.[5] In retaliation, the same text states, Harold Harefoot kept away from services, and when others entered the church to hear mass he filled the surrounding glades with hunting dogs to drown out the service with their noise. This is a one-sided source, weighted entirely towards Harthacnut's case. Moreover, it crosses the line into slander, as it repeats, or perhaps starts, a rumour that Harold was the son of a servant rather than of Cnut, and suggests that he turned away from

---

[3] ASC 1036 E (Irvine, p. 76).
[4] ASC 1035 CD (O'Brien O'Keeffe, p. 105), and John of Worcester, *Chronicon*, s.a. 1035 (Darlington and McGurk, p. 520).
[5] Campbell, *Encomium Emmae Reginae*, III:1 (Campbell, p. 40).

Christianity as a whole as well as from Æthelnoth.[6] We must bear in mind that if accounts had survived from the supporters of Harold Harefoot's side they would probably tell a different story, perhaps focusing on his being older than Harthacnut, not preoccupied with Denmark, and foregrounding his strong familial ties to the English aristocracy. The evidence of coin-minting shows a more equal split in support, with most mints on the northern side of the Thames minting in the name of Harold Harefoot immediately after Cnut's death, and those south of the Thames doing so for Harthacnut.[7] London, Oxford, Southwark and Wallingford appear to have sat between the two, and struck coins for both candidates.[8] However, this relatively neat division collapsed quickly, and within a year or so Harold Harefoot's name can be found on the majority of coins produced throughout England. The Anglo-Saxon Chronicle explains this sea change in its entry for 1037: 'in this year Harold was chosen as king everywhere, and Harthacnut was deserted because he was too long in Denmark; and his mother . . . was driven out without any mercy to face the raging winter [i.e. exiled]'.[9]

Earl Godwine was now left exposed, having backed the losing side, and quickly did his best to demonstrate his new-found loyalty to Harold. He met Alfred, one of Emma's sons by Æthelred, while the prince and potential heir was on course to visit his mother, and gave him a military escort and guided him to Guildford.[10] There Alfred was arrested and handed over to Harold and Ælfgifu, and subsequently blinded and

---

[6] A similar statement about Harold Harefoot, 'who said he was the son of Cnut and the other Æthelgifu – although it was not true', is given by the C and D texts of the Anglo-Saxon Chronicle, s.a. 1035 (O'Brien O'Keeffe, p. 105, Cubbin, p. 65). John of Worcester (*Chronicon*, s.a. 1035 [Darlington and McGurk, p. 520]) is uncharacteristically adamant about this, declaring Harold Harefoot's claims as 'quite untrue, for some say he was the son of a certain cobbler' smuggled to Ælfgifu as a newborn baby.

[7] Talvio, 'Harold I and Harthacnut's Jewel Cross'.

[8] Ibid., p. 283.

[9] ASC 1037 CD (O'Brien O'Keeffe, p. 106).

[10] *Encomium Emmae Reginae*, III:2–6 (Campbell, pp. 40–6). William of Malmesbury, *Gesta Regum*, ii, 188 (p. 334), and John of Worcester, *Chronicon*, s.a. 1036 (p. 522). Note I have not entered into discussion of the difficult problem of the supposedly forged letter that invited Alfred to England from Normandy. See Keynes, 'Introduction', pp. xxxiii–xxxiv, for discussion of this.

incarcerated at Ely. Likewise, the English aristocracy appear to have accepted the new royal candidate and his mother, and began to form relationships and court their favour as with any royal succession. She is most probably the 'my lady' (*mire hlefdigen*, a term normally employed for royal wives or mothers) who received a mark of gold alongside Harold (also described there as *mine cynelaforde*, 'my royal lord', and given two marks of gold) in the will of Bishop Ælfric of Elmham, who died in 1038.[11] Emma took up residence in Bruges, at the heart of neutral Flanders, and awaited her moment.

She did not have to wait very long. On 17 March 1040 Harold died suddenly. A document from the archive of Christ Church, Canterbury, which was either written or copied during the early Anglo-Norman years and intended to play some part in the bitter dispute over the ownership of the port of Sandwich, gives an apparently accurate record of a visit by a monk of that house named Ælfgar to the royal court, then at Oxford.[12] He arrived as Harold lay 'very ill, so that he lay despairing of his life' with Bishop Lyfing of Devon in attendance, presumably preparing for the end. Harold was buried in Westminster, but his body was later exhumed, desecrated and cast into the Thames, probably on Harthacnut's orders.[13] There is some evidence which suggests that his mother fled into exile alongside a son of his named Ælfwine, in an early twelfth-century cartulary from the monastery of Sainte Foi at Conques in Aquitaine.[14] That account notes that an Englishman named Alboynus (Old English cognate: Ælfwine), who was born in London and was the son of a King Heroldus (a Latinized version of Harold) and of Alveva (a Latinized version of Ælfgifu), came to the region before 1060, during

[11] S. 1489; edited in Whitelock, *Wills*, pp. 181–4.

[12] S. 1467. A reproduction of the single-sheet manuscript (British Library, Cotton MS. Augustus ii, 90) is given in this volume.

[13] John of Worcester, *Chronicon*, s.a. 1040 (Darlington and McGurk, p. 530), reports that Harthacnut had his half-brother's body exhumed, thrown into a marsh, and then dumped into the Thames. William of Malmesbury, *Gesta Regum*, II:188.4 (Mynors, Thomson and Winterbottom, p. 336), reports a variant of this story, in which Harthacnut has Harold's body exhumed, decapitated, and the head cast into the Thames.

[14] See Stevenson, 'An Alleged Son', p. 113, for an edition of the text.

a pilgrimage, and persuaded the local authorities to rebuild the church and grant him the office of prior there. The 'Alveva' here may be an unknown consort of Harold, or his own mother, with a southern French scribe slightly garbling the finer details of the interrelationships of this part of the Anglo-Danish dynasty.

Within weeks of Harold Harefoot's death, Harthacnut was with his mother in Bruges, where the English aristocracy contacted him, inviting him to take up the vacant throne.[15] He arrived in June 1040, two and a half months after the death of his half-brother. Harthacnut is chiefly remembered for high levels of taxation on his arrival, and in the case of Worcester the use of violence to ensure his will was enforced after two of his *huscarls* were murdered while trying to collect the tax. Once again parts of the Anglo-Saxon Chronicle become a litany of wrongful and shameful acts, with the C text even noting that Harthacnut had Earl Eadwulf of Northumbria killed while under his safe conduct, making himself 'a pledge breaker'.[16] However, Harthacnut did have some supporters and began to key himself into the English elites, and he made grants of land to monastic houses in Winchester and perhaps Abingdon, and an apparent restitution to Ramsey Abbey of rights and privileges they had had during Cnut's day.[17]

Despite Harthacnut's apparent loathing of his half-brother, there are unlikely to have been major personnel changes at the head of the administration, and he seems to have been forced to accept many of his half-brother's followers as if they were his own. Sources are few, but John of Worcester's record of who took part in the exhumation of Harold's body, and its desecration, reveals much. He lists Archbishop Ælfric of York, Earl Godwine, Styr, who is given the high-ranking title of 'master of his household', Eadric his steward and Thrond/Þróndr his executioner, as well as many other unnamed dignitaries. The

---

[15] ASC 1040 CD (O'Brien O'Keeffe, p. 107); *Encomium Emmae Reginae*, III:10–11 (Campbell, p. 50).
[16] ASC 1041 C (O'Brien O'Keeffe, p. 107).
[17] S. 994, 993 and 996.

political affiliations of several of these men are not now known, and the last two survive in no other record, but Earl Godwine had only recently turned from his support of Harthacnut and thrown in his lot with Harold, and Styr is elsewhere recorded as 'a royal councillor' who held a position of local prominence in Kent during Harold's reign.[18] Godwine and his family were clearly too powerful to punish in 1040, and even other less well known figures, such as Styr, appear to have remained at the centre of political life rather than retiring to their estates. Perhaps they were offered a chance to demonstrate their new loyalty to Harthacnut in the exhumation of his half-brother.

The same impression is given by the confirmation in Harthacnut's name of a grant of land at Brede and Rammesleah, with 'two parts' of the tolls at Winchelsea, Sussex, for Fécamp Abbey in Normandy.[19] The text survives only in an eighteenth-century copy and may be suspect, but it most probably dates to the eleventh century, and the confirmation in Harthacnut's name which is attached to it has a witness-list that perfectly accords with others from the 1040s. Here Harthacnut attests alongside his mother ('Aeleva regis mater'), Earls Godwine and Siward, two names ('Ansgoth, Clapp') that are clearly a copyist's error for Osgot clapa, and five names ('Stigan capellanus, Etwolth, Herman, Alwinesmelt, Spiritus') that are again obvious errors for six royal priests who also witness Cnut

---

[18] He is recorded as such in S. 1467, where he is said to have held the 'third penny of the toll of Sandwich' for some time, presumably in the same fashion that Earl Godwine held the third penny of the shire of Kent during part of the eleventh century. The name is of extreme rarity in Anglo-Saxon England, appearing elsewhere only for the Yorkshire land-owner, Styr Ulfsson, noted above on pp. 69–70 and in Domesday Book for Yorkshire, Lincolnshire and Hampshire. I think we can be certain that these two occurrences in John of Worcester and S. 1467 are of the same man, and his sudden appearance in the 1040s at such a high level argues that he had come from Scandinavia with Harold Harefoot. He may have returned there late in the eleventh century, or he may be identifiable with the 'Sterre' who held the manor of Lockerley in Hampshire from King Edward the Confessor (DB, Hampshire, 23.40). It should be noted that the English form *Sterre* is commonly associated with the separate Old Norse name Stóri (see Björkmann, *Nordische Personenamen in England*, pp. 131–2, for the two names), but the ambiguous spelling of English scribes often muddies the clear distinction. We find an unambiguous 'Styr maiorem domus' in John of Worcester, but a form 'Steorran . . . þæs kings rædesmann' in S. 1467.

[19] S. 982, surviving only in Paris, Bibliothèque Nationale, Moreau MS. 21, pp. 18–19, which was copied before the French Revolution by Dom Jacques Lenoir from the now lost twelfth-century cartulary of the house.

and Edward the Confessor's charters: Stigand, Eadwold, Hermann, Ælfwine and Smelt (here joined to form a single composite name), and Spiritus.[20] Four very garbled names follow ('Osbert, Acchiersum, Bricsih, Geron'), only the third of which is even identifiable (as Bryxsige, a minister who attests another charter from 1042: S. 994). The list ends with seven Scandinavian names ('Aizor, Turchil, Swen, Theustul, Eusten, Tovi, Turgil'), some of whom are not attested anywhere else in English sources and must be Scandinavians who arrived with Harthacnut.[21] 'Aizor' is probably Azor Thoredsson, who held estates in Wiltshire and whose father consistently attested Cnut's charters in a position suggesting great importance at court.[22] Azor appears in two other charters for 1042 (alongside a Thored in the first, who must be his ageing father), as well as with the grand title 'regis dapifer' (royal seneschal) in one from 1062.[23] Thus, Harthacnut appears to have used the priests attached to the court who had worked for his father and most probably also his half-brother, and key figures such as Earl Godwine, Earl Siward, Osgot clapa and Azor Thoredsson appear to have remained close to the king. A handful of new men with Scandinavian names are probably those who accompanied Harthacnut from Denmark and may have been members of his personal retinue or trusted figures drawn from his government there.

Like his grandfather, father and half-brother before him, Harthacnut died suddenly, on 8 June 1042, only two years after his arrival in England, in the words of the C text of the Anglo-Saxon Chronicle: 'as he stood at his drink, and he suddenly fell to the earth with an awful convulsion . . . and he spoke no word afterwards'.[24] John of Worcester is more explicit and informs us that Harthacnut was at the wedding-feast of one of his father's most prominent Anglo-Scandinavian ministers, Tovi

---

[20] For their attestations see Keynes, *Atlas of Attestations*, table lxix.
[21] On these Scandinavians see p. 182 above.
[22] See above, pp. 101–2 and 175–6.
[23] S. 994, 1396 and 1036.
[24] ASC 1042 C (O'Brien O'Keeffe, p. 107).

pruða, in Lambeth.[25] His half-brother Edward (later 'the Confessor'), one of Emma's sons by Æthelred, had returned to England in 1041, and appears to have been welcomed back by Harthacnut into the court. This Edward seamlessly took up the reins of command after the burial of Harthacnut in the Old Minster, Winchester, next to Cnut.[26]

Thus the line of the Anglo-Danish kings ended as it had begun, with an apparently exasperated aristocracy – pushed to their limits either through constant raiding and warfare, or a quick succession of royal deaths and political about-turns – accepting the only candidate who could offer peace and stability. The prevalence of sudden deaths amongst the men in this family has been noted above, as well as the likelihood that they shared an inherited genetic defect.[27] It is ironic that had the rumours circulating in Emma's court – namely, that Harold Harefoot was the son of a lowly man other than Cnut – been true, then Anglo-Scandinavian rule in England might well have endured, and the subsequent history, culture and languages of both England and Denmark been very different.

That said, the legacy of Cnut's rule extended beyond his own life and those of his sons. An Anglo-Scandinavian elite had been formed or implanted, and had had some decades to develop as a powerful bloc within English politics, and presumably also within Denmark. In England at least, these men would remain in positions of power and influence far into the reign of Edward the Confessor, and in a handful of cases up until the Norman Conquest. The most influential family amongst these new elites was that of Earl Godwine. As noted above, Godwine had married the sister of a Danish nobleman, Jarl Ulf, and the first two sons from this union were named after Cnut's father and grandfather in a clear statement of their claim to kinship with Cnut's line and their mark of allegiance to him. They commanded great power

---

[25] John of Worcester, *Chronicon*, s.a. 1042 (Darlington and McGurk, pp. 532–4). In this Tovi pruða married the daughter of Osgot clapa, his long-time associate.

[26] See Biddle and Kjølbye-Biddle, 'Danish Royal Burials in Winchester'.

[27] See above at p. 195.

as a kin group throughout the reigns of Harold Harefoot, Harthacnut and Edward the Confessor, and they exercised sufficient authority to return from exile in the 1050s and force their own reinstatement. Their final end came only after briefly seizing the crown for themselves in 1066. Despite living in England, their Scandinavian connections remained strong up to the Norman Conquest. Sweyn, Godwine's eldest son, was sent to Denmark (via Bruges) in 1047 to escape the wrath of Edward the Confessor, and the surviving members of this family fled there in the aftermath of 1066.[28]

Other high-ranking Scandinavian émigrés also stayed on in England after the downfall of the Anglo-Danish dynasty, and Gunhild, Cnut's niece and wife of Earl Hákon Eiríksson, remained on her English estates until her exile in 1044.[29] Biorn, Swen Estrithsson's younger brother, held an earldom in the region of Huntingdonshire between c. 1045 and his death in 1049/50, and if Adam of Bremen is not mistaken he may have been joined in England by another brother, Esbiorn.[30] I have argued elsewhere that Earl Siward of Northumbria (held office 1032/3–55) was also a prominent member of this family, and he and his son Earl Waltheof (d. 1076) should probably be added to this group.[31]

Cnut's ministers also continued in office, or at least in positions of power and influence. Osgot clapa retained power until he was suddenly exiled before Christmas 1046.[32] He went to Flanders with a fleet of thirty-nine ships, which he used to raid along the Sussex

---

[28] John of Worcester, *Chronicon*, s.a. 1049 (Darlington and McGurk, p. 548); and on the family's later flight to Denmark see my 'English Political Refugees'.

[29] John of Worcester, *Chronicon*, s.a. 1044 (Darlington and McGurk, p. 540). She may also have later been the wife of Harald Thorkelsson, on whom see Keynes, 'Cnut's Earls', p. 66, but note also Williams, 'Thorkell the Tall', p. 157, n. 82.

[30] ASC 1049 CDE (O'Brien O'Keeffe, p. 110); Adam of Bremen, *Gesta*, III:9 (Schmeidler, p. 155).

[31] See Bolton, 'Was the Family'.

[32] ASC 1046 CD (O'Brien O'Keeffe, p. 109); John of Worcester, *Chronicon*, s.a. 1046 (Schmeidler, p. 542).

coastline.[33] He appears to have been restored to his English estates, and is reported as dying in his bed in 1054.[34] His daughter had married his associate, Tovi pruða, in the ceremony at which Harthacnut collapsed and died, and his grandson, Esgar, remained in control of London until the Norman Conquest.[35] Cnut's royal court minister Thored held office until the mid-1040s, with Edward the Confessor making him a grant in 1045, and the witness of his son Azor must be amongst the attestations of the same name in the witness-lists of Edward the Confessor's charters.[36] Azor appears with his full name in a document dated 28 February 1072, in which he transferred ownership of his estates to Bishop Giso of Wells, presumably under duress from the new Norman lords.[37] In the localities, the men Cnut may have implanted into the 'Western Provinces' and East Anglia survived long into the eleventh century, with Urk recorded into the 1050s, only being certainly dead when Edward the Confessor issued a writ in favour of his widow 'Tole' (Tola) sometime in 1058–66.[38] Thorkell of Harringworth remained on his estates until sometime in 1069–71, when he is recorded as revolting against the Normans.[39]

These vestiges of Cnut's administration also continued to act in the interests of a united England and Denmark. In 1047 and again in 1048, Cnut's nephew and Harthacnut's successor on the Danish throne, Swen Estrithsson, called on England to send military aid to Denmark to repel the invasions of King Magnús of Norway and his successor, King Haraldr Hardráði. England had apparently also feared attack from Norway, and had collected a large defensive fleet that stood anchored at

---

[33] ASC 1049 C (O'Brien O'Keeffe, p. 110). Note John of Worcester, *Chronicon*, s.a. 1049 (Schmeidler, p. 550), gives the number as twenty-nine not thirty-nine, perhaps from a misreading or bad note-taking.
[34] See ASC 1054 CD (O'Brien O'Keeffe, p. 115) for his death. If he was exiled for aiding Sweyn Godwinesson he may have shared in Sweyn's reinstatement in 1050.
[35] See pp. 110–11 above, and Lewis, 'Danish Landowners in Wessex', pp. 185–6.
[36] Keynes, *Atlas of Attestations*, table lxxv.
[37] Pelteret, Catalogue, no. 56, p. 83.
[38] See Williams, 'A Place in the Country'.
[39] See p. 125 above.

Sandwich.[40] John of Worcester adds to the Anglo-Saxon Chronicle's account that on both occasions Earl Godwine advised that fifty ships be sent, but he was opposed by Earl Leofric and the people.[41] Edward the Confessor's own views are not recorded here, but having spent his child-hood in the Norman court due to Cnut's invasion and his eventual hostility to the power of the Godwine family, it was unlikely that he would have regarded the Anglo-Scandinavian lords as trusted supporters.[42]

We cannot know the fate of the English elites and royal servants sent to Denmark, but again it seems unlikely that the events of 1035–42 caused them to return home *en masse*.[43] Presumably, having made careers as skilled royal servants in Denmark, they continued in those roles under Swen Estrithsson and his heirs. Certainly, moneyers with the distinctly English names Godwine, Leofwine, Ælfnoth and Ælfweard minted coins for Cnut. All these except Godwine continued to do so for Harthacnut and Magnús 'the Good'. All four minted for Swen Estrithsson, and two or three of them did so for Swen's sons, Harald Hein, Knut 'the Holy' and Erik 'the Good'.[44]

Moreover, amongst these elites, the idea of England and Denmark as linked political entities endured throughout much of the eleventh century. Cnut's successors in Denmark clearly maintained claims to rule in England after 1042.[45] Both Adam of Bremen and the *Vita Ædwardi regis* indicate that Swen Estrithsson made some form of claim to England in the initial years of Edward the Confessor's rule: Adam recorded that immediately after Harthacnut's death Swen travelled to England to petition Edward for the throne, and accepted a promise

---

[40] ASC 1045 CD (O'Brien O'Keeffe, p. 108). ASC D records that the fleet was collected because of a threat from Magnús.

[41] ASC 1048–9 D (Cubbin, pp. 67–8); John of Worcester, *Chronicon*, s.a. 1047–1048 (Darlington and McGurk, p. 544).

[42] For comprehensive discussion of this period of Edward's life see Keynes, 'The Æthelings in Normandy'.

[43] One potential future avenue of research would be to use isotope testing on the teeth of the skeletons excavated at Lund and other Danish sites to see whether these people spent their childhoods in Scandinavia or England.

[44] Hauberg, *Myntforhold*, and Becker, 'Coinages of Harthacnut'.

[45] See Larson, 'The Efforts of the Danish Kings'.

that the kingdom would revert to him in the event of Edward's death without heirs; the *Vita Ædwardi* places the Danish king amongst the ambassadors who travelled to England to pay their respects to Edward after his coronation.[46] With its focus on Edward and praise of him, this account makes Swen choose Edward as a father, and submit himself to him. However, the text is forced to concede that what was agreed between them was settled by oath and the exchange of hostages, suggesting a tense political settlement rather than the relationship of a king and a willing vassal.

In the later eleventh century, the Danish kings tried on three occasions to make good these claims. The first saw the launching of a fleet in 1069 under the command of Swen's brother Esbiorn, three of Swen's sons, an otherwise unknown Jarl Thorkell, and Bishop Kristian of Århus.[47] John of Worcester records that this invasion was brought to a standstill by its commander Esbiorn, who accepted payment from William the Conqueror to desist.[48] The attack was joined in 1070 by Swen himself, but the momentum had been lost and the fleet returned to Denmark. Crucially, John of Worcester notes that Swen immediately exiled his brother on their return to Denmark, 'because he had received money from King William against the wishes of the Danes'.[49] Clearly the aim was not raiding and tribute, but conquest, and the loss of this was insult enough for Swen to exile his own brother. The second attempt on England was launched under the command of two of Swen's sons in 1075, and was intended to add military might to the so-called 'revolt

[46] Adam of Bremen, *Gesta*, II:78 (Schmeidler, p. 136). There are numerous other examples of such arrangements in the period, especially where Scandinavians are concerned. On this see A. Williams, 'Some Notes and Considerations on Problems', for some discussion. *Vita Ædwardi regis*, I:1 (Barlow, pp. 16–17); and as Barlow (ibid., p. 17, n. 37) notes, '[t]his statement has caused endless trouble'. Freeman, *A History of the Norman Conquest*, 2, p. 18, interpreted it to be a mistaken reference to King Magnús of Norway. I concur here with Barlow that the king intended is Swen Estrithsson.

[47] ASC 1068 D (Cubbin, p. 84) and 1070 E (Irvine, p. 88). This last name, Kristian, is unattested in Petersen, *Nordiskt Runnamenslexikon*, but is attested in West Norse saga narratives as 'Kristiann'. Clearly the man here was Danish and so I have used the name 'Kristina' in the *Nordiskt Runnamenslexikon* as a guide to produce the form here.

[48] John of Worcester, *Chronicon*, s.a. 1069–1070 (McGurk, pp. 10–15).

[49] Ibid.

of the three earls' there. The offensive may have been ill-judged, and the revolt collapsed before they arrived, leaving the Danish forces to raid St Peter's minster at York before returning home. The third and final offensive came in 1083, and was under the command of one of the two brothers, King Knut 'the Holy', who had led the expedition of 1075. The Danes assembled a fleet and secured promises of military support from Norway and Flanders. They posed a significant enough threat for William the Conqueror to return from his own campaign in Maine, northern France, bringing hordes of continental mercenaries with him, and causing him to lay waste large areas of the eastern coast-line to slow the invaders' progress.[50] However, luck was not on the Danish side. Pope Gregory VII suddenly died as the Scandinavian forces were beginning to gather, and Emperor Henry IV invaded Saxony, driving his rival for power, Henry of Salm, and his supporters, the archbishop of Magdeburg and the bishop of Halberstadt, across the southern Danish border to seek refuge. Knut was left holding a political hot potato that could incite the Emperor to lead the imperial forces across his border days before Knut was due to sail for England.[51] He was delayed at Hedeby-Schleswig, whereupon the various fleets tired of waiting and disbanded before he arrived.

The rapid succession of deaths in the period 1034–42 removed Cnut and his three sons from the political stage, and began the collapse of the Anglo-Scandinavian rule that Cnut had established. However, that collapse was gradual and took another fifty years to happen, falling away incrementally as each major Anglo-Scandinavian figure in the government or landscape of England and Denmark died or was exiled. Only by the last years of the eleventh century were they all a thing of the past.

[50] ASC 1085 E (Irvine, pp. 93–4).
[51] As argued by Larson, 'The Efforts of the Danish Kings', p. 80.

CONCLUSION

In the chapters above, Cnut emerges in several complementary roles. He was an intelligent and pragmatic diplomacist, an energetic and active ruler, a cunning and resourceful military leader, and most probably a devout Christian.

His life falls into three main phases. His early life appears to have been shaped by the instabilities of his family and its hold on Denmark, namely his position as second son to Swen 'Forkbeard', and the scandalous regicide/patricide that had brought the latter to power there. These probably caused Cnut to seek his own kingdom in the conquest of England, and sharpened his resolve to succeed there. However, luck also played its part in his seizure of power in England, and he could not have predicted or caused the disastrously timed feud that would break out between Æthelred and his son Edmund 'Ironside', or the former's untimely illness and death. Cnut's skill here was, perhaps, in realizing that these situations could be turned to his advantage.

The middle years of his life, those between the invasion of 1016 and the conquest of Norway in 1028, reveal a period of rapid activity characterized by Cnut's responses to various threats. This period is so densely packed with actions and decisions that it is exhausting just to read about. He began by balancing the interests of the most important of the English against the demands of his Scandinavian mercenary armies, paradoxically succeeding in reassuring the one that this was no viking raid while supplying the other with booty. This was immediately followed by apparent challenges to Cnut's authority by an English ealdorman and then an overmighty Danish warlord, both of which were dealt with in quick succession either side of his going to Denmark to receive the crown there. While in Denmark he must have taken steps to ensure the continuation of government, as well as pushing forward the building of governmental and ecclesiastical infrastructure using English wealth and English men at a previously unseen pace. The ongoing problem of Thorkell the Tall in Denmark seems to have led to a military show of force in the region c. 1023, and once Thorkell had apparently died and arrangements there were settled, the region descended into chaos again with the local uprising and invasion by Norway and Sweden, leading to the decisive Battle of Helgeå in 1026. Against this backdrop, Cnut seems to have been meddling in the imperial succession, attempting to get a candidate elected whose interests were least in conflict with his own, and this resulted in his invitation to Conrad II's imperial coronation in Rome at Easter 1027. Finally, on Cnut's return from Rome, Norway's level of political centralization and organization ensured that the attack on Denmark of some months before could not pass without reaction, so he took a fleet to settle matters there, before placing Norway under his rule in 1028.

The years of his mature life, those after 1028, saw the fruits of this labour in the development of a stable court around Cnut, which appears to have fostered a distinct and new Anglo-Danish identity. This period saw the greatest outpouring of his piety in gift-giving to the Church. We might wish that the years of his mature life had been longer, if only to see what such an energetic ruler could produce when not pinned down by threats to his authority, but he died only seven years later in 1035, some months after his control over Norway had collapsed.

A key question, in my mind at least, concerns the partisan nature of our two sets of sources and the man who stood behind them. Often in the English sources Cnut is a model king of late Anglo-Saxon England, producing in his Letter of 1019–20 statements so ideal that they could evidently be used for preaching by Archbishop Wulfstan.[1] Conversely,

---

[1] See pp. 15–16.

our best sources from the Scandinavian material reflect a very different image of him. While there are adaptations of ideology and outlook in skaldic verse that must reflect those of his English- or imperial-influenced court, overwhelmingly he is the ideal Viking-Age ruler, demonstrating his success and continuing divine support through battles and excesses of bloodshed. We appear on first inspection to have two Cnuts, and so are forced to ask ourselves whether one or more of these representations was the creation of the composers of our sources, each working in highly conservative genres and with their own expectations of what the ruler should be; or whether instead these are accurate reflections of aspects of his persona that Cnut revealed to different groups of his followers and subjects at different times. Whichever conclusion we prefer, the man himself stands some distance behind both representations, and we must accept that our sources obscure as much as they reveal.

There seems to be an important similarity in the way that two of the key sources, one from each side of this ethnic divide and both apparently as close to Cnut's own wishes as we can possibly get, appear to affect ignorance of certain of his actions. I have already referred to the controversy caused by the statement of Cnut's Letter of 1019–20 that he had spent his wealth freely to avert hostility to the English, and had then gone to Denmark to ensure that future hostility from there would not trouble the English again.[2] As Niels Lund notes, '[i]t seems a bit rich on Cnut's part to claim he had spent his money averting the dangers that he himself had brought in', and more so since this wealth is very likely to have been part of that extracted from the English only months before.[3] The same apparent ignorance of Cnut's motives can be found in an extant verse from Sigvatr Þórðarson's *Knútsdrápa*, which describes his visit to Rome as that of a pilgrim.[4] The only passing allusion to the presence of Conrad II there is the four-word distillation of Cnut's new alliances in the final statement that he was 'dear to the Emperor, close

[2] Lund, 'Cnut's Danish Kingdom', p. 31.
[3] Ibid.
[4] It is edited by Whaley, p. 661, and given in translation above at pp. 191–2.

to [St] Peter [ie. the Pope]', without any mention of the coronation
ceremony. We are certainly missing verses from this poem, and the ones
in question here survive only in a single text (*Fagrskinna*, with another
related verse which notes that 'few ring-distributors [i.e. generous rulers]
will have measured the route south with their steps', following there,
and also recorded in *Knytlinga saga*). Thus, we might infer that other
unrecorded verses discussed the coronation ceremony.[5] However, this is
unlikely, as the whole poem was almost certainly known to the writers
of the saga accounts in which the relevant parts of it survive, and their
narratives are demonstrably based on it, yet neither mentions the coronation. *Fagrskinna* has Cnut set off on his pilgrimage to Rome with staff
and scrip (satchel) and walk south, in words loosely echoing the content
of the verse, with the Emperor coming to meet him en route and
escorting him to the city, and Cnut taking what he needed from the
Emperor's money in addition to the treasure he brought with him.
Knytlinga saga has him set off on a journey southward to Rome, walking
from Flanders to the Holy City, in which the role of the Emperor is
reduced to one of a patron, in that Cnut was free to use the Emperor's
money.[6]

I am struck in the case of Cnut's letter by an impression of spin-
doctoring, in which the English are given a version of events that would
be most acceptable to them and one centred on them and their needs.
Perhaps the same is true for Sigvatr, who while creating notable breaks
with skaldic tradition, presents Cnut as the friend of the Pope and
the Emperor rather than subordinate to them in a ceremony. These
are only slight indications, but these sources are some of the closest to
Cnut himself. If my suspicions are correct, then these separate attempts
to portray events in the best possible light for the English and the
Scandinavians accord well with Cnut's pragmatism and diplomacy, and

[5] For these verses see Whaley, pp. 661–3. On *Fagrskinna* in general see the excellent introduction to the new translation by Finlay, *Fagrskinna*. The remaining extant verses survive in
six narrative sources (see Whaley, p. 649).

[6] *Fagrskinna*, ch. 40 (Bjarni Einarsson, pp. 204–5) and *Knytlinga saga*, ch. 17 (Bjarni
Guðnason, p. 123).

they suggest that his direct agency may have lain behind these different representations of him.

This is not to say that Cnut did not strongly feel himself to be Scandinavian or that he did not really wish to embrace Englishness, but it suggests a fluidity of identity on his part. The events of his life placed him in a nearly unique position to question some of the overlapping and clashing edges of the cultures in which he lived. He came from a society that did not entirely share his own religious views, and one which had seen his dynasty change that society dramatically. In addition, much of his life was spent in another culture, learning about it in order to succeed, while apparently still engaging with some aspects of a more traditional Scandinavian way of life transplanted on occasion into that host culture. This may have been influenced by the lack of strong social anchors in the form of Scandinavian male familial influences after 1019. Moreover, his wife Emma in the same period may have been almost equally fluid in her ethnic outlook, being of Danish-Norman stock and having spent much of her life in England. An apparent freedom from some of the social norms of English and Scandinavian elite behaviour would explain Cnut's actions in western France, if I have interpreted those correctly, as well as his adoption and development of a new ideology of rule after 1027.[7] He began life as the second son of a Danish king, but appears to have ended it as culturally neither Scandinavian nor English, but something in between, constructed according to what suited him best on each occasion. In that respect, if I am correct, Cnut was surprisingly modern.

[7] On these see pp. 163–71 and 189–92 above.

Appendix I

THE STORY OF CNUT AND THE WAVES

Sharp-eyed readers will note that I have avoided any mention beyond the few words in the introduction of the story of Cnut and the tide, and yet it is perhaps unavoidable. I beg my reader's forgiveness for irascibility on this front, but when one spends the better part of one's adult life researching Cnut, it is the first thing anybody asks you about, and it can become as irritating as a stuck record.

The famous story about Cnut, that he sat enthroned on a beach and commanded the waves to go back, thus receiving wet feet for his trouble, is slightly misunderstood and cut short by most modern retellings.[1] It was first told in the second quarter of the twelfth century by the Anglo-Norman chronicler Henry of Huntingdon in his *Historia Anglorum*, and it must be read in its full version and understood within the context of contemporary tales of Anglo-Saxon saints who could control nature. What most modern readings lop off the end is a flourish that has Cnut reveal himself as the wise man of the story rather than the buffoon, as he declares that this stunt reveals his power to be nothing before that of the Lord of all creation.[2] Thus, he is piously demonstrating through this act that he cannot control nature, and that God and his immediate representatives in the saints will always be more powerful than him. The story ends with Cnut surrendering his crown to an effigy of

---

[1] See p. 1 above.

[2] *Historia Anglorum*, VI:17 (Greenway, pp. 368–9). From here it passes to the writers Ralph Diceto (d. 1201), Henry Knighton (d. 1396), and the Chronicle of John of Brompton (fl. 1436).

Christ in a nearby church. The events are not localized any more than
'by the sea'.[3]

However, these passages were written sometime after the events of
Cnut's life, by a writer not afraid to change details where they did not
fit with his agenda, and as an example for the correct behaviour of the
princes whom his work addresses. Yet this is not to say that some form
of public devotional ceremony does not stand behind the writer's
artistic licence and exaggeration. The hagiographer Goscelin, in his
Translatio Sancte Mildrethe, has Cnut give a crown to a church in
Winchester. He similarly recorded that the king laid a crown on the
altar of Christ Church, Canterbury, but a later record from c. 1400
mentions that the crown was laid on a cross in the nave.[4] Cnut's servant,
Tovi pruða, is also recorded as giving a crown and other ornaments to
Waltham Priory.[5]

The story of Cnut and the waves was certainly popular in the twelfth
century, and, as C. E. Wright noted, another version was told by
Geoffrei Gaimar around 1140.[6] Gaimar locates the story in Westminster,
and he omits the throne, having Cnut stand on the shore. Both he and
Henry of Huntingdon drew on oral material from the Eastern Danelaw,
and perhaps the common origin should be looked for there.

As a final observation, it should be noted that the years following the
death of Henry I in 1135 were markedly uncertain ones, which saw the
difficult and contested reign of Stephen. While there may be a kernel

[3] The location of the episode at Bosham in Sussex is more antiquarian than medieval,
and may be due to the identification of a damaged funerary monument in a local church
as containing a daughter of Cnut. The monument is several centuries later than Cnut or
his offspring. See Peckham, 'The Bosham Myth of Canute's Daughter', and Marwood,
Stone Coffins of Bosham.

[4] Goscelin, *Translatio Sancte Mildrethe*, ch. 6, ed. Rollason, 'Translatio Sancte Mildrethe
Virginis', p. 163.

[5] *Waltham Chronicle*, ch. 7 (Watkiss and Chibnall, p. 12).

[6] Wright, *Cultivation of Saga*, p. 177. Wright also cites a Welsh analogue in a legend about
a King Maelgwn Gwynedd who died in 549. Here this king's throne is made of waxed bird
wings and floats when the tide comes in. However, this legend is only extant in an addition
to a legal tract in one manuscript of the Laws of Hywel Dda (Aberystwyth, National
Library of Wales, MS. Peniarth 32), which dates to c. 1400, and this may be an obscure
descendant of the Cnut legend.

of truth in the story, its capacity to remind a ruler that his power was nothing before that of God and the Church must have appealed greatly to Henry of Huntingdon and Gaimar. It is also telling that the part of the story in which Cnut presents his crown to an effigy of Christ was added to Henry's account after the initial composition of the text around 1130 and in a later edition from c. 1140.

Appendix II

CONCORDANCE OF CHARTERS CITED IN THIS VOLUME

The charters are given here with their relevant place of publication in the new British Academy series of editions or, if not yet published in that series, an archive is indicated (in parentheses) and an earlier place of publication of an edition where available.

S. 877: Miller, *Charters of the New Minster, Winchester*, no. 31, pp. 144–57

S. 896: Kelly, *Charters of Abingdon Abbey*, II, no. 128, pp. 497–503

S. 906: Sawyer, *Charters of Burton Abbey*, no. 28, pp. 48–53

S. 915: Kelly, *Charters of Abingdon Abbey*, II, no. 134, pp. 522–5

S. 921: (Athelney) Kemble, *Codex Diplomaticus*, no. 1306

S. 922: Sawyer, *Charters of Burton Abbey*, no. 32, pp. 60–4

S. 930: Sawyer, *Charters of Burton Abbey*, no. 35, pp. 67–9

S. 931: (Thorney) Kemble, *Codex Diplomaticus*, no. 1308

S. 931b (Barking); unpublished

S. 933: O'Donovan, *Charters of Sherborne*, no. 15, pp. 51–4

S. 934: Kelly, *Charters of Abingdon Abbey*, II, no. 137, pp. 535–40

S. 947: Kelly, *Charters of Peterborough*, no. 19, pp. 284–7

S. 948: (Thorney) Kemble, *Codex Diplomaticus*, no. 1153

S. 949: (Fécamp) Haskins, 'A Charter of Cnut', p. 344

S. 950: Brooks and Kelly, *Charters of Christ Church, Canterbury*, II, no. 144 pp. 1052–7

S. 951: (Exeter, ex. St Germans) Kemble, *Codex Diplomaticus*, no. 728

S. 952: Brooks and Kelly, *Charters of Christ Church, Canterbury*, II, no. 146, pp. 1062–4

S. 953: (Exeter, ex. St Germans) reproduced in Sanders, *Facsimiles of Anglo-Saxon Manuscripts*, II, Exeter 10

S. 954: (Exeter) Kemble, *Codex Diplomaticus*, no. 729

S. 955: Kelly, *Charters of Shaftesbury Abbey*, no. 30, pp. 122–7

S. 956: Miller, *Charters of the New Minster, Winchester*, no. 33, pp. 159–64

S. 958: (Ely) Kemble, *Codex Diplomaticus*, no. 734

S. 959: Brooks and Kelly, *Charters of Christ Church, Canterbury*, II, no. 151, pp. 1079–93

S. 960: (Winchester, Old Minster) Kemble, *Codex Diplomaticus*, no. 739

S. 961: (Abbotsbury) Kemble, *Codex Diplomaticus*, no. 741

S. 962: (Winchester, Old Minster) Kemble, *Codex Diplomaticus*, no. 743

S. 964: Kelly, *Charters of Abingdon Abbey*, II, no. 138, pp. 540–3

S. 967: Kelly, *Charters of Abingdon Abbey*, II, no. 139, pp. 544–5

S. 968: Woodman, *Charters of Northern Houses*, no. 8, pp. 148–57

S. 969: O'Donovan, *Charters of Sherborne*, no. 20, pp. 68–70

S. 970: (Winchester, Old Minster) Kemble, *Codex Diplomaticus*, no. 752

S. 972: (Winchester, Old Minster) Kemble, *Codex Diplomaticus*, no. 750

S. 973: Kelly, *Charters of Abingdon Abbey*, II, no. 140, p. 546

S. 975: O'Donovan, *Charters of Sherborne*, no. 16, pp. 55–8

S. 976: (Winchester, Old Minster) Kemble, *Codex Diplomaticus*, no. 753

S. 979: (Athelney) Kemble, *Codex Diplomaticus*, no. 1324

S. 980: (Bury St Edmunds) Kemble, *Codex Diplomaticus*, no. 735

S. 981: Brooks and Kelly, *Charters of Christ Church, Canterbury*, II, no. 154, pp. 1110–16

S. 982: (Fécamp) Haskins, 'A Charter of Cnut', pp. 343–4

S. 984: (St Benet of Holme) Kemble, *Codex Diplomaticus*, no. 740

S. 989: Kelly, *Charters of St Augustine's Abbey, Canterbury*, no. 32, pp. 119–21

S. 991: (Evesham) Harmer, *Writs*, no. 48

S. 992: Kelly, *Charters of St Paul's, London*, no. 27, pp. 203–6

S. 993: Kelly, *Charters of Abingdon Abbey*, II, no. 141, pp. 549–53

S. 994: (Winchester, Old Minster) Kemble, *Codex Diplomaticus*, no. 763

S. 996: (Ramsey) Kemble, *Codex Diplomaticus*, no. 1331

S. 998: O'Donovan, *Charters of Sherborne*, no. 21, pp. 74–7

S. 1004: (Abbotsbury) Kemble, *Codex Diplomaticus*, no. 772

S. 1010: (Wilton) Kemble, *Codex Diplomaticus*, no. 778

S. 1021: (Exeter) Kemble, *Codex Diplomaticus*, no. 791

S. 1033: (Rouen, St Mary's) Kemble, *Codex Diplomaticus*, no. 810

S. 1034: (Bath) Kemble, *Codex Diplomaticus*, no. 811

S. 1036: (Waltham) Kemble, *Codex Diplomaticus*, no. 813

S. 1222: Brooks and Kelly, *Charters of Christ Church, Canterbury*, II, no. 159, pp. 1134–5

S. 1423: (Worcester) Robertson, *Charters*, no. 81, pp. 156–7

S. 1463: (Peterborough) Kemble, *Codex Diplomaticus*, no. 733

S. 1467: Brooks and Kelly, *Charters of Christ Church, Canterbury*, II, no. 164, pp. 1147–53

S. 1474: O'Donovan, *Charters of Sherborne*, no. 17, pp. 59–61

S. 1489: (Bury St Edmunds) Whitelock, Brett and Brooke, *Councils and Synods*, no. 66, pp. 514–16

S. 1503: Brooks and Kelly, *Charters of Christ Church, Canterbury*, II, no. 142, pp. 1037–50

BIBLIOGRAPHY

MANUSCRIPTS

Cambridge, Corpus Christi College, MS. 201
Cambridge, Jesus College, MS. C.23
London, British Library, Additional MS. 26,788
London, British Library, Additional MS. 49,598
London, British Library, Cotton MS. Galba E iii, 2
London, British Library, Cotton MS. Vespasian A. viii
London, British Library, Royal MS. I. D, ix
Rochester, Cathedral Library MS. A. 3. 5
York, Minster Library, Additional MS. 1

PRIMARY SOURCES

Adam of Bremen, *Gesta Hammaburgensis Ecclesiae Pontificum*, ed. B. Schmeidler, Monumenta Germaniae Historica, Scriptores Rerum Germanicarum in usum Scholarum Separatim Editi 2, Hanover, 1917

Adémar of Chabannes, *Sermones Tres*, ed. J. P. Migne, *Patrologiae Cursus Completus. Series Latina*, 141 (1844–64), cols 111–12 and 115–24

Adémar of Chabannes, *Chronicon aquitanicum et francicum* or *Historia Francorum*, ed. J. Chavanon, Collection des textes pour servir à l'étude et à l'enseignement de l'histoire 20, Alphonse Picard et Fils, Paris, 1897

Ágrip af Nóregskonungasǫgum: A Twelfth-Century Synoptic History of the Kings of Norway, ed. and trans. M. J. Driscoll, Viking Society for Northern Research Text Series, 10, London, 1995

Anglo-Saxon Charters, ed. A. J. Robertson, 2nd edn, Cambridge University Press, 1956

The Anglo-Saxon Chronicle, trans. M. Swanton, Dent, London, 1996

The Anglo-Saxon Chronicle: A Collaborative Edition. Vol. 1: MS. F: Facsimile Edition, ed. D. Dumville, Boydell, Cambridge, 1995

The Anglo-Saxon Chronicle: A Collaborative Edition. Vol. 3: MS. A: A Semi-Diplomatic Edition with Introduction and Indices, ed. J. M. Bately, Boydell, Cambridge, 1986

The Anglo-Saxon Chronicle: A Collaborative Edition. Vol. 4: MS. B: A Semi-Diplomatic Edition with Introduction and Indices, ed. S. Taylor, Boydell, Cambridge, 1983

The Anglo-Saxon Chronicle: A Collaborative Edition. Vol. 5: MS. C: A Semi-Diplomatic Edition with Introduction and Indices, ed. K. O'Brien O'Keeffe, Boydell, Cambridge, 2001

The Anglo-Saxon Chronicle: A Collaborative Edition. Vol. 6: MS. D, ed. G. P. Cubbin, Boydell, Cambridge, 1996

The Anglo-Saxon Chronicle: A Collaborative Edition. Vol. 7: MS. E: A Semi-Diplomatic Edition with Introduction and Indices, ed. S. Irvine, Cambridge University Press, 2004

The Anglo-Saxon Chronicle: A Revised Translation, trans. D. Whitelock, D. C. Douglas and S. I. Tucker, Eyre & Spottiswoode, London, 1961

Anglo-Saxon Wills, ed. D. Whitelock, Cambridge Studies in English Legal History, Cambridge University Press, 1930

Anglo-Saxon Writs, ed. F. E. Harmer, Manchester University Press, 1952

Annales Cambriae, ed. J. Williams (ab Ithel), Rolls Series, Longman, London, 1860

Annales Ryenses, in E. Kroman, et al. (eds.), *Danmarks Middelalderlige Annaler*, Selskabet for Udgivelse af Kilder til Dansk Historie, Copenhagen, 1980, pp. 149–253

Brut y Tywysogyon or The Chronicle of the Princes: Red Book of Hergest Version. Critical Text and Translation with Introduction and Notes, ed. and trans. T. Jones, Board of Celtic Studies, University of Wales History and Law Series, 16, Cardiff University Press, 1955

The Carmen de Hastingae Proelio of Guy, Bishop of Amiens, ed. and trans. F. Barlow, Oxford Medieval Texts, Clarendon Press, Oxford, 1999

Cartularium Monasterii de Rameseia, ed. W. H. Hart and P. A. Lyons, Rolls Series, Longman, London, 1884–93

Charters of Abingdon Abbey, ed. S. E. Kelly, Anglo-Saxon Charters 8, published for The British Academy by Oxford University Press, 2001

Charters of Burton Abbey, ed. P. H. Sawyer, Anglo-Saxon Charters 2, published for The British Academy by Oxford University Press, 1979

Charters of Christ Church Canterbury, ed. N. P. Brooks and S. E. Kelly, Anglo-Saxon Charters 17–18, published for The British Academy by Oxford University Press, 2013

Charters of the New Minster, Winchester, ed. S. Miller, Anglo-Saxon Charters 9, published for The British Academy by Oxford University Press, 2001

Charters of Northern Houses, ed. D. A. Woodman, Anglo-Saxon Charters 16, published for The British Academy by Oxford University Press, 2012

Charters of Peterborough Abbey, ed. S. E. Kelly, Anglo-Saxon Charters 14, published for The British Academy by Oxford University Press, 2009

Charters of St Augustine's Abbey, Canterbury, and Minster-in-Thanet, ed. S. E. Kelly, Anglo-Saxon Charters 4, published for The British Academy by Oxford University Press, 1995

Charters of St Paul's, London, ed. S. E. Kelly, Anglo-Saxon Charters 10, published for The British Academy by Oxford University Press, 2004

Charters of Shaftesbury Abbey, ed. S. E. Kelly, Anglo-Saxon Charters 5, published for The British Academy by Oxford University Press, 1996

Charters of Sherborne, ed. M. A. O'Donovan, Anglo-Saxon Charters 3, published for The British Academy by Oxford University Press, 1988

Chronici Willelmi Thorne, ed. R. Twysden, *Historiae Anglicanae Scriptores X, Simeon Monachus Dunelmensis, Johannes Prior Hagustaldensis, Ricardus Prior Hagustaldensis, Ailredus Abbas Rievallensis, Radulphus de Diceto Londoniensis, Johannes Brompton Jornallensis, Gervasius Monachus Dorobornensis, Thomas Stubbs Dominicanus, Guilielmus Thorn Cantuariensis, Henricus Knighton Leicestrensis, ex Vetustis Manuscriptis, Nunc primum in Lucem Editi*, London, 1652

The Chronicle Attributed to John of Wallingford, ed. R. Vaughan, Camden Miscellany 21, London, 1958

Chronicle of the Bishops of Ribe, in E. Jørgensen, 'Ribe Bispekrønike', *Kirkehistoriske Samlinger* 6 (1933–5), pp. 23–33

Chronicon Abbatiae de Evesham ad annum 1418, ed. W. D. Macray, Rolls Series, Longman, London, 1863

Chronicon Abbatiae Rameseiensis, ed. W. D. Macray, Rolls Series, Longman, London, 1886

Chronicon Monasterii de Abingdon, ed. J. Stevenson, Rolls Series, Longman, London, 1858

Chronicon Roskildense, in M. C. Gertz (ed.), *Scriptores Minores Historiae Danicae Medii Aevi, ex Codicibus Denuo Recensuit*, Selskabet for Udgivelse af Kilder til Dansk Historie, Copenhagen, 1917–18

Codex Caesareus Upsaliensis: An Echternach Gospel Book of the Eleventh Century, ed. C. A. J. Nordenfalk, Almqvist & Wiksell, Stockholm, 1971

Codex Diplomaticus Aevi Saxonici, ed. J. M. Kemble, 6 vols., London, 1839–48

Councils and Synods with Other Documents Relating to the English Church. Vol. I: A.D. 871–1204, ed. D. Whitelock, M. Brett and C. N. L. Brooke, Clarendon Press, Oxford, 1981

Danakonunga Sǫgur: Skjöldunga Saga, Knýtlinga Saga, Ágrip af Sǫgu Danakonunga, ed. Bjarni Guðnason, Íslenzk Fornrit 35, Hið Íslenska Bókmenntafélag, Reykjavík, 1982

Danmarks Runeindskrifter, ed. L. Jacobsen and E. Moltke, Einar Munksgaard Forlag, Copenhagen, 1941–2

De Obsessione Dunelmi, in T. Arnold (ed.), *Symeonis Monachi Opera Omnia: Historia Ecclesiae Dunhelmensis*, Rolls Series, Longman, London, 1882–5

Domesday Book, 7, Dorset, ed. and trans. C. Thorn, F. Thorn and M. Newman, History from the Sources, Phillimore, Chichester, 1983

Domesday Book, 15, Gloucestershire, ed. and trans. J. Morris, History from the Sources, Phillimore, Chichester, 1975

Domesday Book, 19, Huntingdonshire, ed. and trans. J. Morris and S. Harvey, History from the Sources, Phillimore, Chichester, 1975

Domesday Book, 32, Essex, ed. and trans. J. Morris, History from the Sources, Phillimore, Chichester, 1983

Egils saga skallagrimsonar, Sigurður Nordal, Íslenzk Fornrit 2, Hið Íslenska Bókmenntafélag, Reykjavík, 1933

Den Eldre Gulatingslova, ed. B. Eithun, M. Rindal and T. Ulset, Riksarkivet Norrøne Tekster 6, Riksarkivet, Oslo, 1994

Ely Calendar in Cambridge, Trinity College, MS. O. 2, I, in B. Dickins (ed.), 'The Day of Byrhtnoth's Death and Other Obits from a Twelfth-Century Ely Kalender', *Leeds Studies in English*, 3 (1937), pp. 14–24

Encomium Emmae Reginae, ed. and trans. A. Campbell, Camden Society 3rd Series, 72, Royal Historical Society, London, 1949; reprinted with a supplementary introduction by S. Keynes as Camden Classic Reprints 4, Cambridge, 1998

Facsimiles of Anglo-Saxon Manuscripts, ed. W. B. Sanders, 3 vols., Ordnance Survey, Southampton, 1878–84

Fagrskinna, edited as *Ágrip af Nóregskonungasogum: Fagrskinna – Nóregs konunga tal*, ed. Bjarni Einarsson, Íslenzk Fornrit 29, Reykjavik, 1984

John Flete, *History of Westminster Abbey*, in J. Armitage Robinson (ed.), *The History of Westminster Abbey by John Flete*, Notes and Documents Relating to Westminster Abbey 2, Cambridge University Press, 1909

Gaimar, *Lestorie des Engles*, ed. A. Bell, Anglo-Norman Texts Society, Oxford, 1960

Die Gedenküberlieferung der Angelsachsen, ed. J. Gerchow, Arbeiten zur Frühmittelalterforschung 20, Walter de Gruyter, Berlin, 1988

Die Gesetze der Angelsachsen, ed. F. Liebermann, Max Niemeyer, Halle, 1898–1916

The Gesta Normannorum Ducum of William of Jumièges, Orderic Vitalis and Robert of Torigni, ed. and trans. E. M. C. Van Houts, Oxford Medieval Texts, Clarendon Press, Oxford, 1995

Goscelin, *De Vita Sancti Wlsini*, in C. H. Talbot (ed.), 'The Life of Saint Wulsin of Sherbourne by Goscelin', *Revue Bénédictine*, 69 (1959), pp. 68–85

Goscelin, *Liber Confortatorius*, ed. C. H. Talbot, Analecta Monastica, 3rd Series, 37 (1955), pp. 1–117

Goscelin, *Vita S. Edithe*, in A. Wilmart (ed.), 'La Légende de Ste Édith en Prose et Vers par le Moine Goscelin', *Analecta Bollandiana*, 56 (1938), pp. 5–101 and 265–307

Hemingi Chartularium Ecclesiæ Wigorniensis, ed. T. Hearne, Oxford, 1723

Henry of Huntingdon, *Historia Anglorum: The History of the English People*, ed. and trans. D. E. Greenway, Oxford Medieval Texts, Clarendon Press, Oxford, 1996

Herman, *Liber de Miraculis*, in T. Arnold (ed.), *Memorials of St Edmund's Abbey*, Rolls Series, Longman, London, 1890–6

Historia Ecclesie Abbendonensis: The History of the Church of Abingdon, ed. J. Hudson, 2 vols., Oxford University Press, 2002–7

Historia de Sancto Cuthberto: A History of Saint Cuthbert and a Record of his Patrimony, ed. and trans. T. Johnson South, Anglo-Saxon Texts 3, Brewer, Cambridge, 2002

Holinshed, R., J. Hooker et al., *The first and second volumes of Chronicles . . . now newlie augmented and continued (with manifold matters of singular note and worthie memorie) to the yeare 1586*, Henry Denham, London, 1587

Hugh Candidus, *Chronica*, in W. T. Mellows (ed.), *The Chronicle of Hugh Candidus, A Monk of Peterborough*, Oxford University Press on behalf of the Friends of Peterborough Cathedral, London, 1949

Joannis Lelandi Antiquarii, De Rebus Britannicus Collectanea, ed. T. Hearne, 2nd edn, London, 1774

John of Worcester, *The Chronicle of John of Worcester. Vol. II: The Annals from 450 to 1066*, ed. R. R. Darlington and P. McGurk, trans. J. Bray and P. McGurk, Oxford Medieval Texts, Clarendon Press, Oxford, 1995

The Letters and Poems of Fulberht of Chartres, ed. and trans. F. Behrends, Oxford Medieval Texts, Clarendon Press, Oxford, 1976

Liber Eliensis, ed. E. O. Blake, Camden Society 3rd Series, 92, Royal Historical Society, London, 1962

Liber Ruber, in H. H. E. Craster (ed.), 'The Red Book of Durham', *English Historical Review*, 40 (1925), pp. 504–35

Liber Vitæ Ecclesiæ Dunelmensis; nec non Obituaria duo ejusdem Ecclesiae, ed. J. Stevenson, Surtees Society, Nichols and Son, Edinburgh, 1834

The Liber Vitae of the New Minster and Hyde Abbey, Winchester: British Library Stowe 944: together with leaves from British Library Cotton Vespasian A. VIII and British Library Cotton Titus D. XXVII, ed. S. D. Keynes, Rosenkilde and Bagger, Copenhagen, 1996

Den Norsk-Isländske Skjaldedigtning, ed. and trans. Finnur Jónsson, 4 vols., Nordisk Forlag, Copenhagen and Kristiania (Oslo), 1912–15

Den Norsk-Isländska Skjaldedigtningen, ed. E. A. Kock, Gleerup, Lund, 1949–50

Norske Middelalder Dokumenter, ed. and trans. S. Bagge, S. H. Smedsdal and K. Helle, Universitetsforlaget, Bergen, 1974

Olafs Saga hins Helga: Die 'Legendarische Saga' über Olaf den Heiligen (Hs. Delagard. saml. nr. 8II), ed. and trans. into German, A. Heinrichs, Germanische Bibliothek, Vierte Reihe, Texte, Winter, Heidelberg, 1982

Osbern, *Translatio Sancti Ælfegi*, ed. A. R. Rumble and R. Morris, 'Textual Appendix: Translatio Sancti Ælfegi Cantuariensis Archepiscopi et Martiris (BHL 2519): Osbern's Account of the Translation of St Ælfheah's Relics from London to Canterbury, 8–11 June 1023', in A. R. Rumble (ed.), *The Reign of Cnut, King of England, Denmark and Norway*, Studies in the Early History of Britain, Leicester University Press, London/New York, 1994, pp. 283–315

The Parker Chronicle and Laws, a Facsimile, ed. R. Flower and A. H. Smith, Early English Text Society, Original Series, 208, London, 1941

Passio Olaui, in G. Storm (ed.), *Monumenta Historica Norvegiae. Latinske Kildeskrifter til Norges Historie i Middelalderen*, Norsk-Historisk Kjeldeskrift-Institutt, Kristiania (Oslo), 1880, pp. 125–44

Peterborough Chronicle, 1070–1154, ed. C. Clark, Oxford University Press, 1958

The Peterborough Chronicle: The Bodleian Manuscript Laud Misc. 636, ed. D. Whitelock, with an appendix by C. Clark, Early English Manuscripts in Facsimile 4, Rosenkilde and Bagger, Copenhagen, 1954

Poetry from the King's Sagas, Vol. 1, ed. D. Whaley, Skaldic Poetry of the Scandinavian Middle Ages, Brepols, Turnhout, 2012

Poetry from the King's Sagas, Vol. 2, ed. K. E. Gade, Skaldic Poetry of the Scandinavian Middle Ages, Brepols, Turnhout, 2009

The Poetry of Arnórr jarlaskáld: An Edition and Study, ed. D. Whaley, Brepols, Turnhout, 1998

'Red Book of Thorney', in J. Caley, H. Ellis and B. Bandinel (eds.), *Monasticon Anglicanum: A History of Abbies and other Monasteries, Hospitals, Frieries, and Cathedral and Collegiate Churches*, *with their Dependencies, in England and Wales; Also of All Such Scotch, Irish, and French Monasteries As Were in Any Manner Connected With Religious Houses in England. Together With a Particular Account of Their Respective Foundations, Grants, and Donations, and a Full Statement of Their Possessions, As Well Temporal As Spiritual. Originally Published in Latin by Sir William Dugdale, Kt. Garter Principal King at Arms. A New Edition, Enriched with a Large Accession of Materials Now First Printed from Ledger Books, Chartularies, Rolls, and other Documents Preserved in the National Archives, Public Libraries, and other Repositories; The History of each Religious Foundation in English Being Prefixed to its Respective Series of Latin Charters*, London, 1817–30, II, pp. 594–7

Die Regesten des Kaiserreiches unter Konrad II, 1024–1039, ed. J. F. Böhmer, ed. and newly revised by H. Appelt, Böhlau, Graz, 1951

Reyner, C., *Apostulatus Benedictinorum in Anglia, sive Disceptatio Historica de Antiquitate Ordinis Monachorum Nigrorum S. Benedicti in Regno Angliae*, Douai, 1626

Rimbert, *Vita Anskarii auctore Rimberto*, ed. G. Waitz, Monumenta Germaniae Historica, Scriptores Rerum Germanicarum 55, 1884

Robert of Torigni's *Chronica*, in R. Howlett (ed.), *Chronicles of the Reigns of Stephen, Henry II and Richard I*, Rolls Series, Longman, London, 1844–89

S. 949 and 982, in C. H. Haskins (ed.), 'A Charter of Cnut for Fécamp', *English Historical Review*, 33 (1918), pp. 342–4

Skáldatal, in Finnur Jónsson (ed.), *Snorra Edda Sturlusonar*, Gyldendalske Boghandel, Copenhagen, 1931

Slayter, W., *The History of Great Britanie from the first peopling of this island to this plesant raigne of o[u]r hapy and peacefull monarke K. James*, W. Stansby for Richard Meighen, London, 1621

Snorre Sturlasons Edda, Uppsala-Handskriften DG 11, ed. A. Grape, G. Kallstenius and O. Thorell, Almqvist & Wiksell, Stockholm, 1977

Snorri Sturluson, *Heimskringla*, ed. Bjarni Aðalbjarnarson, Íslenzk Fornrit 26–8, Hið Íslenska Bókmenntafélag, Reykjavík, 1941–51

'Supplement to *Jómsvíkinga saga*', in A. Campbell (ed.), *Encomium Emmae Reginae*, Camden Society 3rd Series, 72, Royal Historical Society, London, 1949; reprinted with a supplementary introduction by S. Keynes as Camden Classic Reprints 4, Cambridge, 1998, pp. 92–4

Symeon of Durham, *Historia Dunelmensis Ecclesiae*, in T. Arnold (ed.), *Symeonis Monachi Opera Omnia*, Rolls Series, Longman, London, 1882–5

Tewkesbury Chronicle, in J. Caley, H. Ellis and B. Bandinel (eds.), *Monasticon Anglicanum: A History of Abbies and other Monasteries, Hospitals, Frieries, and Cathedral and Collegiate Churches, with their Dependencies, in England and Wales; Also of All Such Scotch, Irish, and French Monasteries As Were in Any Manner Connected With Religious Houses in England. Together With a Particular Account of Their Respective Foundations, Grants, and Donations, and a Full Statement of Their Possessions, As Well Temporal As Spiritual. Originally Published in Latin by Sir William Dugdale, Kt. Garter Principal King at Arms. A New Edition, Enriched with a Large Accession of Materials Now First Printed from Ledger Books, Chartularies, Rolls, and other Documents Preserved in the National Archives, Public Libraries, and other Repositories; The History of each Religious Foundation in English Being Prefixed to its Respective Series of Latin Charters*, London, 1817–1830, II, pp. 59–65

Thangmarus Presbyter Hildesheimensis, *Vita Sancti Bernwardi episcopi Hildesheimensis, auctore Thangmaro*, ed. G. H. Pertz, *Patrologie Cursus Completus. Series Latina*, 140 (1844), cols. 393–436

Theodoricus Monachus, *Historia de Antiquitate*, ed. G. Storm, *Monumenta Historica Norvegiae. Latinske Kildeskrifter til Norges Historie i Middelalderen*, Norsk-Historisk Kjeldeskrift-Institutt, Kristiania (Oslo), 1880, pp. 1–68

Thietmari Merseburgensis Episcopi Chronicon. Die Chronik des Bischofs Thietmar von Merseburg und ihre Korveier Überarbeitung, ed. R. Holtzmann, Monumenta Germaniae Historica, Scriptores Rerum Germanicarum, Nova Series, Tomus 9, Berlin, 1935

Die Urkunden der Deutschen Könige und Kaiser, Bd. 2, Tl. 2. Die Urkunden Otto des III, ed. T. Sickel, Monumenta Germaniae Historica, Diplomatum Regum et Imperatorum Germaniae, Hanover, 1893

Vita Ædwardi regis qui apud Westmonasterium requiescit: The Life of King Edward who Rests at Westminster, ed. F. Barlow, Oxford Medieval Texts, Clarendon Press, Oxford, 1992

The Waltham Chronicle: An Account of the Discovery of Our Holy Cross at Montacute and its Conveyance to Waltham, ed. and trans. L. Watkiss, L. and M. Chibnall, Oxford Medieval Texts, Clarendon Press, Oxford, 1994

Widukindi Monachi Corbeiensis Rerum Gestarum Saxonicarum Libri Tres. Die Sachsengeschichte des Widukind von Korvei, ed. H. E. Lohmann and P. Hirsch, *Monumenta Germaniae Historica*. Scriptores Rerum Germanicarum in usum Scholarum ex Monumentis Germanicae Historicis Separatim Editi, Hanover, 1935

William of Malmesbury, *De Antiquitate Glastoniensis Ecclesiae*, in J. Scott (ed. and trans.), *The Early History of Glastonbury: An Edition, Translation and Study of William of Malmesbury's De Antiquitate Glastonie Ecclesie*, Boydell, Woodbridge, 1981

— *Gesta Pontificum Anglorum: The History of the English Bishops. Vol I: Text and Translation*, ed. and trans. M. Winterbottom and R. M. Thomson, Oxford Medieval Texts, Clarendon Press, Oxford, 2007

— *Gesta Regum Anglorum*, ed. and trans. R. A. B. Mynors, R. M. Thomson and M. Winterbottom, Oxford Medieval Texts, Clarendon Press, Oxford, 1987–99

— *Vita Wulfstani*, ed. R. R. Darlington, Camden Society 3rd Series, 40, Royal Historical Society, London, 1928

William Thorne, *Chronica*, in R. Twysden (ed.), *Historiae Anglicanae Scriptores X, Simeon Monachus Dunelmensis, Johannes Prior Hagustaldensis, Ricardus Prior Hagustaldensis, Ailredus Abbas Rievallensis, Radulphus de Diceto Londoniensis, Johannes Brompton Jornallensis, Gervasius Monachus Dorobornensis, Thomas Stubbs Dominicanus, Guilielmus Thorn Cantuariensis, Henricus Knighton Leicestrensis, ex Vetustis Manuscriptis, Nunc primum in Lucem Editi*, London, 1652

Wiponis Opera. Die Werke Wipos, ed. H. Bresslau, Monumenta Germaniae Historica. Scriptores Rerum Germanicarum in usum Scholarum Separatim Editi 59, Hanover, 1915, and reprinted 1977

Wolfhere, *Vita Godehardi episcopi posterior*, ed. G. H. Pertz, Monumenta Germaniae Historica, Scriptores (in Folio) 11, Hanover, 1854, pp. 196–218

Wulfstan, *Sermo Lupi ad Anglos*, ed. D. Whitelock, Methuen's Old English Library, London, 1976

The York Gospels, a Facsimile with Introductory Essays, ed. N. Barker, Roxburghe Club, London, 1986

SECONDARY SOURCES

Abrams, L., 'The Anglo-Saxons and the Christianization of Scandinavia', *Anglo-Saxon England*, 24 (1995), pp. 213–49

Almqvist, B., *Norrön Niddiktning: Traditionshistoriska Studier i Versmagi*, Almqvist & Wiksell, Stockholm, 1974

Andersen, M., M. Højog and S. A. Sørensen, 'Et Vikingetidshus fra Bredgade i Roskilde', *Romu* (Roskilde) (1986), pp. 33–50

Andersen, P. S., *Samlingen av Norge og Kristningen av Landet 800–1130*, Handbok i Norges Historie 2, Universitetsforlaget, Bergen/Oslo/Tromsø, 1977

Andrén, A., 'Stadsbilden', in A. W. Mårtensson (ed.), *Uppgrävt förflutet för PKbanken i Lund. En Investering i Arkeologi*, Archaeologica Lundensia: Investigationes de Antiquitatibus Urbis Lundae 7, Kulturhistoriska Museet, Lund, 1976, pp. 21–40

Angenendt, A., 'How Was a Confraternity Made? The Evidence of Charters', in D. and L. Rollason (eds.), *The Durham 'Liber Vitae' and its Context*, Regions and Regionalism in History, 1, Boydell, Woodbridge, 2004, pp. 207–19

Arnskov, P., *Bogen om Slagelse. Historiske og Topografiske Skildringer af Slagelse Gennem Aarene*, Age Bøggild, Slagelse, 1931

Arup, E., 'Kong Svend 2.s Biografi', *Scandia, Tidskrift för Historisk Forskning*, 4:1 (1931), pp. 55–101

Astås, R., 'Óláfr, St.', in P. Pulsiano, *Medieval Scandinavia: An Encyclopedia*, Garland Reference Library of the Humanities 934 and Garland Encyclopedias of the Middle Ages 1, Garland, New York, 1993, pp. 445–6

Balle, S., 'Ulf Jarl og Drabet i Roskilde', *Historisk Årbog for Roskilde Amt* (1983), pp. 23–59

Barlow, F., *Edward the Confessor*, English Monarchs Series, Yale University Press, London, 1970

— *The English Church 1000–1066: A History of the Anglo-Norman Church*, 2nd edn, Longman, London, 1979

— *The Godwins: The Rise and Fall of a Noble Dynasty*, Pearson/Longman, London, 2003

— 'Two Notes: Cnut's Second Pilgrimage and Queen Emma's Disgrace in 1043', *English Historical Review*, 73 (1958), pp. 649–56

— *William Rufus*, Methuen, London, 1990

Barnes, M., 'Towards an Edition of the Scandinavian Runic Inscriptions of the British Isles: Some Thoughts', *Northern Studies/Scottish Society for Northern Studies*, 29 (1992), pp. 32–42

Bates, D., J. Crick and S. Hamilton, *Writing Medieval Biography: Essays in Honour of Frank Barlow*, Boydell, Woodbridge, 2006

Baxter, S., *The Earls of Mercia: Lordship and Power in Late Anglo-Saxon England*, Oxford Historical Monographs, Oxford University Press, 2007

Becker, C. J., 'The Coinages of Harthacnut and Magnus the Good at Lund c.1040–1046', in C. J. Becker (ed.), *Studies in Northern Coinages of the Eleventh Century*, Det kongelige Videnskabernes Selskab, Historisk-Filosofiske Skrifter 9:4, Copenhagen, 1981, pp. 119–74

Beech, G., 'Biography and the Study of Eleventh-Century Society: Peter II of Poitiers (1087–1115)', *Francia: Forschungen zur Westeuropaischen Geschichte*, 7 (1979), pp. 101–21

— 'England and Aquitaine in the Century before the Norman Conquest', *Anglo-Saxon England*, 19 (1990), pp. 81–101

Bethurum, D., *The Homilies of Wulfstan*, Clarendon Press, Oxford, 1957

Biddle, M. and B. Kjølbye-Biddle, 'Danish Royal Burials: Cnut and his Family', in R. Lavelle and S. Roffey, *Danes in Wessex: The Scandinavian Impact on Southern England, c.800–c.1100*, Oxbow, Oxford/Philadelphia, 2016, pp. 212–49

Bill, J. and A. Daly, 'The Plundering of the Ship Graves from Oseberg and Gokstad: An Example of Power Politics?', *Antiquity*, 86 (2012), pp. 808–24

Birch, D. J., *Pilgrimage to Rome in the Middle Ages: Continuity and Change*, Boydell, Woodbridge, 2000

Birkebæck, F. A., 'Det Ældste Roskilde', in F. A. Birkbæck (ed.), *13 Bidrag til Roskilde By og Egn's Historie. Udgivet i Andledning af Roskilde's Museum's 50 Års Jubilæum*, Roskilde Museum, 1979, pp. 80–92

Birkedahl, P., 'Sebbersund – en Handelsplads med Trækirke ved Limfjorden – Forbindelser til Norge', in *Havn og Handel i 1000 År, Karmøyseminaret 1997*, Dreyer Bok, Stavanger, 2000, pp. 31–9

Bjarni Guðnason, 'Theodoricus og íslenskir Sagnaritarar', in E. G. Pétursson and J. Kristjánsson (eds.), *Sjötíu Ritgerðir Helgaðar Jakobi Benediktssyni*, Stofnun Árna Magnússonar, Reykjavík, 1977, pp. 107–20

— *Um Skjöldungasögu*, Bókaútgáfa Menningarsjóðs, Reykjavík, 1963

Björkmann, E., *Nordische Personenamen in England in Alt- und Frühmittel-Englischer Zeit*, Studien zur Englischen Philologie, 37, Max Niemeyer, Halle, 1910

Blackburn, M. A. S., 'Do Cnut the Great's First Coins as King of Denmark Date from Before 1018?', in K. Jonsson and B. Malmer (eds.), *Sigtuna Papers: Proceedings of the Viking-Age Coinage Symposium at Sigtuna, 1989, Commentationes de nummis saeculorum IX–XI in Suecia repertis*. Nova Series, 6, Stockholm/London, 1990, pp. 52–65

Blomkvist, R., *Tusentalets Lund*, Det Gamla Lund, Lund, 1941

Bolton, T., 'Ælfgifu of Northampton: Cnut the Great's "other woman" ', *Nottingham Medieval Studies*, 51 (2007), pp. 247–68

— *Conquest and Controversy: The Early Career of Odda of Deerhurst*, Deerhurst lecture for 2006, Deerhurst, 2010
— *The Empire of Cnut the Great: Conquest and Consolidation of Power in Northern Europe in the Early Eleventh Century*, The Northern World 40, Brill, Leiden/Boston, 2009
— 'English Political Refugees at the Court of Sveinn Ástríðarson, King of Denmark (1042–76)', *Mediaeval Scandinavia*, 15 (2005), pp. 17–36
— 'A Newly Emergent Mediaeval Manuscript Containing *Encomium Emmae Reginae* with the Only Known Complete Text of the Recension Prepared for King Edward the Confessor', *Mediaeval Scandinavia*, 19 (2009), pp. 205–21
— 'Preliminary Investigations into the Scholia of Adam of Bremen's *Gesta Hammaburgensis ecclesiae pontificum*', *Mediaeval Scandinavia* (forthcoming)
— 'A Textual Historical Response to Adam of Bremen's Witness to the Activities of the Uppsala-Cult', in G. Steinsland (ed.), *Transformasjoner i Vikingtid og Norrøn Middelalder*, Unipub forlag, Oslo, 2006, pp. 61–91
— 'Was the Family of Earl Siward and Earl Waltheof a Lost Line of the Ancestors of the Danish Royal Family?', *Nottingham Medieval Studies*, 51 (2007), pp. 41–71
Boyle, E., 'A Welsh Record of an Anglo-Saxon Political Mutilation', *Anglo-Saxon England*, 35 (2006), pp. 245–9
Branca, A. et al., 'Detektorfunna föremål från Järnåldern. Översikt av Materialiet vid Årsskriftet 1998/1999', in B. Hårdh (ed.), *Fynden i Centrum: Keramik, Glas och Metal från Uppåkra*, Uppåkrastudier 2, Acta Archaeologica Lundensia Series in 8° 30, Almqvist & Wiksell International, Häftad, 1999, pp. 59–66
Bresslau, H., 'Ein Beitrag zur Kenntnis von Konrads II: Beziehungen zu Byzanz und Dänemark', *Forschungen zur deutschen Geschichte*, 10 (1870), pp. 607–13
— *Jahrbücher des Deutschen Reichs unter Konrads II, erster Band, 1024–1031*, Dunder und Humblot, Leipzig, 1879
Brett, M., 'John of Worcester and his Contemporaries', in R. H. C. Davis and J. M. Wallace Hadrill (eds.), *The Writing of History in the Middle Ages: Essays Presented to R. W. Southern*, Oxford University Press, 1981, pp. 101–26
Brooks, N., *The Early History of the Church of Canterbury: Christ Church from 597 to 1066*, Studies in the Early History of Britain, Leicester University Press, 1984
Campbell, A., 'Knúts Saga', *Saga-Book of the Viking Society*, 13 (1946–53), pp. 238–48
— *Skaldic Verse and Anglo-Saxon History*, Dorothea Coke Memorial Lecture, Constable, London, 1970
Campbell, J., 'The Late Anglo-Saxon State: A Maximum View', *Proceedings of the British Academy*, 87 (1994), pp. 39–65
— 'Some Agents and Agencies of the Late Anglo-Saxon State' in J. C. Holt (ed.), *Domesday Studies: Papers Read at the Novocentenary Conference of the Royal Historical Society and the Institute of British Geographers, Winchester, 1986*, Boydell, Woodbridge, 1987, pp. 201–25
Christiansen, E., 'The Churches of St. Clemens in Scandinavia', *Archaeologia Lundensia*, 3 (1968), pp. 103–16
— *Saxo Grammaticus, Danorum Regum Heroumque Historia, Books X–XVI: The Text of the First Edition with Translation and Commentary in Three Volumes*, BAR International Series, 84 and 118, Oxford, 1980–1
— (trans.), *The Works of Sven Aggeson: Twelfth-Century Danish Historian*, Viking Society for Northern Research, Text Series, 9, London, 1992
Christensen, T., 'Lejre Beyond Legend – The Archaeological Evidence', *Journal of Danish Archaeology*, 10 (1991), pp. 163–85
Christensen, T., A. C. Larsen, S. Larsson and A. Vince, 'Early Glazed Ware from Medieval Denmark', *Medieval Ceramics*, 18 (1994), pp. 67–76
Christensen, T. and N. Lynnerup, 'Kirkegården i Kongemarken', in N. Lund (ed.), *Kristendommen i Danmark før 1050. Et Symposium i Roskilde den 5–7 Februar 2003*, Roskilde Museums Forlag, Roskilde, 2004, pp. 142–52
Cinthio, M., *De Första Stadsborna: Medeltida Graver och Människor i Lund*, Brutus Östlings Bokförlag, Stockholm/Stehag, 2002

— 'Myntverk och Myntare i Lund', *Kulturen: En Årsbok till Medlemmarna av Kulturhistoriska Föreningen för Södra Sverige* (1990), pp. 48–53

— 'Trinitatiskyrkan, Gravarna och de förste Lundboarna', in N. Lund (ed.), *Kristendommen i Danmark før 1050. Et Symposium i Roskilde den 5–7 Februar 2003*, Roskilde Museums Forlag, Roskilde, 2004, pp. 159–73

Clarke, H. and B. Ambrosiani, *Towns in the Viking Age*, rev. repr., Leicester University Press, 1995

Clarke, P. A., *The English Nobility under Edward the Confessor*, Oxford Historical Monographs, Clarendon Press, Oxford, 1994

Classen, A. (ed.), *Childhood in the Middle Ages and the Renaissance: The Results of a Paradigm Shift in the History of Mentality*, Walter de Gruyter, Berlin, 2005

Cotgrave, J., *The English Treasury of Wit and Language collected out of the most, and best of our English drammatick poems; methodically digested into common places for generall use*, Humphrey Moseley, London, 1655

Crawford, B., 'The Cult of Clement of Denmark', *Historie*, 2 (2006), pp. 236–82

Crook, J., ' "A Worthy Antiquity": The Movement of King Cnut's Bones in Winchester Cathedral', in A. R. Rumble (ed.), *The Reign of Cnut, King of England, Denmark and Norway*, Studies in the Early History of Britain, Leicester University Press, London/New York, 1994, pp. 165–91

Davidson, D. L., 'Hákon jarl ("earl") Sigurðarson', in P. Pulsiano, *Medieval Scandinavia: An Encyclopedia*, Garland Reference Library of the Humanities 934 and Garland Encyclopedias of the Middle Ages 1, Garland, New York, 1993, p. 259

Demidoff, L., 'The Death of Sven Forkbeard – in Reality and Later Tradition', *Mediaeval Scandinavia*, 11 (1978–9), pp. 30–47

Deshman, R., 'Kingship and Christology in Ottonian and Anglo-Saxon Art', *Fruhmittelalterliche Studien*, 10 (1976), pp. 367–405

Dickins, B., 'The Cult of S. Olave in the British Isles', *Saga-Book of the Viking Society*, 12 (1939), pp. 53–80

Dumville, D. N., 'Some Aspects of Annalistic Writing at Canterbury in the Eleventh and Early Twelfth Centuries', *Peritia*, 2 (1983), pp. 23–57

Edwards, D., 'Christian and Pagan References in Eleventh-Century Norse Poetry: The Case of Arnórr Jarlaskáld', *Saga-Book of the Viking Society*, 21 (1982–3), pp. 34–53

Ellehøj, S., *Studier over den ældste norrønne Historieskrivning*, Bibliotheca Arnamagnæana, 26, Copenhagen, 1965

Erdmann, C., *The Origin of the Idea of Crusade* (trans. W. Goffart from *Die Entstehung des Kreuzzugsgedankens*, 1935), Princeton University Press, 1977

Felitzen, O. von, and revised by J. Insley, 'The Onomasticon', in L. Rollason (ed.), *The Thorney Liber Vitae: London, British Library, Additional MS 40,000, fols. 1–12r, Edition, Facsimile and Study*, Boydell, Woodbridge, 2015, pp. 125–210

— *The Pre-Conquest Personal Names of Domesday Book*, Nomina Germanica, Arkiv för Germansk Namnforskning, 3, Jöran Sahlgren, Uppsala, 1937

Feveile, C., *Ribe Studier – Det ældste Ribe. Udgravninger på nordsiden af Ribe Å 1984–2000*, Jysk Arkæologisk Selskabs Skrifter, 51, Højberg, 2006

Fidjestøl, B., *Det Norrøne Fyrstediktet*, Nordisk Institutts Skriftserie, Universitetet i Bergen, 11, Bergen, 1982

— ' "Have you heard a poem worth more?" A Note on the Economic Background of Early Skaldic Praise-Poetry', in O. E. Haugen and E. Mundal (eds.) and P. Foote (trans.), *Bjarne Fidjestøl: Collected Papers*, The Viking Collection: Studies in Northern Civilization, 9, Odense University Press, 1997, pp. 117–32

— 'Norse-Icelandic Composition in the Oral Period', in O. E. Haugen and E. Mundal (eds.) and P. Foote (trans.), *Bjarne Fidjestøl: Collected Papers*, The Viking Collection: Studies in Northern Civilization, 9, Odense University Press, 1997, pp. 303–32

Finberg, H. P. R., 'The House of Ordgar and the Foundation of Tavistock Abbey', *English Historical Review*, 58 (1943), pp. 190–201

— *Lucerna. Studies of Some Problems in the Early History of England*, Macmillan, London, 1964

Finlay, A., *Fagrskinna: A Catalogue of the Kings of Norway: A Translation with Introduction and Notes*, The Northern World Series, 7, Brill, Leiden, 2004

Finnur Jónsson, *Den Oldnorske og Oldislandske Litteraturs*, G. E. C. Gads forlag, Copenhagen, 1858–1934

Fleming, R., 'Christchurch's Sisters and Brothers: An Edition and Discussion of Canterbury Obituary Lists', in M. A. Meyer (ed.), *The Culture of Christendom: Essays in Medieval History in Commemoration of Denis L. T. Bethell*, Hambleton, London, 1993, pp. 115–54

Fletcher, R., *Bloodfeud: Murder and Revenge in Anglo-Saxon England*, Allen Lane, London, 2002

Foot, S., *Athelstan: The First King of England*, English Monarchs Series, Yale University Press, New Haven/London, 2011

Foote, P. (trans.), *Bjarne Fidjestøl: Collected Papers*, The Viking Collection: Studies in Northern Civilization, 9, Odense University Press, 1997, pp. 303–32

Foote, P. G., 'Wrecks and Rhymes', in T. Andersson and K. I. Sandred (eds.), *The Vikings: Proceedings of the Symposium of the Faculty of Arts of Uppsala University June 6–9, 1977*, Acta Universitatis Upsaliensis, 8, Almqvist & Wiksell, Stockholm, 1978, pp. 57–66; reprinted in M. Barnes, H. Bekker-Nielsen and G. W. Weber, *Aurvandilstá: Norse Studies*, Odense University Press, 1984, pp. 222–35

Frank, R., 'King Cnut in the Verse of his Skalds', in A. R. Rumble (ed.), *The Reign of Cnut, King of England, Denmark and Norway*, Studies in the Early History of Britain, Leicester University Press, London/New York, 1994, pp. 106–24

— 'When Poets Address Princes', in Gísli Sigurðsson, Guðrún Kvaran and Sigurgeir Steingrímsson (eds.), *Sagnaþing Helgað Jónasi Kristjánssyni Sjötugum 10. Apríl 1994*, Hið Íslenska Bókmenntafélag, Reykjavík, 1994, pp. 189–95

Freeman, E. A., *A History of the Norman Conquest of England, its Causes and its Results*, 6 vols., 3rd edn, Oxford University Press, 1877–9

Fuglesang, S. H., *Some Aspects of the Ringerike Style: A Phase of 11th-Century Scandinavian Art*, Mediaeval Scandinavia Supplements, 1, Odense University Press, 1980

Gade, K., *The Structure of Old Norse Dróttkvætt Poetry*, Islandica, 49, Cornell University Press, Ithaca, NY/London, 1995

Gade, K. and E. Marold (eds.), *Skaldic Poetry of the Scandinavian Middle Ages*, Brepols, Turnhout, forthcoming.

Gallén, J., 'Vem var Ulf Jarl, Sven Estridsens Far?', *Scandia, Tidskrift för Historisk Forskning*, 58:1 (1992), pp. 13–30

Gameson, R., 'Planning, Production and Paleography', in L. Rollason (ed.), *The Thorney Liber Vitae: London, British Library, Additional MS 40,000, fols. 1–12r, Edition, Facsimile and Study*, Boydell, Woodbridge, 2015, pp. 115–24

Gelting, M. H., 'Elusive Bishops: Remembering, Forgetting, and Remaking the History of the Early Danish Church', in S. Gilsdorf (ed.), *The Bishop: Power and Piety at the First Millennium*, Neue Aspekte der Europäischen Mittelalterforschung, 4, Münster/Hamburg/Berlin, 2004, pp. 169–200

— 'Un Évêque danois élève de Fulbert de Chartres?', in M. Rouche (ed.), *Fulbert de Chartres: Précurseur de l'Europe médiévale?*, Université Paris-Sorbonne, 2008, pp. 63–75

— 'Forholdet mellem Liber Daticus og Memoriale Fratrum', in Eva Nilsson Nylander (ed.), *Mellan Evighet Och Vardag: Lunds Domkyrkas Martyrologium Liber Daticus Vetustior (den Äldre Gåvoboken): Studier Och Faksimilutgåva*, Skrifter Utgivna av Universitetsbiblioteket i Lund, 2015, pp. 131–49

— 'Poppo's Ordeals: Courtier Bishops and the Success of Christianization at the Turn of the Millennium', *Viking and Medieval Scandinavia*, 6 (2010), pp. 101–33

— 'Saxo Grammaticus in the Archives', in L. Melve and S. Sønnesyn (eds.), *The Creation of Medieval Northern Europe: Christianisation, Social Transformations, and Historiography*, Dreyer, Oslo, 2012, pp. 322–5

— 'Uløste Opgaver: Adam af Bremen, Saxo Grammaticus og Knytlinga Saga', *Scandia,*
   Tidskrift för Historisk Forskning, 77:2 (2011), pp. 126–43
Gerchow, J., 'Prayers for King Cnut: The Liturgical Commemoration of a Conqueror', in
   C. Hicks (ed.), *England in the Eleventh Century: Proceedings of the 1990 Harlaxton Symposium,*
   Harlaxton Medieval Studies, 2, Paul Watkins Medieval Studies, 12, Stamford, 1992, pp.
   219–38
Gillingham, J., 'Chronicles and Coins as Evidence for Levels of Tribute and Taxation in
   Late Tenth- and Early Eleventh-Century England', *English Historical Review,* 105 (1990),
   pp. 939–50
— '"The Most Precious Jewel in the English Crown"': Levels of Danegeld and Heregeld in
   the Early Eleventh Century', *English Historical Review,* 104 (1989), pp. 373–84
Graham-Campbell, J., *Viking Art,* Thames & Hudson, London, 2013
Gransden, A., *Historical Writing. Vol. I: c.550–c.1307,* Routledge, London, 1996
Gräslund, B., 'Knut den Store och Sveariket: Slaget vid Helgeå i Ny Belysning', *Scandia,*
   Tidskrift för Historisk Forskning, 52 (1986), pp. 211–38
Grierson, P., 'Domesday Book, the Geld de Moneta and Monetagium: A Forgotten Minting
   Reform', *British Numismatic Journal,* 55 (1986), pp. 84–94
Grinder-Hansen, K., 'Ringsted som Møntsted', in J. S. Jensen (ed.), *Tusindtallets Danske
   Mønter fra den Kongelige Mønt- og Medaillesamling: Danish Coins from the 11th Century in the Royal
   Collection of Coins and Medals,* Nationalmuseet, Copenhagen, 1995, pp. 42–3
Gustin, I., 'Vikter och Varuutbyte i Uppåkra', in B. Hårdh (ed.), *Fynden i Centrum: Keramik,
   Glas och Metal från Uppåkra,* Uppåkrastudier, 2, Acta Archaeologica Lundensia Series in 8°
   30, Almqvist & Wiksell International, Häftad, 1999, pp. 243–70
Guðrún Nordal, 'Skáldatal and its Manuscript Context in Kringla and Uppsalaedda', in
   J. R. Haglund (ed.), *Sagas and the Norwegian Experience: "Sagene og Noreg",* Preprints of the
   10th International Saga Conference, Trondheim, 3–9 August 1997, Noregs Teknisk-
   Naturvitskaplege Universitet, Trondheim, 1997, pp. 205–12
— *Tools of Literacy: The Role of Skaldic Verse in Icelandic Textual Culture of the Twelfth and Thirteenth
   Centuries,* Toronto University Press, 2001
Haki Antonsson, 'The Cult of St. Óláfr in the Eleventh Century and Kievan Rus',
   Middelalderforum, Tverrfaglig Tidsskrift for Middelalderstudier, 1–2 (2003), pp. 143–60
Hare, M., 'Cnut and Lotharingia: Two Notes', *Anglo-Saxon England,* 29 (2000), pp. 261–78
Harris, J. D., 'The Site of Alney, AD 1016', *Glevensis: The Gloucester and District Archaeological
   Research Group Review,* 26 (1992), pp. 11–12
Hart, C. J. R., *Early Charters of Eastern England,* Leicester University Press, 1966
Hauberg, P., *Myntforhold og Udmyntninger i Danmark indtil 1146,* Det Kongelige Videnskabernes
   Selskabs Skrifter, 6. Række, Historisk og Filosofisk Afdeling Series, 5.1, Copenhagen,
   1900
Heijne, C. von, 'Viking-Age Hoards and Socio-Political Changes in the Slågarp Area,
   Skåne', *Lund Archaeological Review,* 7 (2003), pp. 109–21
Helgesson, B., 'HELGE – ett Spår av en Tidig Kristen Mission i Uppåkra?', in B. Hårdh
   (ed.), *Fynden i Centrum: Keramik, Glas och Metal från Uppåkra,* Uppåkrastudier, 2, Acta
   Archaeologica Lundensia Series in 8° 30, Almqvist & Wiksell International, Häftad,
   1999, pp. 191–241
Hellberg, S., 'Slaget vid Nesjar och Sven Jarl Håkonsson', *Scripta Islandica,* 23 (1972), pp.
   21–30
Henriksson, V., *St. Olav of Norway: King, Saint – and Enigma,* Tano, Oslo, 1985
Herter, H., 'Effeminatus', in T. Klauser (ed.), *Reallexikon fuer Antike und Christentum: Sachworterbuch
   zur Auxeinandersetzung des Christentums mit der antiken Welt,* Hiersemann, Stuttgart, 1950–
Heslop, T. A., 'The Production of *de luxe* Manuscripts and the Patronage of King Cnut and
   Queen Emma', *Anglo-Saxon England,* 19 (1990), pp. 151–95
Hill, D., 'Trends in the Development of Towns during the Reign of Ethelred II', in D. Hill
   (ed.), *Ethelred the Unready: Papers from the Millenary Conference,* BAR British Series, 59, 1978,
   pp. 213–26

— 'An Urban Policy for Cnut?', in A. R. Rumble (ed.), *The Reign of Cnut, King of England, Denmark and Norway*, Studies in the Early History of Britain, Leicester University Press, London/New York, 1994, pp. 101–5

Hjermind, J., 'Bestemmelse af Proveniens og Brændingstemperatur på Tidligmiddelalderlig Keramik, Lerklining m.v. fra Viborg og Spangsbjerg', in M. Iversen et al., *Viborg Søndersø 1018–1030: Arkæologi og Naturvidenskab i et Værkstedsområde fra Vikingetid*, Jysk Arkæologisk Selskab, Viborg Stiftsmuseum, 2005, pp. 423–38

— 'Keramik', in M. Iversen et al., *Viborg Søndersø 1018–1030: Arkæologi og Naturvidenskab i et Værkstedsområde fra Vikingetid*, Jysk Arkæologisk Selskab, Viborg Stiftsmuseum, 2005, pp. 415–22

Hofmann, D., *Nordisch-Englische Lehnbeziehungen der Wikingerzeit*, Bibliotheca Arnamagnæana, 14, E. Munksgaard, Copenhagen, 1955

Holst, M. K., M. D. Jessen and A. Pedersen, *Runestenens Jelling*, Enogtredivte Tværfaglige Vikingesymposium, Aarhus Universitet, Aarhus, 2012

Holst, M. K., M. D. Jessen, S. W. Andersen and A. Pedersen, 'Kongens Gård i Jelling? Et Nyt Anlæg fra Harald Blåtands Tid', *Nationalmuseets Arbejdsmark* (2011), pp. 170–81

Hooper, N., 'Edgar the Ætheling: Anglo-Saxon Prince, Rebel and Crusader', *Anglo-Saxon England*, 14 (2007), pp. 197–215

— 'Historiography and Hagiography at Saint-Wandrille: The "Inventio et Miracula Sancti Vulfranni"', *Anglo-Norman Studies*, 12 (1989), pp. 233–51

— 'The Housecarls in England in the Eleventh Century', *Anglo-Norman Studies: Proceedings of the Battle Conference*, 7 (1984), pp. 161–76

— 'Military Developments in the Reign of Cnut', in A. R. Rumble (ed.), *The Reign of Cnut, King of England, Denmark and Norway*, Studies in the Early History of Britain, Leicester University Press, London/New York, 1994, pp. 89–100

Houts, E. M. C. van, 'A Note on Jezebel and Semiramis, Two Latin Norman Poems from the Early Eleventh Century', *Journal of Medieval Latin*, 2 (1992), pp. 18–24

— 'The Political Relations between Normandy and England before 1066 according to the "Gesta Normannorum Ducum"', in R. Foreville (ed.), *Les Mutations socio-culturelles au tournant des XIe–XIIe siècles*, Actes du IVe colloque internationale Anselmien, Paris, pp. 85–97

Howard, I., *Swein Forkbeard's Invasions and the Danish Conquest of England, 991–1017*, Warfare in History, Boydell, Woodbridge, 2003

Hunter Blair, P., 'Some Observations on the "*Historia Regum*" attributed to Symeon of Durham', in N. K. Chadwick (ed.), *Celt and Saxon: Studies in the Early British Border*, Cambridge University Press, 1964, pp. 63–118

Hvass, S., 'Viking-Age Villages in Denmark – New Investigations', in S. O. Lindquist (ed.), *Society and Trade in the Baltic during the Viking Age: Papers of the VIIth Visby Symposium held at Gotlands Fornsal, Gotland's Historical Museum, Visby, August 15th–19th, 1983*, Acta Visbyensia 7, Visby, 1985, pp. 211–27

— 'Vikingebebyggelsen i Vorbasse', *Mark og Montre fra Sydvestjyske Museer*, Kulturhistoriske Museer i Ribe amt (1977), pp. 18–29

— 'Vorbasse: The Viking-Age Settlement at Vorbasse, Jutland', *Acta Archaeologica*, 50 (1979), pp. 137–72

Indrebø, G., 'Aagrip', *Edda*, 17 (1922), pp. 18–65

Insley, C., 'The Family of Wulfric Spott: An Anglo-Saxon Mercian Marcher Dynasty?', in D. Roffe (ed.), *The English and their Legacy, 900–1200: Essays in Honour of Ann Williams*, Boydell, Woodbridge, 2012, pp. 115–28

— 'Politics, Conflict and Kinship in Early Eleventh-Century Mercia', *Midlands History*, 25 (2000), pp. 28–42

Jacobsen, L., *Svenskevældets Fald: Studier til Danmarks Oldhistorie i filologisk og runologisk Lys*, Levin and Munksgaard, Copenhagen, 1929

Jensen, J. S., 'Ribes Mønter i 1000-tallet', in J. S. Jensen (ed.), *Tusindtallets Danske Mønter fra den Kongelige Mønt- og Medaillesamling: Danish Coins from the 11th Century in the Royal Collection of Coins and Medals*, Nationalmuseet, Copenhagen, 1995, pp. 48–9

Jeppesen, T. G., *Middelalder-Landsbyens Opståen: Kontinuitet og Brud i den Fynske Agrarbebyggelse mellem Yngre Jernalder og Tidlig Middelalder*, Fynske Studier, 11, Odense, 1981
Jesch, J., 'History in the Political Sagas', *Medium Aevum*, 62:2 (1993), pp. 210–20
— 'Reading the Jelling Inscription', in P. Gammeltoft (ed.), *Beretning fra enogtredivte tværfaglige Vikingesymposium*, Forlaget Wormianum, Højbjerg, 2013, pp. 7–18
Jochens, J., 'The Politics of Reproduction: Medieval Norwegian Kingship', *American Historical Review*, 92 (1987), pp. 327–49
John, E., 'The *Encomium Emmae Reginae* – A Riddle and a Solution', *Bulletin of the John Rylands Library*, 63 (1980), pp. 58–94
Jonsson, K., 'The Coinage of Cnut', in A. R. Rumble (ed.), *The Reign of Cnut, King of England, Denmark and Norway*, Studies in the Early History of Britain, Leicester University Press, London/New York, 1994, pp. 193–230
Jón Viðar Sigurðsson, 'Tendencies in the Historiography on the Medieval Nordic States (to 1350)', in J. S. Amelang and S. Beer (eds.), *Public Power in Europe: Studies in Historical Transformation*, Edizioni Plus, Pisa, 2006, pp. 1–15
Kapelle, W. E., *The Norman Conquest of the North: The Region and its Transformation, 1000–1135*, Croom Helm, London, 1979
Karkov, C. E., *Ruler Portraits of Anglo-Saxon England*, Anglo-Saxon Studies, 3, Boydell, Woodbridge, 2004
Keats-Rohan, K. S. B., 'The Prosopography', in L. Rollason (ed.), *The Thorney Liber Vitae: London, British Library, Additional MS 40,000, fols. 1–12r, Edition, Facsimile and Study*, Boydell, Woodbridge, 2015, pp. 211–68
Kennedy, A., 'Cnut's Law Code of 1018', *Anglo-Saxon England*, 11 (1983), pp. 57–81
Ker, N. R., 'The Additions in Old English', in N. Barker (ed.), *The York Gospels: A Facsimile with Introductory Essays by Jonathan Alexander, Patrick McGurk, Simon Keynes and Bernard Barr*, Roxburgh Club, London, 1986, pp. 81–99
— *Catalogue of Manuscripts Containing Anglo-Saxon*, Clarendon Press, Oxford, 1957
— 'The Handwriting of Archbishop Wulfstan', in P. Clemoes and K. Hughes (eds.), *England before the Conquest: Studies in Primary Sources Presented to Dorothy Whitelock*, Cambridge University Press, 1971, pp. 315–31
Keynes, S. D., *An Atlas of Attestations in Anglo-Saxon Charters c.670–1066. Vol. I: Tables*, ASNC Guides Texts and Studies, 5, Cambridge, 2002; online at http://www.kemble.asnc.cam.ac.uk/node/30
— 'The Æthelings in Normandy', *Anglo-Norman Studies*, 13 (1991), pp. 173–205
— 'The Burial of King Æthelred the Unready at St Paul's', in D. Roffe (ed.), *The English and their Legacy, 900–1200: Essays in Honour of Ann Williams*, Boydell, Woodbridge, 2012, pp. 129–48
— 'Church Councils, Royal Assemblies, and Anglo-Saxon Royal Diplomas', in G. R. Owen-Crocker and B. W. Schneider (eds.), *Kingship, Legislation and Power in Anglo-Saxon England*, Publications of the Manchester Centre for Anglo-Saxon Studies, 2013, pp. 17–182
— 'Cnut's Earls', in A. R. Rumble (ed.), *The Reign of Cnut, King of England, Denmark and Norway*, Studies in the Early History of Britain, Leicester University Press, London/New York, 1994, pp. 43–88
— 'The Declining Reputation of King Æthelred the Unready', in D. Hill (ed.), *Ethelred the Unready: Papers from the Millenary Conference*, BAR British Series, 59, Oxford, 1978, pp. 227–53
— *Deerhurst, A.D. 1016: Eadric Streona and the Danish Conquest of England*, Deerhurst Lecture for 2004 (forthcoming)
— *The Diplomas of King Æthelred the Unready, 978–1016: A Study in their Use as Historical Evidence*, Cambridge Studies in Medieval Life and Thought, 3rd Series, 13, Cambridge University Press, 1980
— 'Giso, Bishop of Wells', *Anglo-Norman Studies: Proceedings of the Battle Conference*, 19 (1997), pp. 202–70
— 'The Lost Cartulary of Abbotsbury', *Anglo-Saxon England*, 18 (1989), pp. 209–44

— 'Manuscripts of the Anglo-Saxon Chronicle', in R. Gameson (ed.), *The Cambridge History of the Book in Britain. Vol. I: c.400–1100*, Cambridge University Press, 2012, pp. 537–52

— 'The Massacre of St. Brice's Day (13 November 1002)', in N. Lund (ed.), *Beretning fra Seksogtyvende tværfaglige Vikingesymposium*, Aarhus Universitet, Afdeling for Middelalder- og Renæssancearkæologi, Hikuin, Højbjerg, 2007, pp. 32–66

— 'Regenbald the Chancellor (*sic*)', *Anglo-Norman Studies: Proceedings of the Battle Conference*, 10 (1987), pp. 185–222

— 'A Tale of Two Kings: Alfred the Great and Æthelred the Unready', *Transactions of the Royal Historical Society*, 5th Series, 36 (1986), pp. 195–217

Keynes, S. D. and R. Love, 'Earl Godwine's Ship', *Anglo-Saxon England*, 38 (2010), pp. 185–223

Keynes, S. D. and R. Naismith, 'The *Agnus Dei* Pennies of King Æthelred the Unready', *Anglo-Saxon England*, 40 (2011), pp. 175–223

King, P., 'The Cathedral Priory of Odense in the Middle Ages', *Kirkehistoriske Samlinger*, 7 (1966), pp. 1–20

— 'English Influence on the Church at Odense in the Early Middle Ages', *Journal of Ecclesiastical History*, 13 (1962), pp. 144–55

Koht, H., 'Haakon Sigurdsson', in E. Bull and E. Jansen (eds.), *Norsk Biografisk Leksikon*, Aschehoug, Kristiania (Oslo), 1931, pp. 187–91

— 'Sagaernes Opfatning av vor gamle Historie', *Historisk Tidsskrift*, 5:2 (1914), pp. 195–206

Körner, S., *Battle of Hastings: England and Europe 1035–1066*, Bibliotheca Historica Lundensis, 14, Gleerup, Lund, 1964

Kristensen, H. K., 'A Viking-Period and Medieval Settlement at Viborg Søndersø, Jutland', *Journal of Danish Archaeology*, 7 (1988), pp. 191–204

— *Middelalderbyen Viborg*, Projekt Middelalderbyen, 4, Centrum, Århus, 1987

Krogh, K. J., *Gåden om Kong Gorms Grav: Historien om Nordhøjen i Jelling*, Poul Kristensen. Herning, 1993

— 'The Royal Viking-Age Monuments at Jelling in the Light of Recent Archaeological Excavations: A Preliminary Report', *Acta Archaeologica*, 53 (1982), pp. 183–216

Krogh, K. J. and B. Leth-Larsen, *Hedensk og Kristent: Fundene fra den kongelige Gravhøj i Jelling*, Vikingekongernes Monumenter i Jelling 2, Nationalmuseet, Copenhagen, 2007

Kuhn, H., *Das Dróttkvætt*, Winter, Heidelberg, 1983

Kürbis, B., 'Die Epistola Mathildis Suevae an Mieszko II. in neuer Sicht Ein Forschungsbericht', *Frühmittelalterliche Studien*, 23 (1989), pp. 318–37

Lang, H. J., "The Fall of the Monarchy of Mieszko II, Lambert', *Speculum: A Journal of Medieval Studies*, 49 (1974), pp. 623–39

Lange, G., 'Die Anfänge der isländisch-norwegischen Geschictschreibung', *Studia Islandica*, 47, Reyjavík, 1989

Larson, L. M., *Canute the Great 995–1035, and the Rise of Danish Imperialism During the Viking Age*, Heroes of the Nations Series, Putnam, London, 1912

— 'The Efforts of the Danish Kings to Recover the English Crown after the Death of Harthacnut', published as an appendix to the *Annual Report of the American Historical Association for the Year 1910* (1912), pp. 71–81

— 'The Political Policies of Cnut as King of England', *American Historical Review*, 15 (1909–10), pp. 720–43

Larsson, L. and B. Hårdh, 'Uppåkra – ett Hövdinga – eller Kungasäte', *Fornvännen. Tidskrift för Svensk Antikvarisk Forkning*, 92 (1997), pp. 139–54

Lawson, M. K., 'Archbishop Wulfstan and the Homiletic Element in the Laws of Æthelred II and Cnut', in A. R. Rumble (ed.), *The Reign of Cnut, King of England, Denmark and Norway*, Studies in the Early History of Britain, Leicester University Press, London/New York, 1994, pp. 141–64

— *Cnut: The Danes in England in the Early Eleventh Century*, Longman, London, 1993
— 'The Collection of Danegeld and Heregeld in the Reigns of Æthelred II and Cnut',
    English Historical Review, 99 (1984), pp. 721–38
— 'Danegeld and Heregeld Once More', *English Historical Review*, 105 (1990), pp. 951–61
— ' "Those Stories Look True": Levels of Taxation in the Reigns of Æthelred II and Cnut',
    English Historical Review, 104 (1989), pp. 385–406
Lee, H., *Virginia Woolf*, Chatto & Windus, London, 1996
Lewis, C. P., 'Danish Landowners in Wessex in 1066', in R. Lavelle and S. Roffey (eds.),
    Danes in Wessex: The Scandinavian Impact on Southern England, c.800–c.1100, Oxbow, Oxford/
    Philadelphia, PA, 2016, pp. 172–211
Liebermann, F., *National Assembly in the Anglo-Saxon Period*, Max Niemeyer, Halle, 1913
Lindkvist, T., 'Early Political Organisation (a) Introductory Survey', in K. Helle (ed.), *The
    Cambridge History of Scandinavia. Vol. 1: Prehistory to 1520*, Cambridge University Press, 2003,
    pp. 160–7
— 'Social and Political Power in Sweden 1000–1300: Predatory Incursions, Royal Taxation,
    and the Formation of a Feudal State', in R. Samson (ed.), *Social Approaches to Viking Studies*,
    Cruithne, Glasgow, 1991, pp. 137–45
Lindqvist, H., *A History of Sweden: From Ice Age to Our Age*, trans. R. Bradbury, Norstedts
    Förlag, Stockholm, 2006
Lund, N., 'The Armies of Swein Forkbeard and Cnut: Leding or Lith?', *Anglo-Saxon England*,
    15 (1986), pp. 105–18
— 'Cnut's Danish Kingdom', in A. R. Rumble (ed.), *The Reign of Cnut, King of England,
    Denmark and Norway*, Studies in the Early History of Britain, Leicester University Press,
    London/New York, 1994, pp. 27–42
— 'The Danish Perspective', in D. Scragg (ed.), *The Battle of Maldon AD 991*, Blackwell,
    Oxford, pp. 114–42
— 'Mission i Danmark før Harald Blåtands Dåb', in N. Lund (ed.), *Kristendommen i Danmark
    før 1050. Et Symposium i Roskilde den 5–7 Februar 2003*, Roskilde Museums Forlag, Roskilde,
    2004, pp. 20–7
— 'Svend Estridsens Blodskam og Skilsmisse', in L. C. A. Sonne and S. Croix (eds.), *Svend
    Estridsen*, Syddansk Universitetsforlag, Viborg, 2016, pp. 39–55
Löfving, C., 'Who Ruled the Region East of the Skagerrak in the Eleventh Century?', in R.
    Samson (ed.), *Social Approaches to Viking Studies*, Cruithne Press, Glasgow, 1991, pp. 147–56
McDougall, D., I. McDougall and P. Foote, *Theodoricus Monachus: Historia de Antiquitate Regum
    Norwagiensium*, Viking Society for Northern Research, Text Series, XI, London, 1998
Mack, K., 'Changing Thegns: Cnut's Conquest and the English Aristocracy', *Albion*, 16
    (1984), pp. 375–87
— 'The Stallers: Administrative Innovation in the Reign of Edward the Confessor', *Journal
    of Medieval History* 12 (1986), pp. 123–34
Madsen, H. J., 'Introduction to Viking Århus', in H. Bekker-Nielsen, P. Foote and O. Olsen
    (eds.), *The Proceedings of the Eighth Viking Congress, Århus, 24th–31st August 1977*, Mediaeval
    Scandinavia Supplements, 2, Odense University Press, 1981, pp. 69–72
Malmer, B., *Nordiska Mynt före År 1000*, Acta Archaeologica Lundensia, Series in 8° Nr. 4,
    Lund, 1966
Marafioti, N., *The King's Body: Burial and Succession in Late Anglo-Saxon England*, Anglo-Saxon
    Series, Toronto University Press 2014
Marten, L., 'The Shiring of East Anglia: An Alternative Hypothesis', *Historical Research*, 81
    (2008), pp. 1–27
Mårtensson, A. W., 'Gravar och Kyrkor', in A. W. Mårtensson (ed.), *Uppgrävt förflutet för
    PKbanken i Lund. En Investering i Arkeologi*, Archaeologica Lundensia: Investigationes de
    Antiquitatibus Urbis Lundae, 7, Kulturhistoriska Museet, Lund, 1976, pp. 87–134
— (ed.), *Uppgrävt förflutet för PKbanken i Lund. En Investering i Arkeologi*, Archaeologica Lundensia:
    Investigationes de Antiquitatibus Urbis Lundae 7, Kulturhistoriska museet, Lund, 1976
Marwood, G. W., *The Stone Coffins of Bosham Church*, privately published, Chichester, 1974

Mason, E., *The House of Godwin: The History of a Dynasty*, Hambledon, London/New York, 2004

Maund, K. L., ' "A Turmoil of Warring Princes": Political Leadership in Ninth-Century Denmark', *Haskins Society Journal*, 6 (1994), pp. 29–47

Melinikova, E., 'The Baltic Policy of Jaroslav the Wise', in U. Fransson et al. (eds.), *Cultural Interaction between East and West: Archaeology, Artefacts and Human Contacts in Northern Europe*, Stockholm Studies in Archaeology, 44, Stockholms Universitet, Stockholm, 2007, pp. 73–7

Metcalf, D. M., 'Can We Believe the Very Large Figure of £72,000 for the Geld Levied by Cnut in 1018?', in K. Jonsson (ed.), *Studies in Late Anglo-Saxon Coinage*, Numismatiska Meddelanden, 35, Stockholm, 1990, pp. 165–76

Moberg, O., 'The Battle of Helgeå', *Scandinavian Journal of History*, 14 (1989), pp. 1–19

— *Olav Haraldsson, Knut den Store och Sverige*, Gleerup, Lund, 1941

Moltke, E., *Runes and their Origin, Denmark and Elsewhere*, Nationalmuseet, Copenhagen, 1985

Molyneaux, G., *The Formation of the English Kingdom in the Tenth Century*, Oxford University Press, 2015

Mortensen, L. B., 'The Nordic Archbishoprics as Literary Centres around 1200', in K. Friis-Jensen and I. Skovgaard-Petersen (eds.), *Archbishop Absalon of Lund and his World*, Roskilde Museums Forlag, 2000

Naismith, R. G. R., 'London and its Mint, c.800–1066: A preliminary Survey', *British Numismatic Journal*, 83 (2013), pp. 44–74

Nelson, J. L., *Charles the Bald*, Longman, London, 1992

Nielsen, I., *Middelalderbyen Ribe*, Projekt Middelalderbyen, 1, Forlaget Centrum, Viby, 1985

Nielsen, J. N., 'Sebbersund – Tidlige Kirker ved Limfjorden', in N. Lund (ed.), *Kristendommen i Danmark før 1050. Et Symposium i Roskilde den 5–7 Februar 2003*, Roskilde Museums Forlag, 2004, pp. 103–22

Nielsen, L. C., 'Hedenskab og Kristendom. Religionsskiftet Afspejlet i Vikingetidens Grave', in P. Mortensen and B. M. Rasmussen (eds.), *Fra Stamme til Stat i Danmark 2. Hovdingesamfund og Kongemagt*, Jysk Arkæologisk Selskabs Skrifter, 22:2, Aarhus Universitetsforlag, 1991, pp. 245–67

— 'Omgård: A Settlement from the Late Iron Age and the Viking Period in West Jutland', *Acta Archaeologica*, 50 (1979), pp. 173–208

— 'Stormænd og bonder. Et Aktuelt Problem i Sydskandinavisk Vikingetid', *Kontaktstencil*, 19 (1981), pp. 63–82

Nightingale, P., 'The Origin of the Court of Husting and Danish Influence on London's Development into a Capital City', *English Historical Review*, 102 (1987), pp. 559–78

Nilsson, B., 'Vikings Deceased in England – Commemorated by Whom? Runic Memorials in Sweden', in J. Hill and M. Swann (eds.), *The Community, the Family and the Saint: Patterns of Power in Early Medieval Europe*, Brepols, Turnhout, 1998, pp. 379–90

Okasha, E., 'An Inscribed Anglo-Saxon Lid from Lund', *Medieval Archaeology*, 28 (1984), pp. 181–3

Oleson, T. J., *The Witenagemot in the Reign of Edward the Confessor: A Study in the Constitutional History of Eleventh-Century England*, Oxford University Press and Toronto University Press, London, 1955

Olrik, H., 'Den Danske Biskop Tymme: (Thietmar) af Hildesheim', *Historisk Tidsskrift* (Copenhagen), Bind 6. række, 3 (1891–2), pp. 692–710

Olsen, O., 'Sankt Ibs Kirke i Vindebode: Et Bidrag til Roskildes Ældste Historie', in *Fra Københavns Amt 1961* (1961), pp. 61–87

— 'St Jørgensbjærg Kirke. Arkæologiske Undersøgelser i Murværk og Gulv', *Aarbøger for Nordisk Oldkyndighed og Historie. Udgivne af det Kongelige Nordiske Oldskriftselskab 1960* (1961), pp. 1–71

Ortenberg, V., *The English Church and the Continent in the Tenth and Eleventh Centuries*, Clarendon Press, Oxford, 1992

Owen-Crocker, G. R., 'Pomp, Piety, and Keeping the Woman in her Place: The Dress of Cnut and Ælfgifu-Emma', in R. Netherton and G. R. Owen-Crocker (eds.), *Medieval Clothing and Textiles*, Boydell, Woodbridge, 2005, pp. 41–52

Peckham, D. W., 'The Bosham Myth of Canute's Daughter', *Sussex Notes and Queries*, 17 (1970), pp. 179–84

Pedersen, A., 'Anglo-Danish Contact across the North Sea in the Eleventh Century: A Survey of the Danish Archaeological Evidence', in J. Adams and K. Holman (eds.), *Scandinavia and Europe 800–1350: Contact, Conflict and Coexistence*, Medieval Texts and Cultures of Northern Europe, 4, Brepols, Turnhout, 2004, pp. 43–67

— 'Jelling im 10. Jahrhundert – Alte Thesen, neue Ergebnisse', in K. P. Hofmann, H. Kamp and M. Wemhoff (eds.), *Die Wikinger und das Fränkische Reich: Identitäten zwischen Konfrontation und Annäherung*, Wilhelm Frink, Paderborn, 2014, pp. 275–96

Pelteret, D. A. E., *Catalogue of English Post-Conquest Vernacular Documents*, Boydell, Woodbridge, 1990

Peterson, L., *Nordiskt Runnamnslexikon*, 5th edn, Institutet för Språk och Folkminnen, Uppsala, 2007; online at http://www.sprakochfolkminnen.se/om-oss/publikationer/institutets-utgivning/sprakpublikationer/namn/personnamn/personnamn/2013-11-24-nordiskt-runnamnslexikon.html

Plummer, C. (ed.), *Two of the Saxon Chronicles Parallel*, Clarendon Press, Oxford, 1892–9

Poetry from Treatises on Poetics, in K. Gade and E. Marold (eds.), *Skaldic Poetry of the Scandinavian Middle Ages*, Brepols, Turnhout, 2017

Pons-Sans, S. M., *Norse-Derived Vocabulary in Late Old English Texts: Wulfstan's Works, a Case Study*, NOWELE Supplement Series, 22, University Press of Southern Denmark, Odense, 2007

Poole, R. G., 'The "Conversion Verses" of Hallfreðr Vandræðaskáld', *Maal og Minne* (2002), pp. 15–37

— 'Skaldic Verse and Anglo-Saxon History: Some Aspects of the Period 1009–1016', *Speculum: A Journal of Medieval Studies*, 62 (1987), pp. 265–98

— *Viking Poems on War and Peace: A Study in Skaldic Narrative*, Toronto Medieval Texts and Translations, 8, University of Toronto Press, Toronto/Buffalo/London, 1991

Pratt, D., 'Kings and Books in Anglo-Saxon England', *Anglo-Saxon England*, 43 (2014), pp. 297–377

Previté-Orton, C. W., *The Early History of the House of Savoy (1000–1233)*, Cambridge University Press, 1912

Raraty, D., 'Earl Godwine of Wessex: The Origins of his Power and his Political Loyalties', *History*, 74 (1989), pp. 3–19

Rasmusson, N. L., 'An Overlooked Type of Coin from the Time of King Anund Jacob', in N. L. Rasmusson and L. O. Lagerqvist (eds.), *Commentationes de Nummis Saeculorum IX–XI in Suecia Repertis*, Kungliga Vitterhets Historie och Antikvitets Akademiens Handligar, Antikvariska Serien 19, Almqvist & Wiksell, Stockholm, 1968, pp. 375–81

Refskou, N., '"In marca vel regno Danorum"', *Kirkehistoriske Samlinger* (1985), pp. 19–33

— 'Ottonernes Missionsvirksomhed', in N. Lund (ed.), *Kristendommen i Danmark før 1050. Et Symposium i Roskilde den 5–7 Februar 2003*, Roskilde Museums Forlag, 2004, pp. 28–42

Renardy, C., 'Les Écoles ligeoises du IXe au XIIe siècle: grandes lignes de leur évolution', *Revue belge de philologie et d'histoire*, 57 (1979), pp. 309–28

Reynolds, L. D., *Texts and Transmissions: A Survey of the Latin Classics*, Clarendon Press, Oxford, 1983

Roach, L., *Æthelred the Unready*, English Monarchs Series, Yale University Press, New Haven/London, 2016

— *Kingship and Consent in Anglo-Saxon England, 871–978: Assemblies and the State in the Early Middle Ages*, Cambridge Studies of Medieval Life and Thought, 4th Series, Cambridge University Press, 2013

Roesdahl, E., 'Aggersborg in the Viking Age', in H. Bekker-Nielsen (ed.), *The Proceedings of the Eighth Viking Congress: Århus, 24–31 August 1977*, Mediaeval Scandinavia Supplements, 2, Odense University Press, 1981, pp. 107–22

— 'Danish Geometrical Viking Fortresses and their Context', *Anglo-Norman Studies: Proceedings of the Battle Conference*, 9 (1986), pp. 209–26

— 'English Connections in the Time of Knut the Great – Material from Viborg', in U. Fransson et al. (eds.), *Cultural Interaction between East and West: Archaeology, Artefacts and Human Contacts in Northern Europe*, Stockholm Studies in Archaeology, 44, Stockholms Universitet, 2007, pp. 276–8

— *Fyrkat. En Jysk Vikingeborg II. Oldsagerne og Glavpladsen*, Afdeling for Middelalder- og Renæssancearkæologi, Nordiske Fortidsminder Serie B, in quarto, Copenhagen, 1977

— 'En Gravplads fra Tidlig Kristen Tid – Fyrkat', in N. Lund (ed.), *Kristendommen i Danmark før 1050. Et Symposium i Roskilde den 5–7 Februar 2003*, Roskilde Museums Forlag, 2004, pp. 153–8

— 'Hvornår blev Kirkerne Bygget?', in N. Lund (ed.), *Kristendommen i Danmark før 1050. Et Symposium i Roskilde den 5–7 Februar 2003*, Roskilde Museums Forlag, 2004, pp. 201–6

— *Viking Age Denmark*, trans. S. Margeson and K. Williams, British Museum Publications, London, 1982

Roach, L. et al., *The Vikings in England and their Danish Homeland*, catalogue for exhibition in Copenhagen, Århus and York, The Anglo-Danish Viking Project, 1981

Rollason, D. W., *The Mildreth Legend: A Study in Early Medieval Hagiography in England*, Leicester University Press, 1982

— (ed.), 'Translatio Sancte Mildrethe Virginis', *Medieval Studies*, 48 (1986), pp. 139–210

Rollason, L. (ed.), *The Thorney Liber Vitae: London, British Library, Additional MS 40,000, fols. 1–12r, Edition, Facsimile and Study*, Boydell, Woodbridge, 2015

Ros, J., *Sigtuna. Staden, Kyrkona och den Kyrkliga Organisationen*, Occasional Papers in Archaeology, Uppsala Universitet, Institutionen för Arkeologi och Antik Historia, 30, Uppsala, 2001

Sawyer, B., 'Appendix: The Evidence of Scandinavian Runic Inscriptions', in A. R. Rumble (ed.), *The Reign of Cnut, King of England, Denmark and Norway*, Studies in the Early History of Britain, Leicester University Press, London/New York, 1994, pp. 23–6

— 'Viking-Age Rune-Stones as a Crisis Symptom', *Norwegian Archaeological Review*, 24 (1991), pp. 97–112

Sawyer, B. and P. H. Sawyer, 'Adam and Eve of Scandinavian History', in P. Magdalino (ed.), *The Perception of the Past in Twelfth-Century Europe*, Hambledon, London, 1992, pp. 37–51

— 'A Gormless Dynasty: The Jelling Dynasty Revisited', *Runica-Germanica Mediaevalia*, 37 (2003), pp. 689–706

Sawyer, P. H., *Anglo-Saxon Charters: An Annotated List and Bibliography*, Royal Historical Society Guides and Handbooks, 8, Royal Historical Society, London, 1968

— 'Cnut's Scandinavian Empire', in A. R. Rumble (ed.), *The Reign of Cnut, King of England, Denmark and Norway*, Studies in the Early History of Britain, Leicester University Press, London/New York, 1994, pp. 10–26

— 'Knut, Sweden and Sigtuna', in S. Tesch (ed.), *Avstamp för en ny Sigtunaforskning. 18 Forskare om Sigtuna. Heldagseminarium kring Sigtunaforskning den 26 November 1987, Gröna Laden, Sigtuna*, Komm. för Sigtunaforskning, Sigtuna Museer, Sigtuna, 1989, pp. 88–93

— 'Konger og Kongemakt', in P. Mortensen and B. M. Rasmussen (eds.), *Fra Stamme til Stat i Danmark 2. Hovdingesamfund og Kongemagt*, Jysk Arkæologisk Selskabs Skrifter, 22:2, Aarhus Universitetsforlag, 1991, pp. 277–85

— *The Making of Sweden*, Viktoria Bokförlag, Alingsås, 1989 (later republished in Swedish as *När Sverige blev Sverige*, 1991)

— 'The Process of Scandinavian Christianization in the Tenth and Eleventh Centuries', in B. Sawyer, P. Sawyer and I. Wood (eds.), *The Christianization of Scandinavia: Report of a Symposium held at Kungälv, Sweden, 4–9 August 1985*, Viktoria Bokförlag, Alsingsås, 1987, pp. 68–87

— 'Swein Forkbeard and the Historians', in I. Wood and G. A. Loud (eds.), *Church and Chronicle in the Middle Ages: Essays Presented to John Taylor*, Hambledon, London/Rio Grande, 1991, pp. 27–40

— *Textus Roffensis: Rochester Cathedral Library Manuscript A. 3. 5.*, *Part I*, Early English Texts in Facsimile, 7, Rosenkilde and Bagger, Copenhagen, 1957

— *The Wealth of Anglo-Saxon England, based on the Ford Lectures delivered in the University of Oxford in Hilary Term 1993*, Oxford University Press, 2013

Sharpe, R., 'The Use of Writs in the 11th Century: A Hypothesis Based on the Archive of Bury St. Edmunds', *Anglo-Saxon England*, 32 (2004), pp. 247–91

Sigurdsson, J. V., *Det Norrøne Samfunnet: Vikingen, Kongen, Erkebiskopen og Bonden*, Pax Forlag, Oslo, 2008

Silvegren, U., 'Mynten från Uppåkra', in B. Hårdh (ed.), *Fynden i Centrum: Keramik, Glas och Metal från Uppåkra*, Uppåkrastudier, 2, Acta Archaeologica Lundensia Series in 8° 30, Almqvist & Wiksell International, Häftad, 1999, pp. 95–112

Snook, B., *The Anglo-Saxon Chancery: The History, Language and Production of Anglo-Saxon Charters from Alfred to Edgar*, Boydell, Woodbridge, 2015

Sprockel, C., *The Language of the Parker Chronicle. Vol. I*, Martinus Nijhoff, The Hague, 1965

Staats, R., 'The Laws of Cnut and the History of Anglo-Saxon Royal Promises', *Anglo-Saxon England*, 10 (1982), pp. 173–90

— *Theologie der Reichskrone: Ottonische "Renovatio Imperii" im Spiegel einer Insignie*, Monographen zur Geschichte des Mittelalters,13, Hiersemann, Stuttgart, 1976

Stafford, P., *Queen Emma and Queen Edith: Queenship and Women's Power in Eleventh-Century England*, Blackwell, Oxford, 1997

— 'The Reign of Æthelred II: A Study in the Limitations on Royal Policy and Action', in D. Hill (ed.), *Ethelred the Unready: Papers from the Millenary Conference*, BAR British Series, 59, 1978, pp. 15–46

Steindorff, E., *Jahrbücher des Deutschen Reichs unter Heinrich III*, Dunder & Humblot, Leipzig, 1839–95

Stenton, F. M., *Anglo-Saxon England*, 3rd edn, Clarendon Press, Oxford, 1971

Stevenson, W. H., 'An Alleged Son of King Harold Harefoot', *English Historical Review*, 28 (1913), pp. 112–17

Ström, F., 'Poetry as an Instrument of Propaganda: Jarl Hákon and his Poets', in U. Dronke, Guðrún P. Helgadóttir, G. W. Weber and H. Bekker-Nielsen (eds.), *Specvlvm Norroenvm: Norse Studies in Memory of Gabriel Turville-Petre*, Odense University Press, 1981, pp. 440–58

Stumman Hansen, S., and K. Randsborg (eds.), *Vikings in the West*, Acta Archaeologica, 71, Acta Archaeologica Supplementa II, Munksgaard, Copenhagen, 2000

Syrett, M., *The Vikings in England: The Evidence of Runic Inscriptions*, Anglo-Saxon, Norse and Celtic Guides, Texts and Studies, 4, Cambridge University Press, 2002

Talvio, T., 'Harold I and Harthacnut's Jewel Cross Type Reconsidered', in M. A. S. Blackburn (ed.), *Anglo-Saxon Monetary History: Essays in Memory of Michael Dolley*, Leicester University Press, 1986, 273–90

Taranger, A., 'De Norske Folkelovbøker (før 1263) – I', *Tidsskrift for Retsvidenskap*, ny. række V, 39 (1926), pp. 183–211

— 'De Norske Folkelovbøker (før 1263) – II', *Tidsskrift for Retsvidenskap*, ny. række V, 41 (1928), pp. 1–68

Thaastrup-Leith, A. K., 'Traekirker i det Middelalderlige Danmark indtil ca. 1100. Hvornår blev de Bygget?', in N. Lund (ed.), *Kristendommen i Danmark før 1050. Et Symposium i Roskilde den 5–7 Februar 2003*, Roskilde Museums Forlag, 2004, pp. 207–14

Thomson, R. M., *William of Malmesbury*, Boydell, Woodbridge, 2003

Townend, M., 'Contextualising the *Knútsdrápur*: Skaldic Praise-Poetry at the Court of Cnut', *Anglo-Saxon England*, 30 (2001), pp. 145–79

— 'Knútr and the Cult of St Óláfr: Poetry and Patronage in Eleventh-Century Norway and England', *Viking and Medieval Scandinavia*, 1 (2005), pp. 251–79

— 'Whatever Happened to York Viking Poetry? Memory, Tradition and the Transmission of Skaldic Verse', *Saga-Book of the Viking Society*, 27 (2003), pp. 48–90

Treharne, E., *Living through Conquest: The Politics of Early English, 1020–1220*, Oxford Textual Perspectives, Oxford University Press, 2012
— 'The Performance of Piety: Cnut, Rome, and England', in F. Tinti (ed.), *England and Rome in the Early Middle Ages: Pilgrimage, Art, and Politics*, Studies in the Early Middle Ages, Brepols, Turnhout, 2014, pp. 343–61
Trillmich, W., *Kaiser Konrad II und seine Zeit*, Europa Union Verlag, Bonn, 1991
Tschan, F. J. (trans.), *History of the Archbishops of Hamburg-Bremen by Adam of Bremen*, Columbia University Press, New York, 1959, reprinted 2002
Uspenskij, F., 'Dynastic Names in Medieval Scandinavia and Russia (Rus'): Family Traditions and International Connections', *Studia Anthroponomica Scandinavica*, 21 (2003), pp. 15–50
Vince, A. G., *Saxon London: An Archaeological Investigation*, Seaby, London, 1990
Vincent, N., *Peter des Roches: An Alien in English Politics 1205–1238*, Cambridge Studies in Medieval Life and Thought, Cambridge University Press, 2002
Weibull, C., *Saxo: Kritiska Undersökningar i Danmarks Historia från Sven Estridsens Död till Knut VI*, Berlingska Boktryckeriet, Lund, 1915
Weibull, L., *Kritiska Undersökningar i Nordens Historia omkring År 1000*, Gleerup, Lund, 1911
Weidhagen-Hallerdt, M., 'St Clemens Kyrka i Helsingborg', in A. Andrén (ed.), *Medeltiden och Arkeologin. Festskrift till Erik Cinthio*, Lund Studies in Medieval Archaeology, 1, Lund Universitets Historiska Museum, 1986, pp. 131–43
Whitelock, D., 'Archbishop Wulfstan, Homilist and Statesman', *Transactions of the Royal Historical Society*, 4th Series, 24 (1942), pp. 25–45
— 'The Dealings of the Kings of England with Northumbria in the Tenth and Eleventh Centuries', in P. Clemoes (ed.), *The Anglo-Saxons: Studies in Some Aspects of their History and Culture Presented to Bruce Dickins*, Bowes and Bowes, London, 1959, pp. 70–88
— 'Scandinavian Personal Names in the Liber Vitae of Thorney Abbey', *Saga-Book of the Viking Society for Northern Research*, 12 (1937–45), pp. 127–53
— 'Wulfstan and the Laws of Cnut', *English Historical Review*, 63 (1948), pp. 433–52
— 'Wulfstan's Authorship of Cnut's Laws', *English Historical Review*, 70 (1955), pp. 72–85
Wilcox, J., 'Wulfstan's *Sermo Lupi ad Anglos* as Political Performance: 16 February 1014 and Beyond', in M. Townend (ed.), *Wulfstan, Archbishop of York: The Proceedings of the Second Alcuin Conference*, Brepols, Turnhout, 2004, pp. 375–96
Williams, A., *Æthelred the Unready: The Ill-Counselled King*, Hambledon, London/New York, 2003
— ' "Cockles amongst the Wheat": Danes and English in the Western Midlands in the First Half of the Eleventh Century', *Midland History*, 11 (1986), pp. 1–22
— *The English and the Norman Conquest*, Boydell, Woodbridge, 1997
— 'The King's Nephew: The Family and Career of Ralph Earl of Hereford', in C. Harper-Bill, C. J. Holdsworth and J. L. Nelson (eds.), *Studies in Medieval History Presented to R. Allen Brown*, Boydell, Woodbridge, 1989, pp. 327–44
— 'Land and Power in the Eleventh Century: The Estates of Harold Godwineson', *Proceedings of the Battle Conference on Anglo-Norman Studies*, 3 (1980), pp. 171–8 and 230–4
— *Land, Power and Politics: The Family and Career of Odda of Deerhurst*, Deerhurst Lecture 1996, Deerhurst, 1997
— 'A Place in the Country: Orc of Abbotsbury and Tole of Tolpuddle, Dorset', in R. Lavelle and S. Roffey (eds.), *Danes in Wessex: The Scandinavian Impact on Southern England, c.800–c.1100*, Oxbow, Oxford/Philadelphia, PA, 2016, pp. 158–71
— 'The Spoilation of Worcester', *Anglo-Norman Studies*, 19 (1996), pp. 383–408
— 'Thorkell the Tall and the Bubble Reputation: The Vicissitudes of Fame', in R. Lavelle and S. Roffey (eds.), *Danes in Wessex: The Scandinavian Impact on Southern England, c.800–c.1100*, Oxbow, Oxford/Philadelphia, PA, 2016, pp. 144–57
— 'A West-Country Magnate of the Eleventh Century: The Family, Estates and Patronage of Beorhtric, Son of Ælfgar', in K. S. B. Keats-Rohan (ed.), *Family Trees and the Roots of*

   Politics: The Prosopography of Britain and France from the Tenth to the Twelfth Century, Boydell, Woodbridge, 1997, pp. 41–68

Wilson, D. M. and O. Klindt-Jensen, *Viking Art*, George Allen & Unwin, London, 1966

Winroth, A., *The Conversion of Scandinavia: Vikings, Merchants, and Missionaries in the Remaking of Northern Europe*, Yale University Press, New Haven/London, 2012

Wolfram, H., *Conrad II 990–1039: Emperor of Three Kingdoms*, trans. D. A. Kaiser, Pennsylvania State University Press, University Park, PA, 2006

Woods, D., 'The Agnus Dei Penny of King Æthelred II: A Call to Hope in the Lord (Isaiah LX)?', *Anglo-Saxon England*, 42 (2013), pp. 299–309

Wormald, F., *The Bendictional of St. Ethelwold*, Faber & Faber, London, 1959

— 'Æthelred the Lawmaker', in D. Hill (ed.), *Ethelred the Unready: Papers from the Millenary Conference*, BAR British Series, 59, 1978, pp. 47–80

Wormald, P., *The Making of English Law: King Alfred to the Twelfth Century. Vol. 1: Legislation and its Limits*, Oxford University Press, 1999

Wright, C. E., *The Cultivation of Saga in Anglo-Saxon England*, Oliver & Boyd, Edinburgh, 1939

Yorke, B., *Kings and Kingdoms of Early Anglo-Saxon England*, Routledge, London/New York, 1990

INDEX